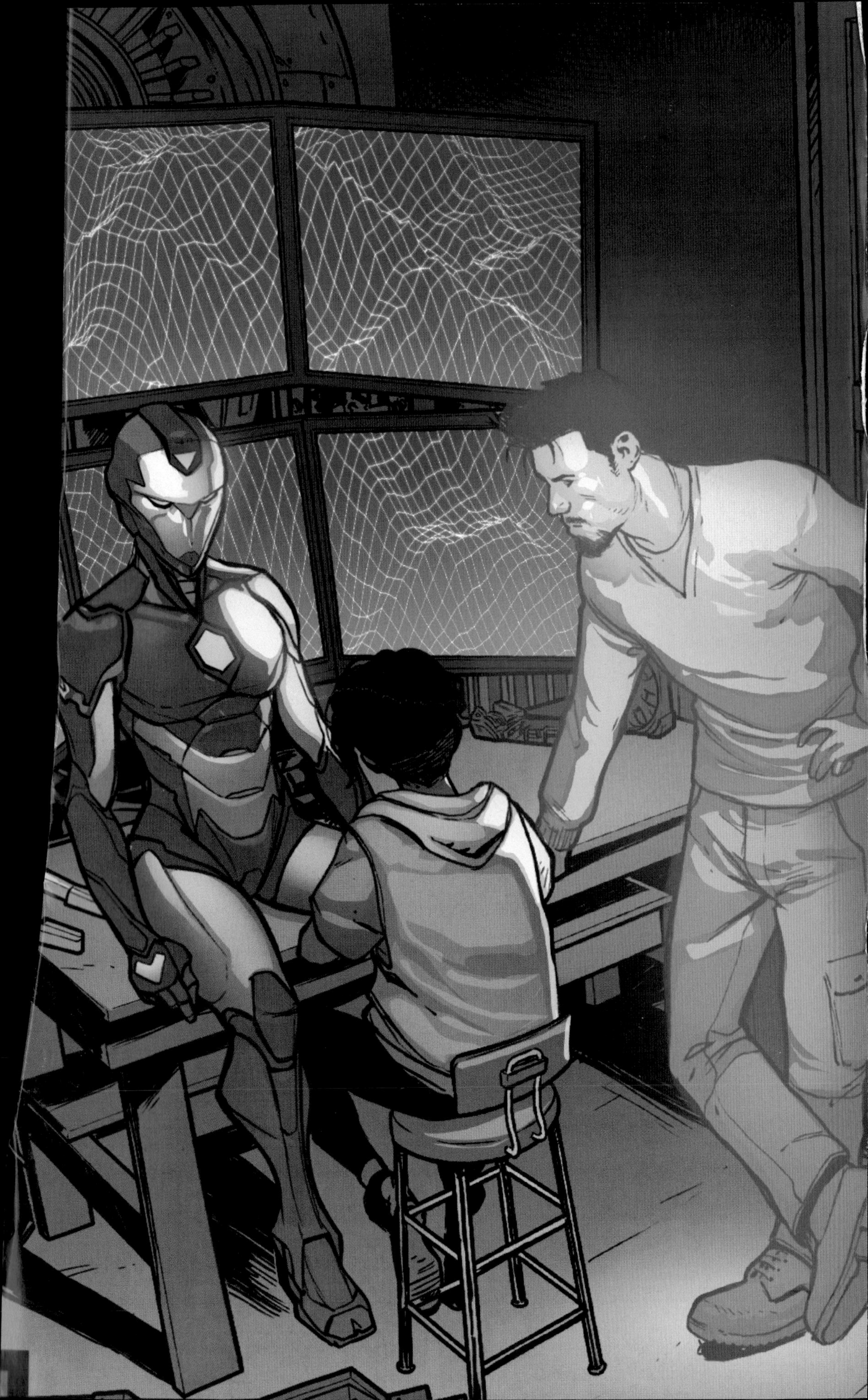

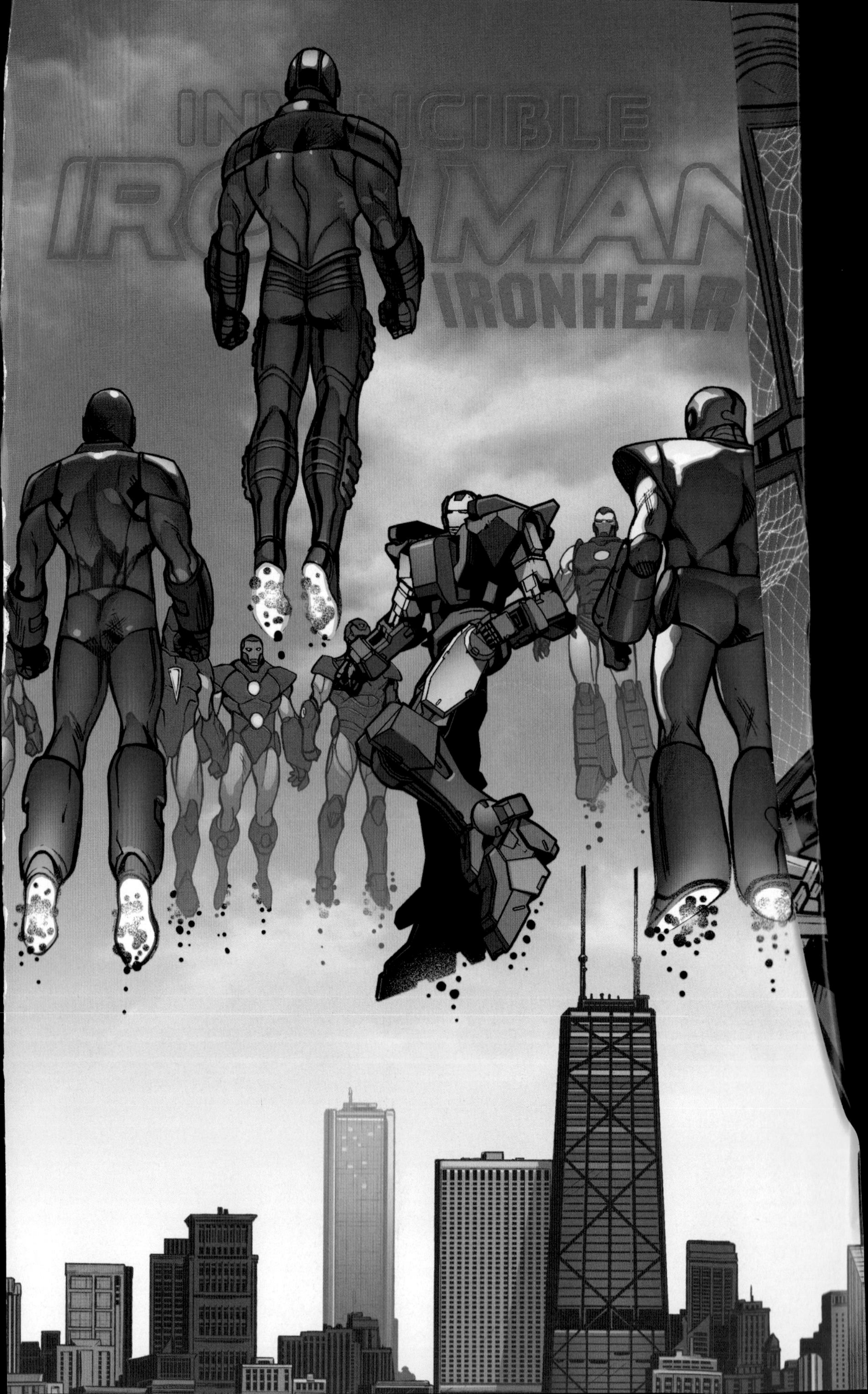

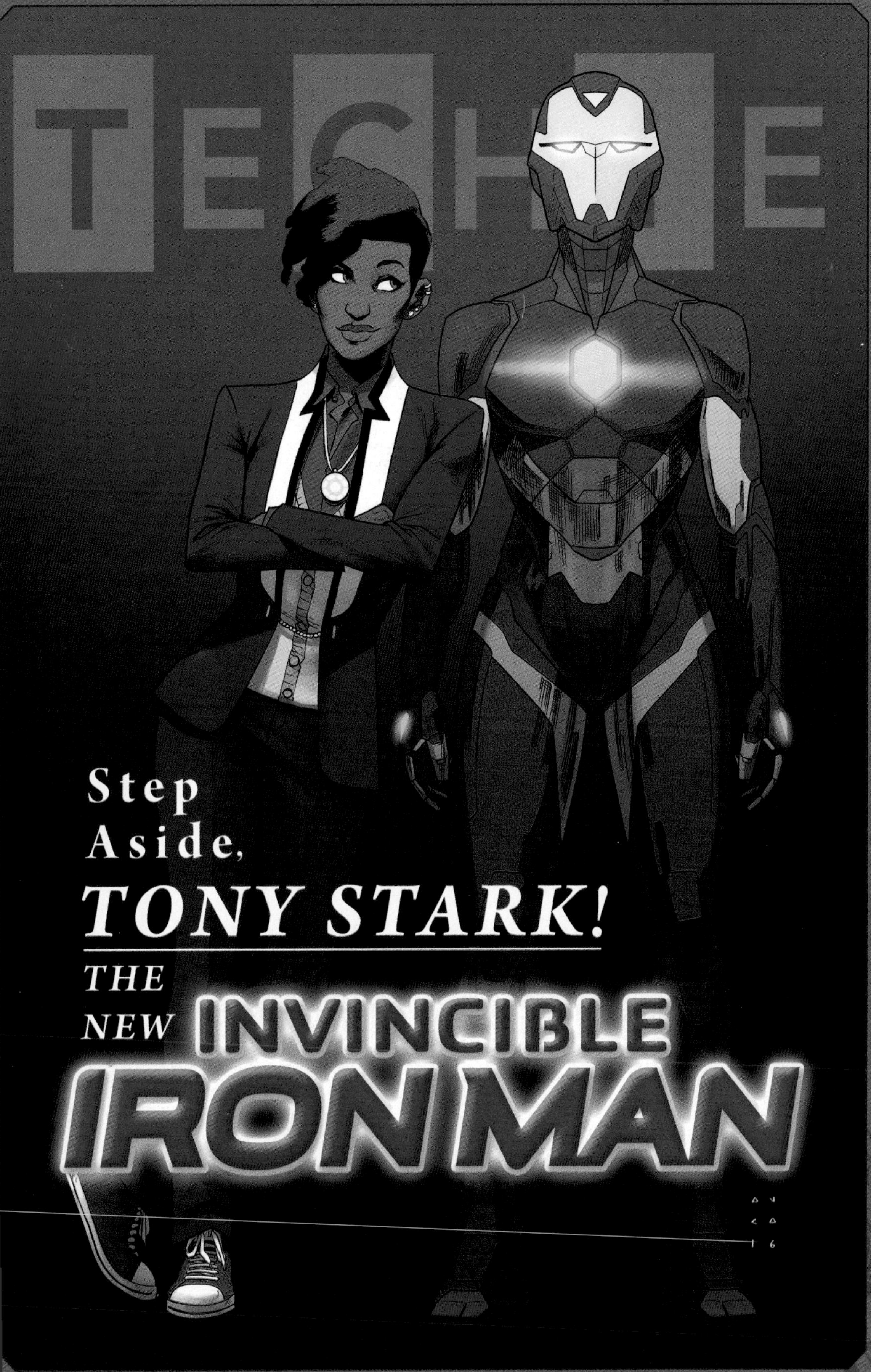
Step
Aside,
TONY STARK!
THE
NEW INVINCIBLE
IRON MAN

KRIS ANKA
3 VARIANT

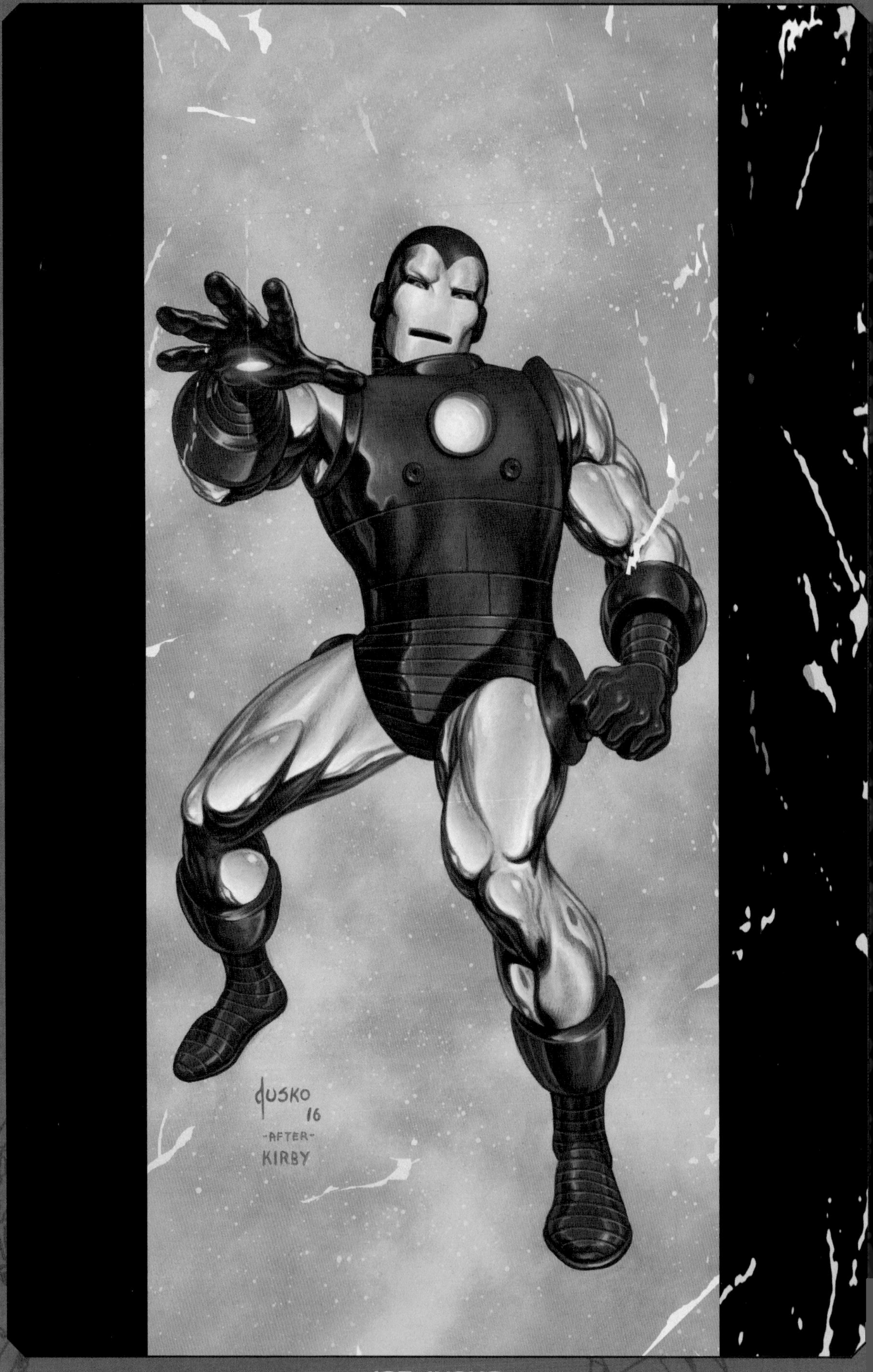
JUSKO 16
-AFTER-
KIRBY

JOE JUSKO
4 CORNER BOX VARIANT

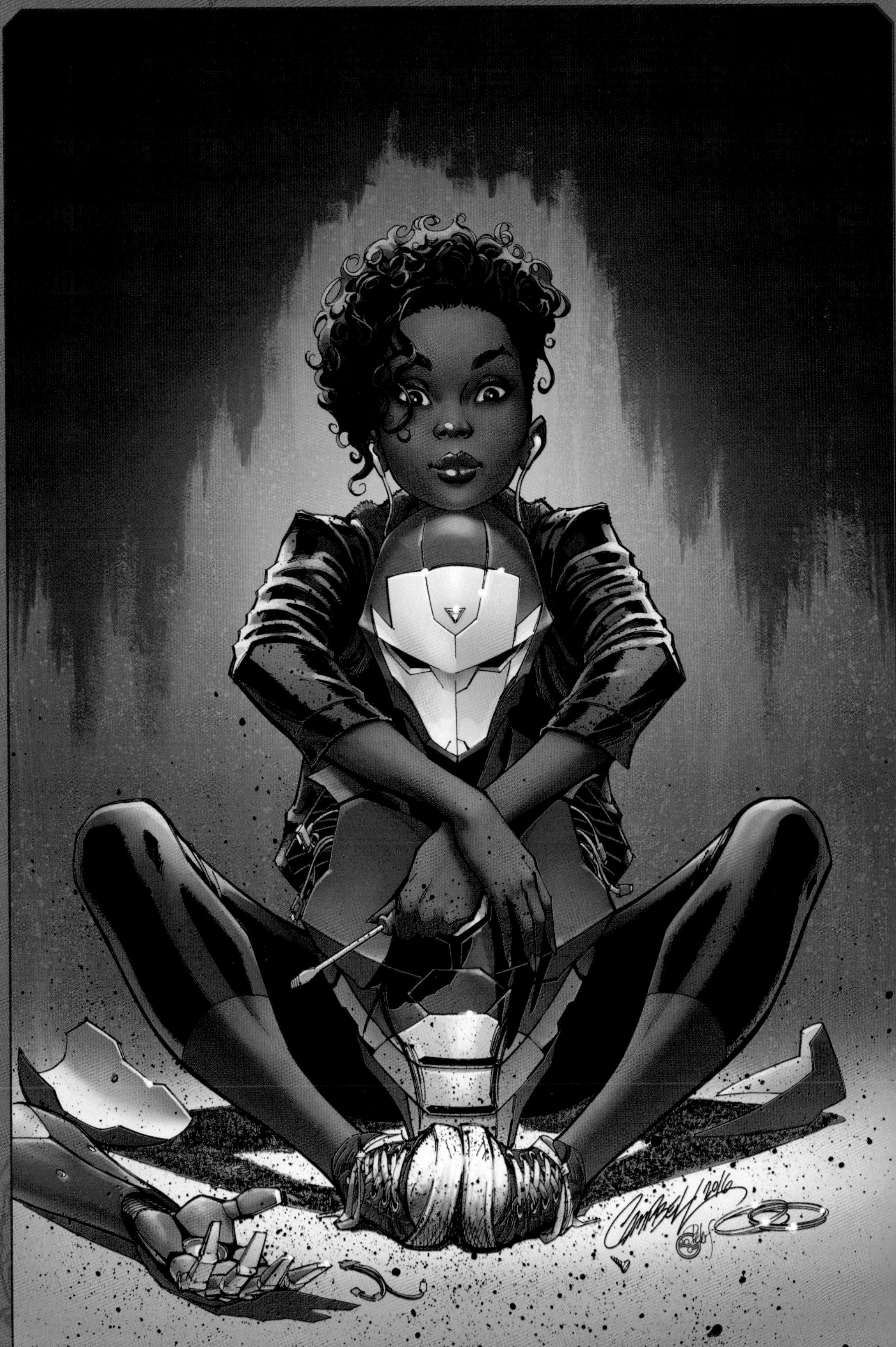

J. SCOTT CAMPBELL

2 VARIANT

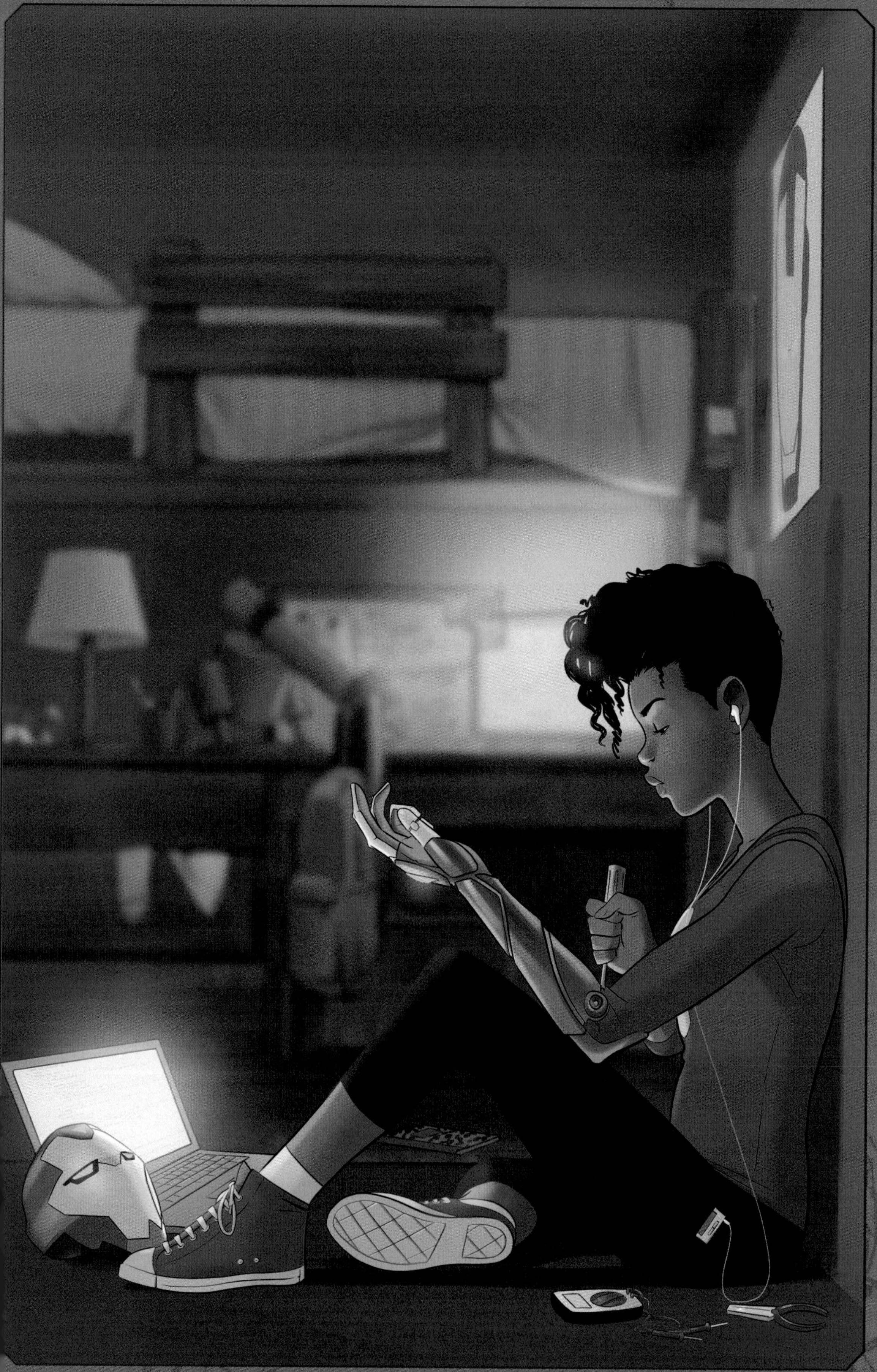

ANTHONY PIPER

2 VARIANT

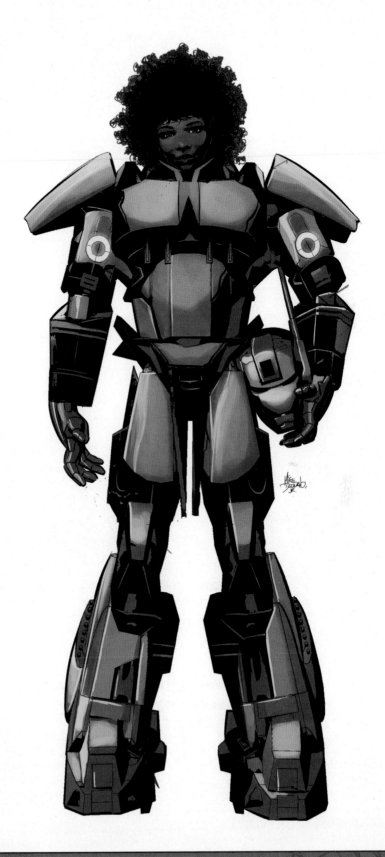

MIKE DEODATO JR. & **FRANK MARTIN**
2 TEASER VARIANT

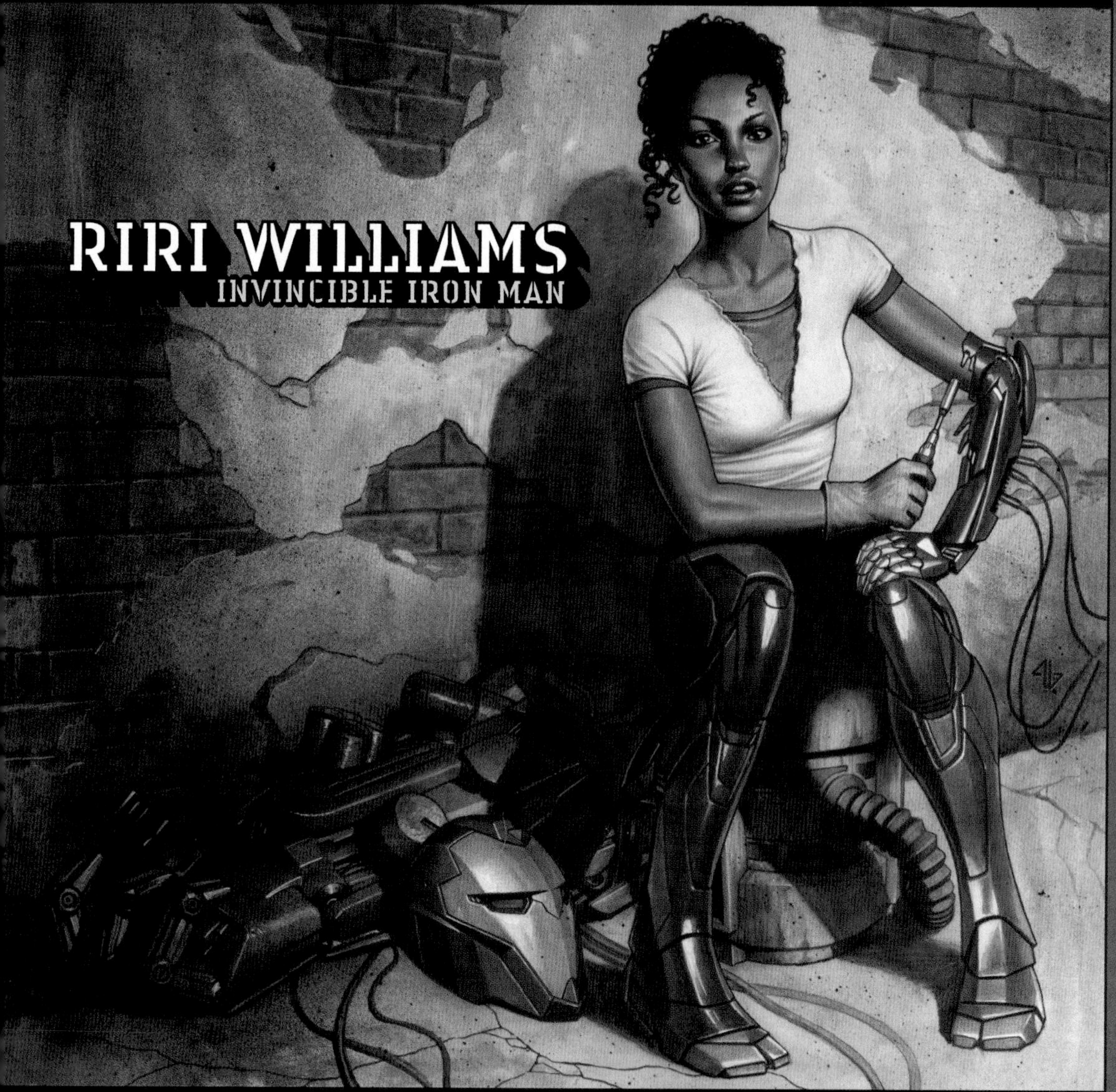

RIRI WILLIAMS
INVINCIBLE IRON MAN

ADI GRANOV
1 HIP-HOP VARIANT

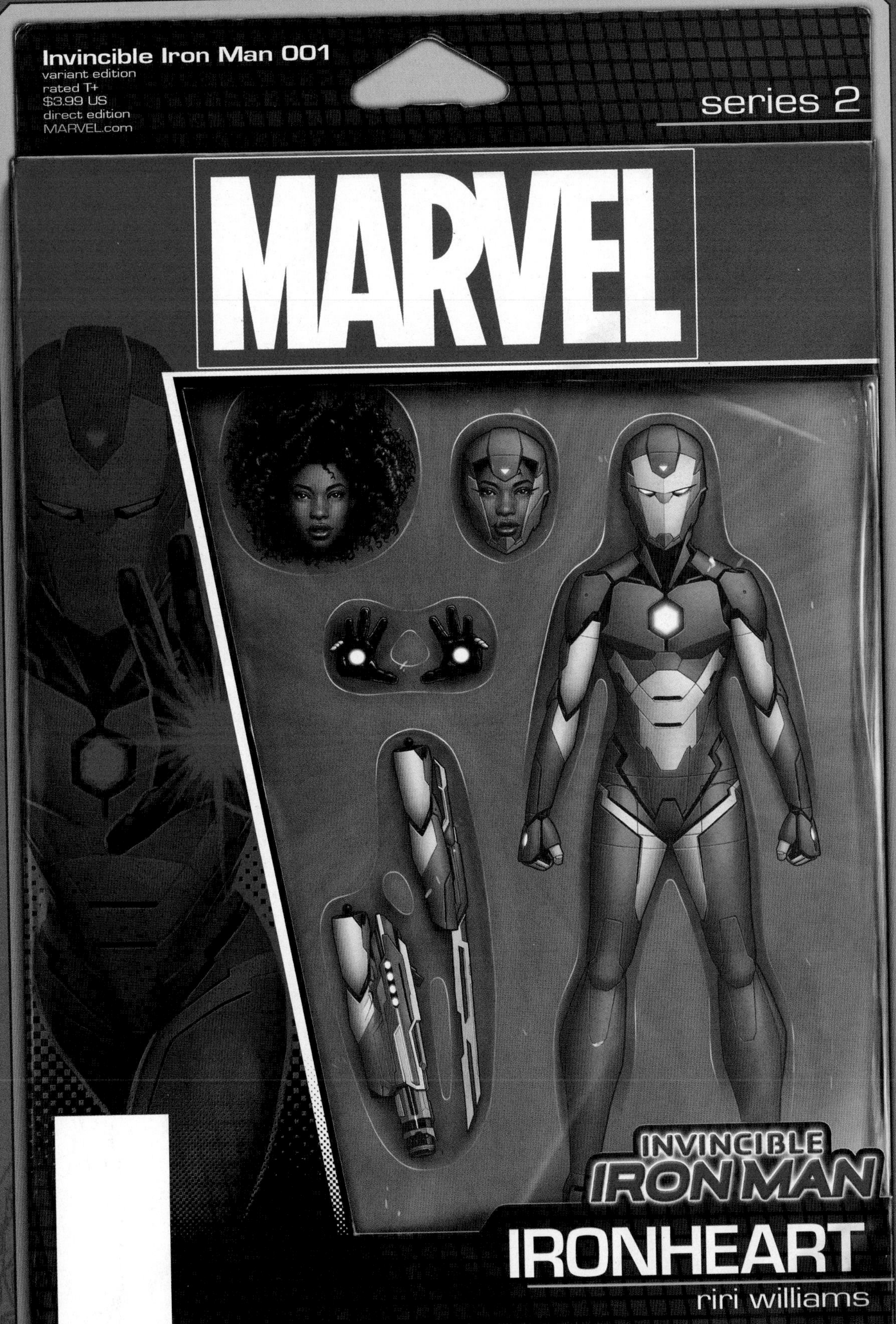

Invincible Iron Man 001
variant edition
rated T+
$3.99 US
direct edition
MARVEL.com
series 2
MARVEL
INVINCIBLE
IRON MAN
IRONHEART
riri williams

JOHN TYLER CHRISTOPHER
1 ACTION FIGURE VARIANT

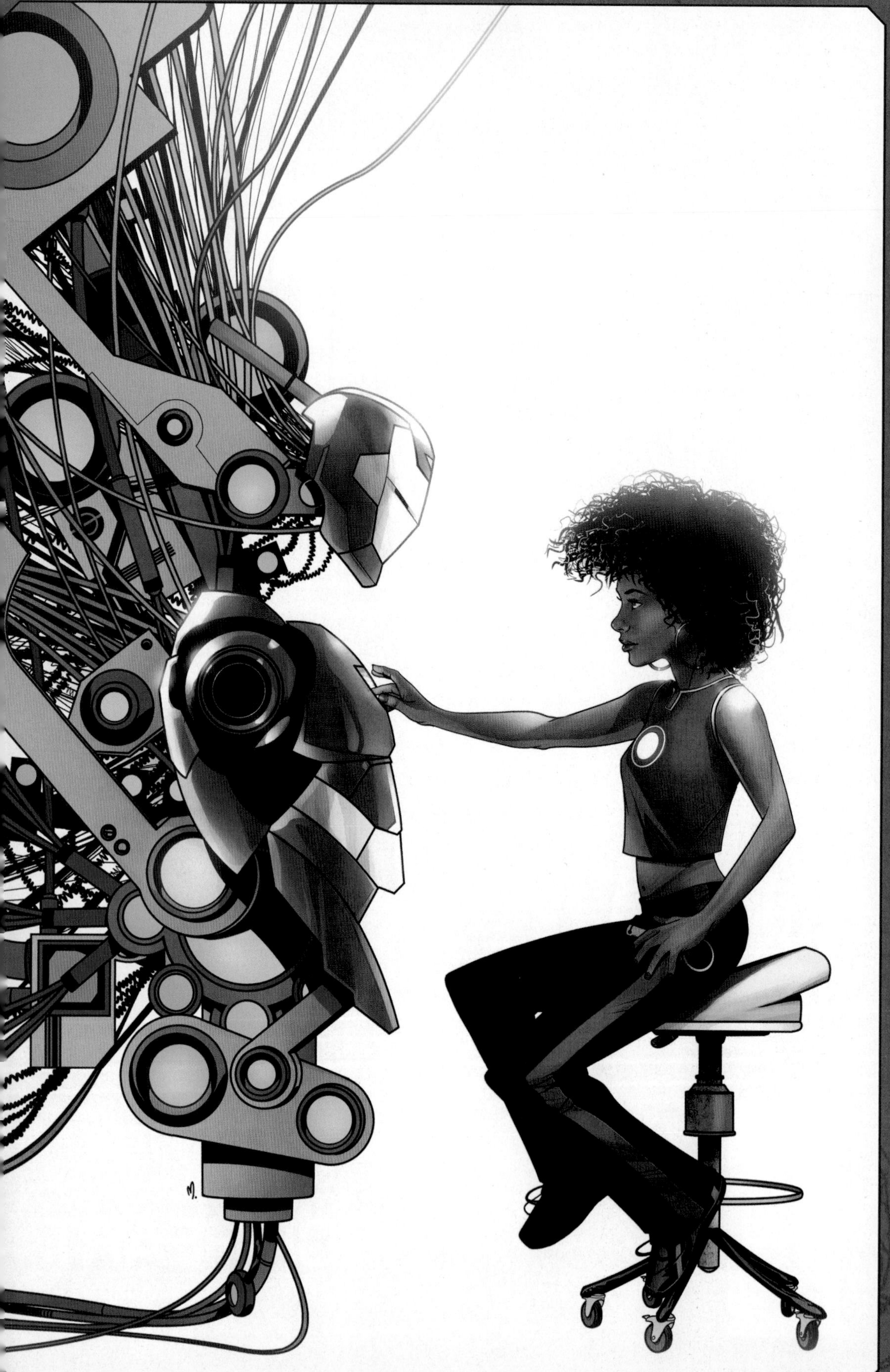

MIKE McKONE & JASON KEITH
1 STEAM VARIANT

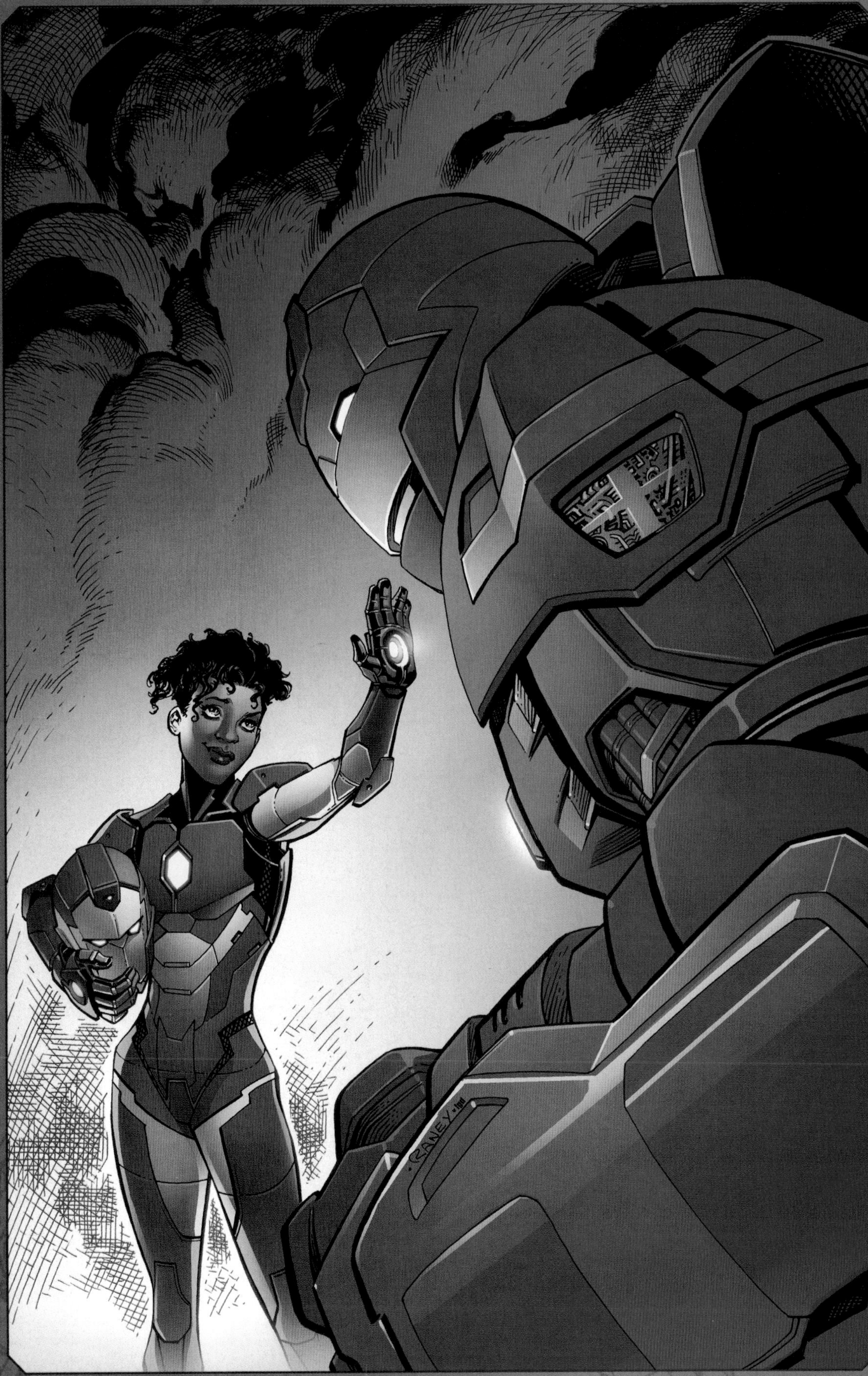
RANEY

TOM RANEY & FRANK D'ARMATA
1 DIVIDED WE STAND VARIANT

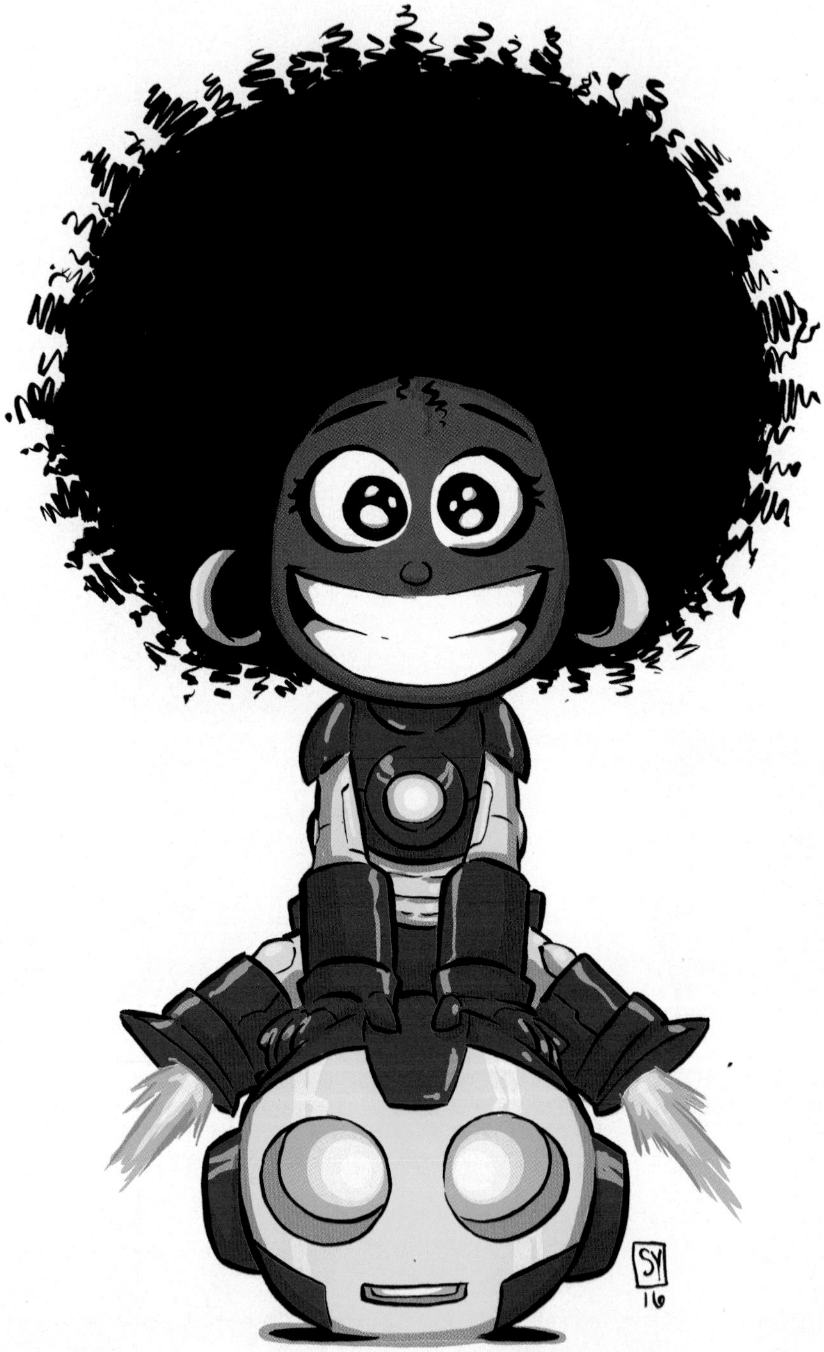
SY
16

SKOTTIE YOUNG
1 VARIANT

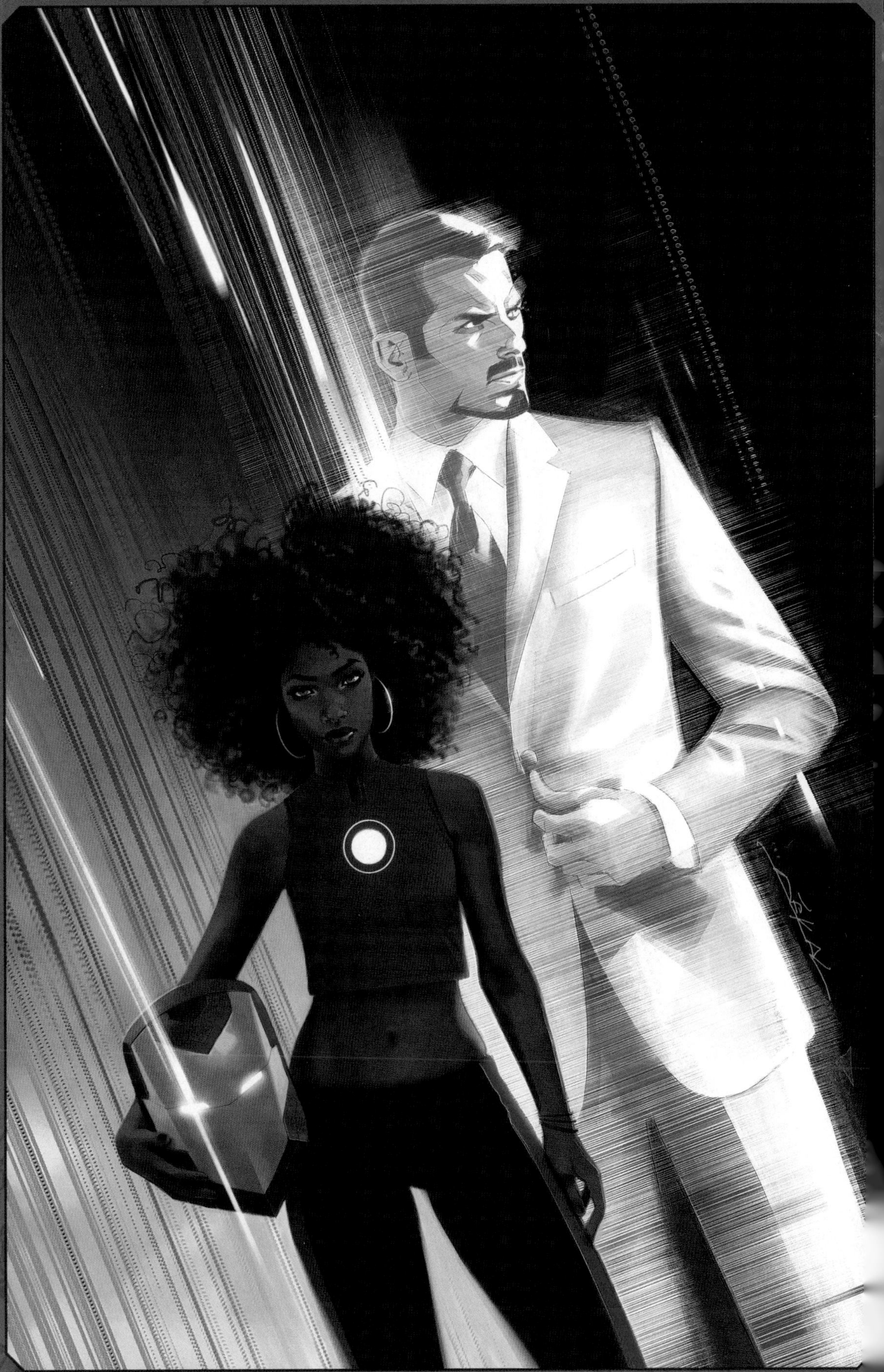

JEFF DEKAL

1 VARIANT

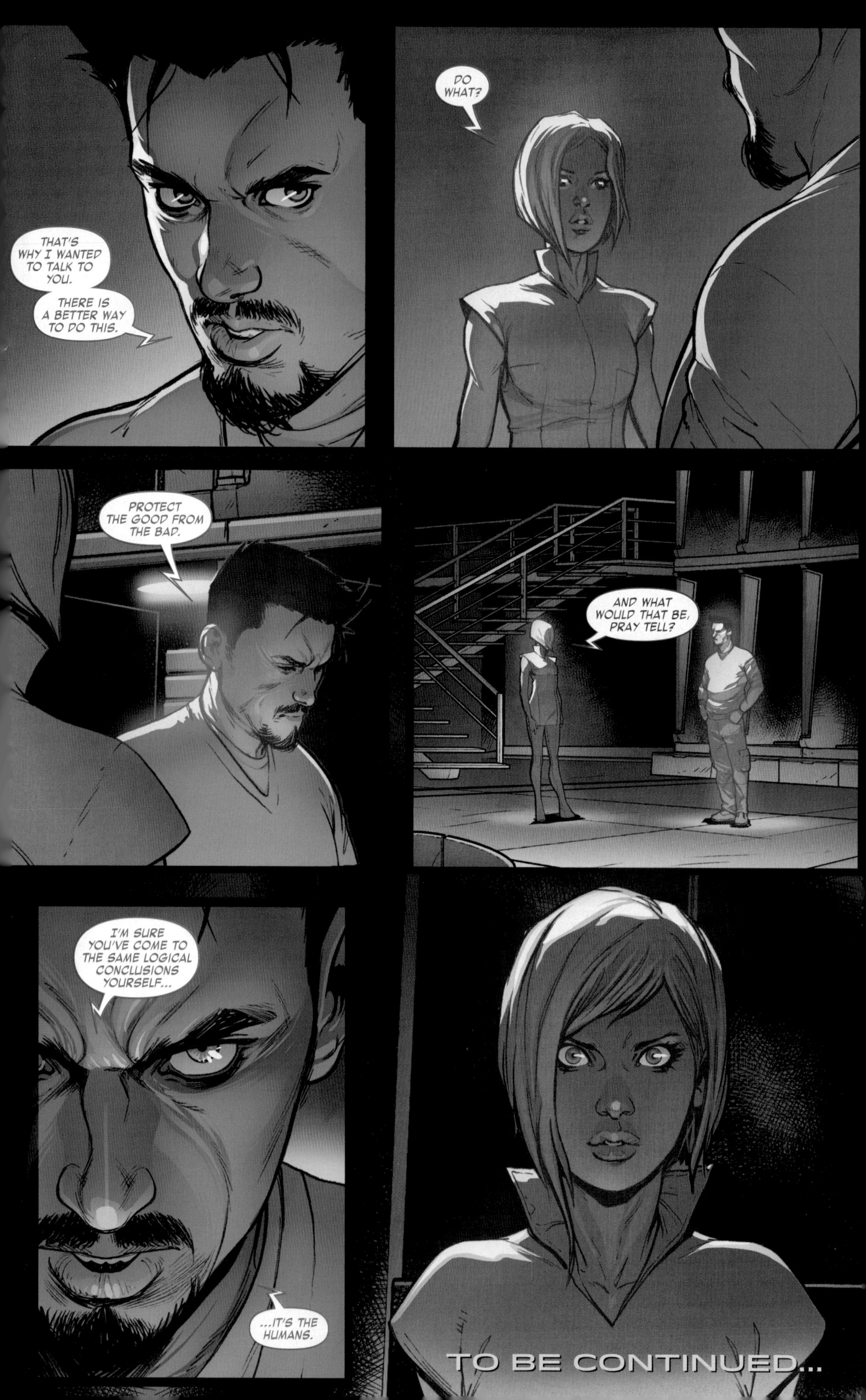
THAT'S WHY I WANTED TO TALK TO YOU.
THERE IS A BETTER WAY TO DO THIS.
DO WHAT?
PROTECT THE GOOD FROM THE BAD.
AND WHAT WOULD THAT BE, PRAY TELL?
I'M SURE YOU'VE COME TO THE SAME LOGICAL CONCLUSIONS YOURSELF...
...IT'S THE HUMANS.
TO BE CONTINUED...

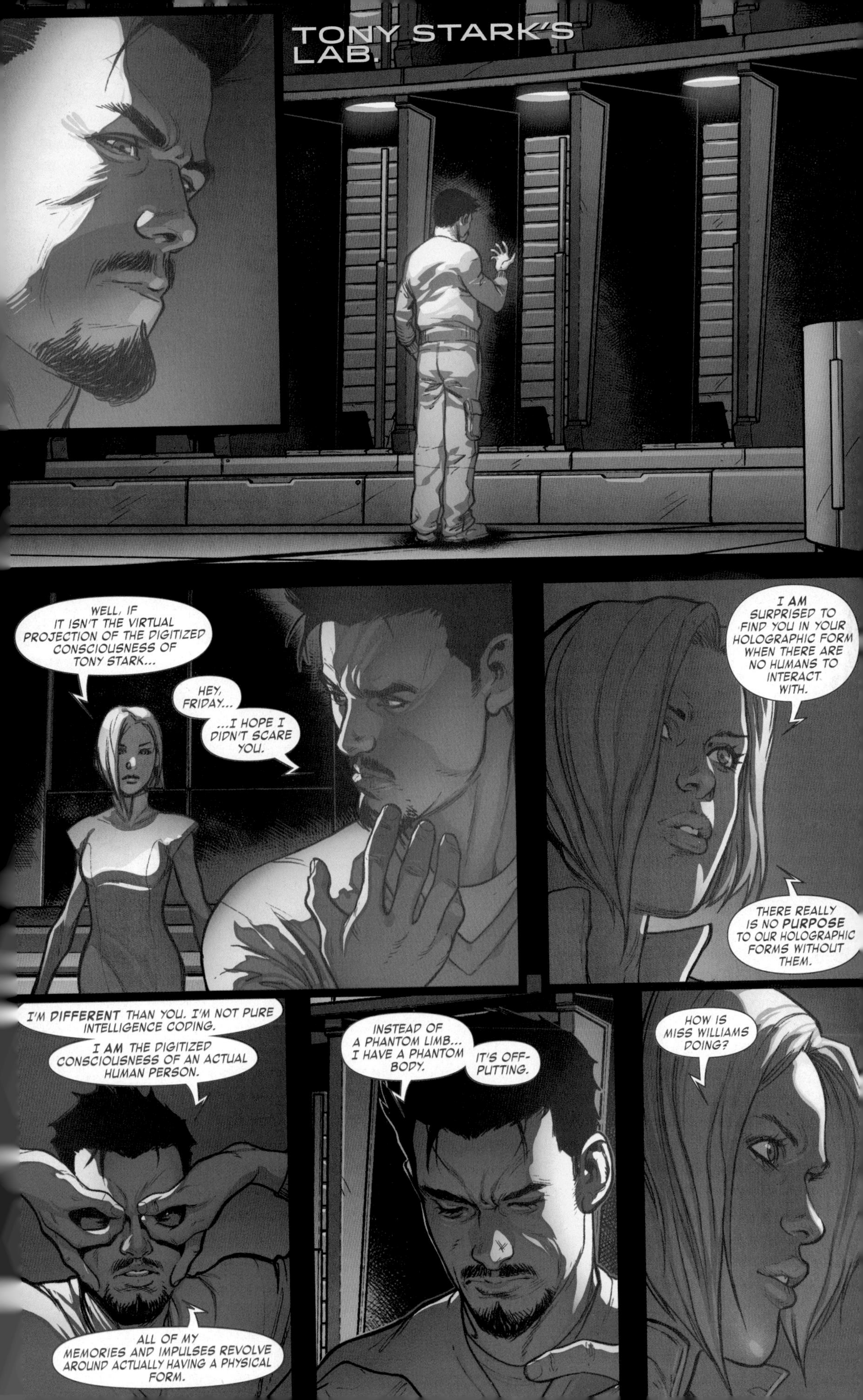
TONY STARK'S LAB.
WELL, IF IT ISN'T THE VIRTUAL PROJECTION OF THE DIGITIZED CONSCIOUSNESS OF TONY STARK...
HEY, FRIDAY...
...I HOPE I DIDN'T SCARE YOU.
I AM SURPRISED TO FIND YOU IN YOUR HOLOGRAPHIC FORM WHEN THERE ARE NO HUMANS TO INTERACT WITH.
THERE REALLY IS NO PURPOSE TO OUR HOLOGRAPHIC FORMS WITHOUT THEM.
I'M DIFFERENT THAN YOU. I'M NOT PURE INTELLIGENCE CODING.
I AM THE DIGITIZED CONSCIOUSNESS OF AN ACTUAL HUMAN PERSON.
ALL OF MY MEMORIES AND IMPULSES REVOLVE AROUND ACTUALLY HAVING A PHYSICAL FORM.
INSTEAD OF A PHANTOM LIMB... I HAVE A PHANTOM BODY.
IT'S OFF-PUTTING.
HOW IS MISS WILLIAMS DOING?

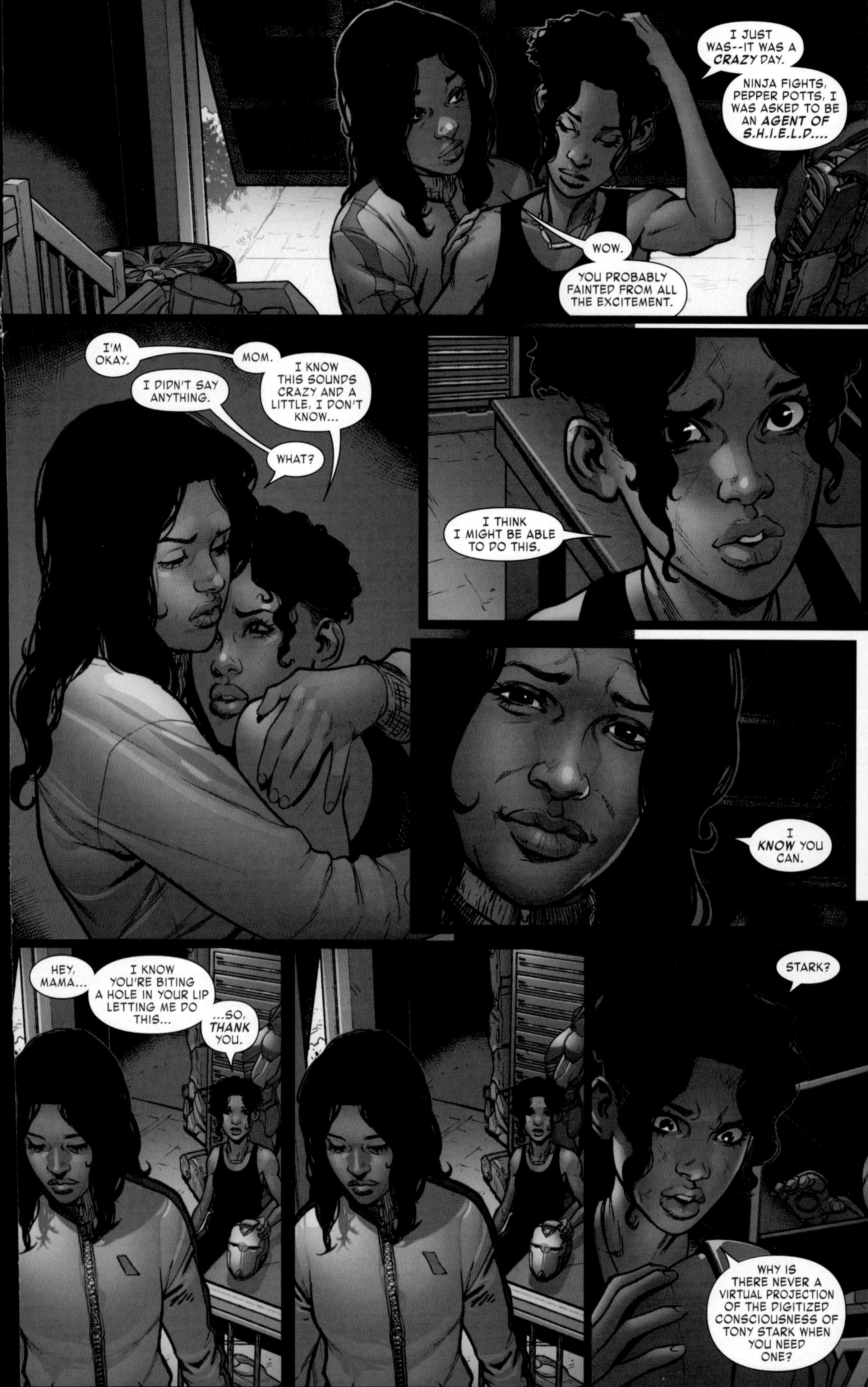

I JUST WAS--IT WAS A CRAZY DAY.
NINJA FIGHTS, PEPPER POTTS, I WAS ASKED TO BE AN AGENT OF S.H.I.E.L.D....
WOW.
YOU PROBABLY FAINTED FROM ALL THE EXCITEMENT.
I'M OKAY.
MOM.
I DIDN'T SAY ANYTHING.
I KNOW THIS SOUNDS CRAZY AND A LITTLE, I DON'T KNOW...
WHAT?
I THINK I MIGHT BE ABLE TO DO THIS.
I KNOW YOU CAN.
HEY, MAMA...
I KNOW YOU'RE BITING A HOLE IN YOUR LIP LETTING ME DO THIS...
...SO, THANK YOU.
STARK?
WHY IS THERE NEVER A VIRTUAL PROJECTION OF THE DIGITIZED CONSCIOUSNESS OF TONY STARK WHEN YOU NEED ONE?

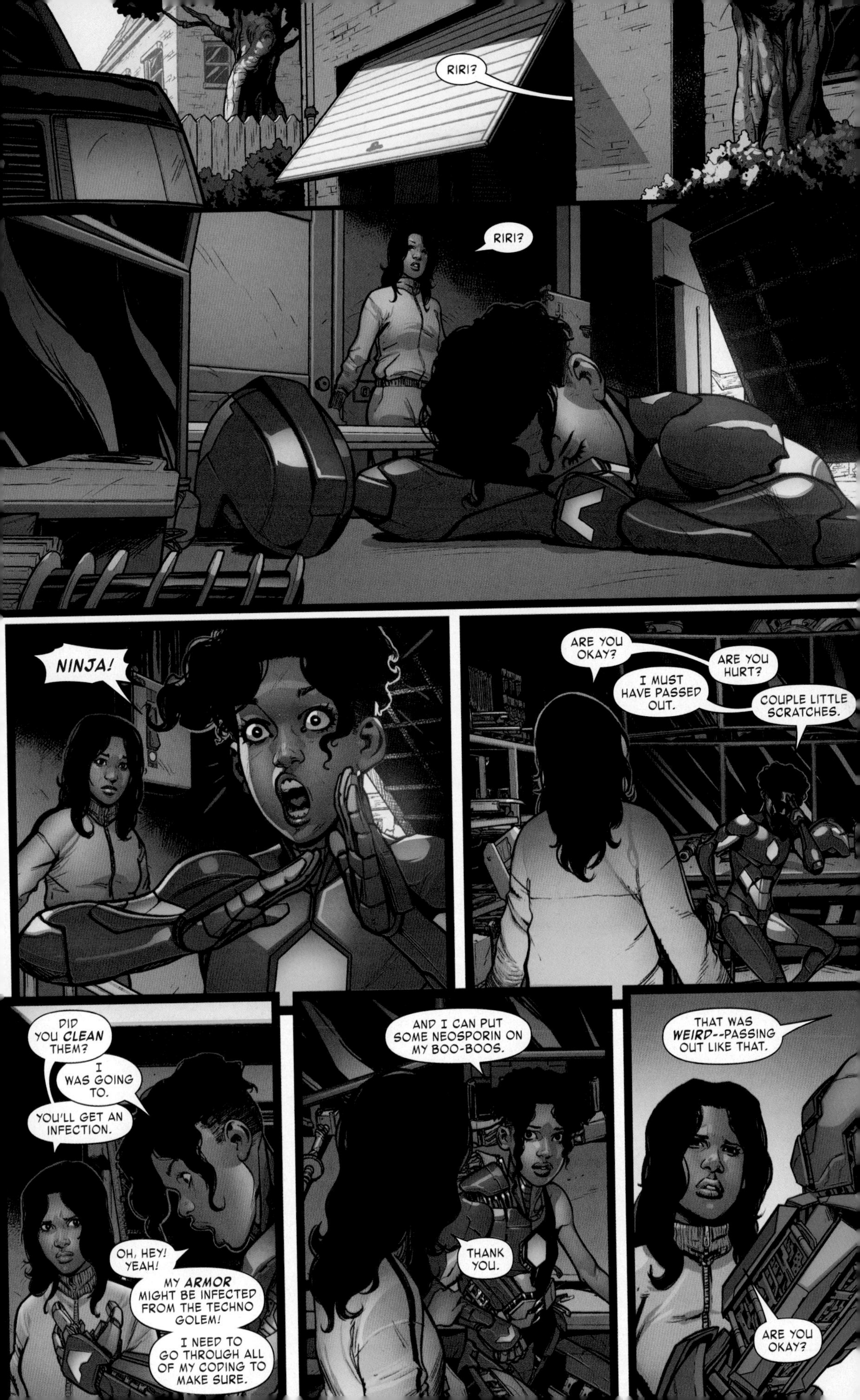
RIRI?
RIRI?
NINJA!
ARE YOU OKAY?
ARE YOU HURT?
I MUST HAVE PASSED OUT.
COUPLE LITTLE SCRATCHES.
DID YOU CLEAN THEM?
I WAS GOING TO.
YOU'LL GET AN INFECTION.
OH, HEY! YEAH!
MY ARMOR MIGHT BE INFECTED FROM THE TECHNO GOLEM!
I NEED TO GO THROUGH ALL OF MY CODING TO MAKE SURE.
AND I CAN PUT SOME NEOSPORIN ON MY BOO-BOOS.
THANK YOU.
THAT WAS WEIRD--PASSING OUT LIKE THAT.
ARE YOU OKAY?

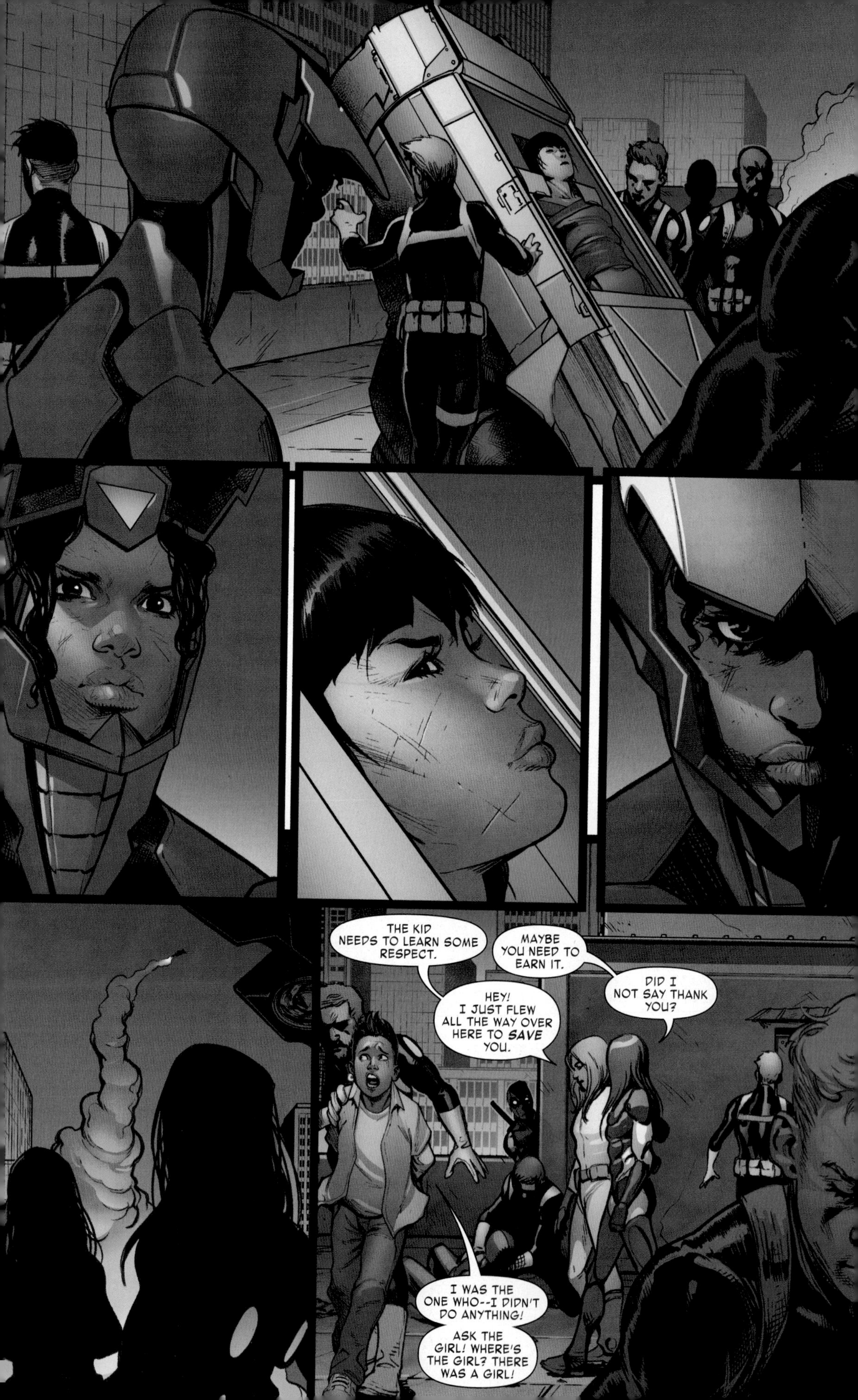
THE KID NEEDS TO LEARN SOME RESPECT.
HEY! I JUST FLEW ALL THE WAY OVER HERE TO SAVE YOU.
MAYBE YOU NEED TO EARN IT.
DID I NOT SAY THANK YOU?
I WAS THE ONE WHO--I DIDN'T DO ANYTHING!
ASK THE GIRL! WHERE'S THE GIRL? THERE WAS A GIRL!

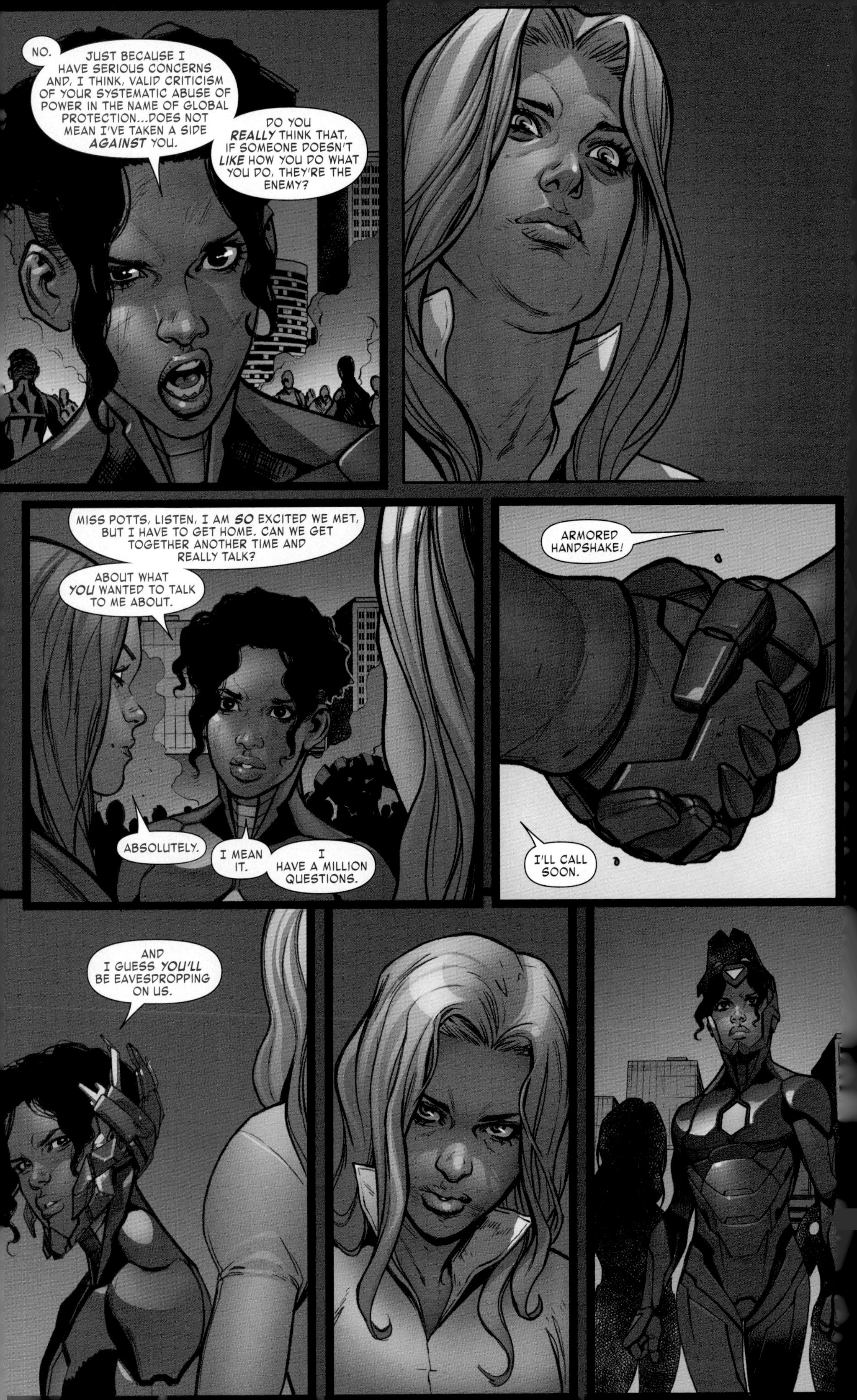
NO.
JUST BECAUSE I HAVE SERIOUS CONCERNS AND, I THINK, VALID CRITICISM OF YOUR SYSTEMATIC ABUSE OF POWER IN THE NAME OF GLOBAL PROTECTION...DOES NOT MEAN I'VE TAKEN A SIDE AGAINST YOU.
DO YOU REALLY THINK THAT, IF SOMEONE DOESN'T LIKE HOW YOU DO WHAT YOU DO, THEY'RE THE ENEMY?
MISS POTTS, LISTEN, I AM SO EXCITED WE MET, BUT I HAVE TO GET HOME. CAN WE GET TOGETHER ANOTHER TIME AND REALLY TALK?
ABOUT WHAT YOU WANTED TO TALK TO ME ABOUT.
ABSOLUTELY.
I MEAN IT.
I HAVE A MILLION QUESTIONS.
ARMORED HANDSHAKE!
I'LL CALL SOON.
AND I GUESS YOU'LL BE EAVESDROPPING ON US.

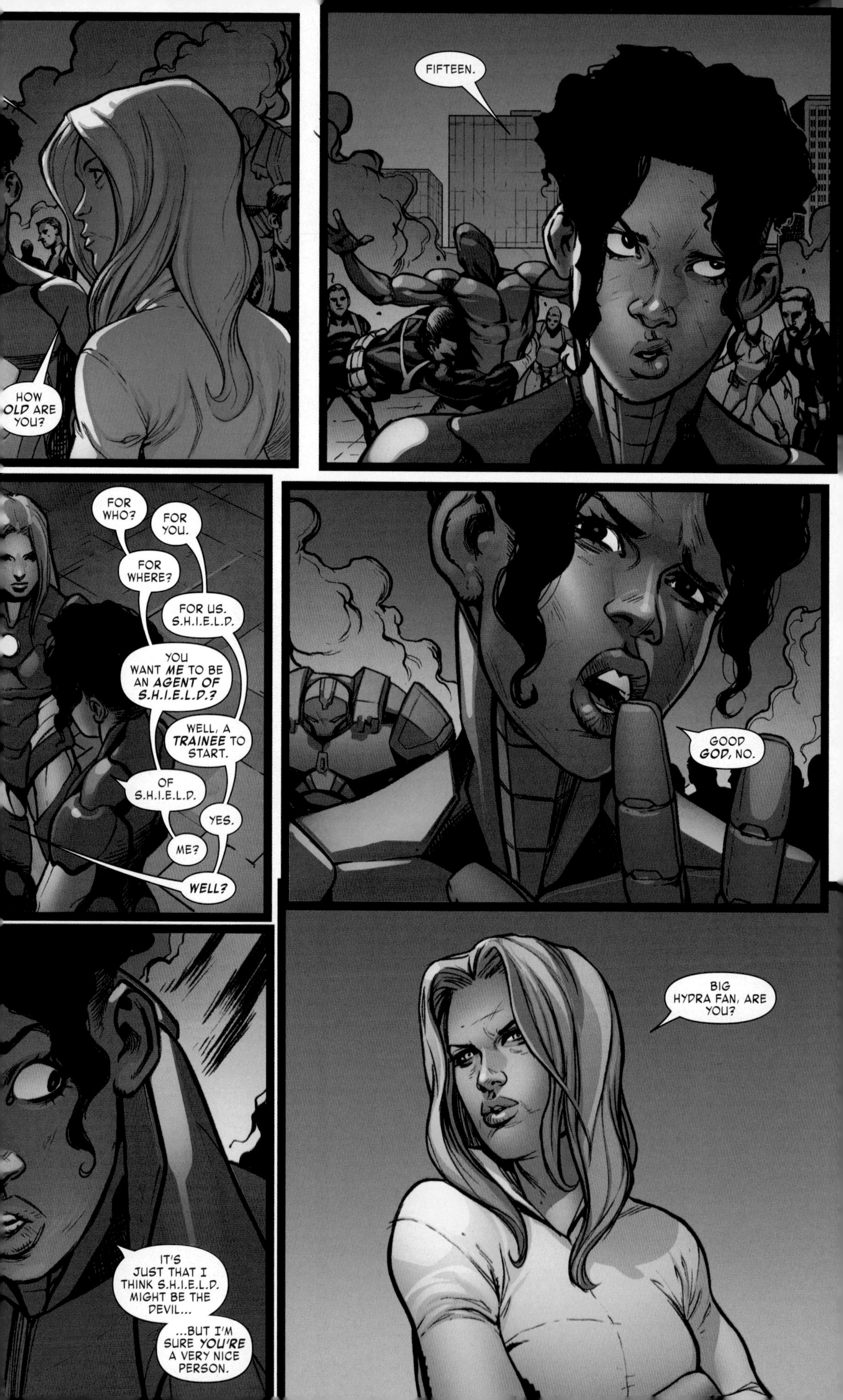
HOW OLD ARE YOU?
FIFTEEN.
FOR WHO?
FOR YOU.
FOR WHERE?
FOR US. S.H.I.E.L.D.
YOU WANT ME TO BE AN AGENT OF S.H.I.E.L.D.?
WELL, A TRAINEE TO START.
OF S.H.I.E.L.D.
YES.
ME?
WELL?
GOOD GOD, NO.
IT'S JUST THAT I THINK S.H.I.E.L.D. MIGHT BE THE DEVIL...
...BUT I'M SURE YOU'RE A VERY NICE PERSON.
BIG HYDRA FAN, ARE YOU?

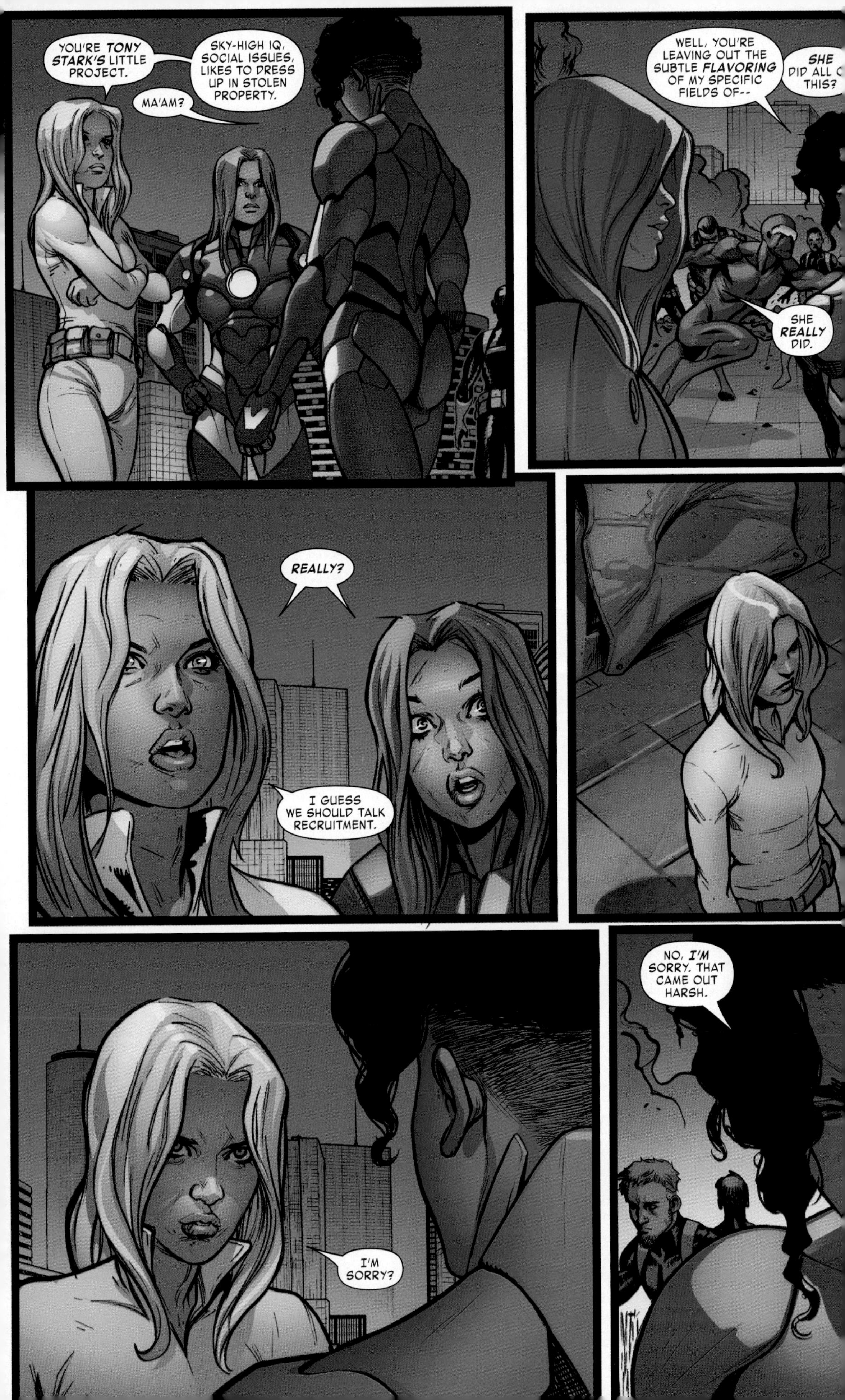
YOU'RE TONY STARK'S LITTLE PROJECT.
SKY-HIGH IQ, SOCIAL ISSUES, LIKES TO DRESS UP IN STOLEN PROPERTY.
MA'AM?
WELL, YOU'RE LEAVING OUT THE SUBTLE FLAVORING OF MY SPECIFIC FIELDS OF--
SHE DID ALL OF THIS?
SHE REALLY DID.
REALLY?
I GUESS WE SHOULD TALK RECRUITMENT.
I'M SORRY?
NO, I'M SORRY. THAT CAME OUT HARSH.

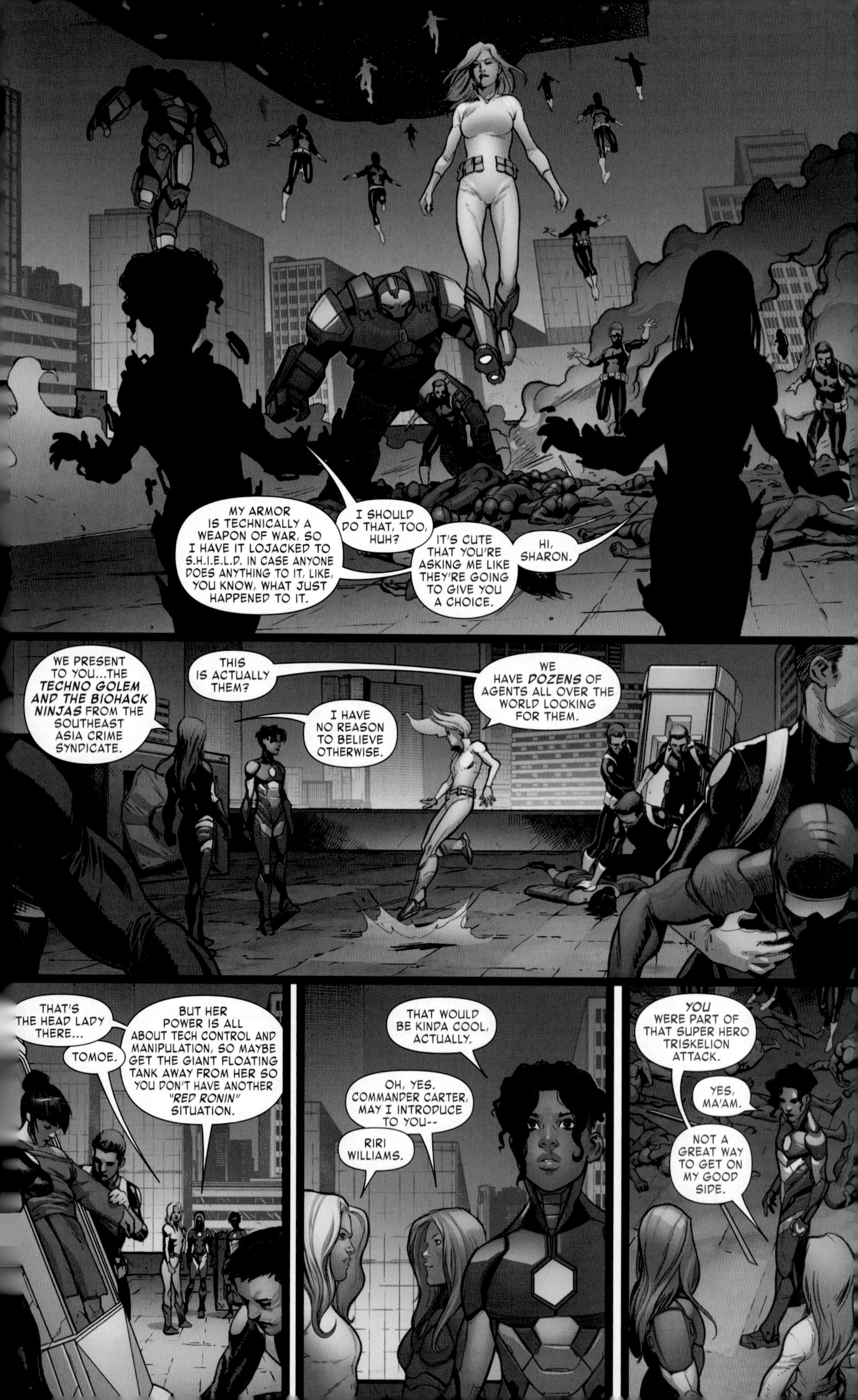
MY ARMOR IS TECHNICALLY A WEAPON OF WAR, SO I HAVE IT LOJACKED TO S.H.I.E.L.D. IN CASE ANYONE DOES ANYTHING TO IT, LIKE, YOU KNOW, WHAT JUST HAPPENED TO IT.
I SHOULD DO THAT, TOO, HUH?
IT'S CUTE THAT YOU'RE ASKING ME LIKE THEY'RE GOING TO GIVE YOU A CHOICE.
HI, SHARON.
WE PRESENT TO YOU...THE TECHNO GOLEM AND THE BIOHACK NINJAS FROM THE SOUTHEAST ASIA CRIME SYNDICATE.
THIS IS ACTUALLY THEM?
I HAVE NO REASON TO BELIEVE OTHERWISE.
WE HAVE DOZENS OF AGENTS ALL OVER THE WORLD LOOKING FOR THEM.
THAT'S THE HEAD LADY THERE...
TOMOE.
BUT HER POWER IS ALL ABOUT TECH CONTROL AND MANIPULATION, SO MAYBE GET THE GIANT FLOATING TANK AWAY FROM HER SO YOU DON'T HAVE ANOTHER "RED RONIN" SITUATION.
THAT WOULD BE KINDA COOL, ACTUALLY.
OH, YES. COMMANDER CARTER, MAY I INTRODUCE TO YOU--
RIRI WILLIAMS.
YOU WERE PART OF THAT SUPER HERO TRISKELION ATTACK.
YES, MA'AM.
NOT A GREAT WAY TO GET ON MY GOOD SIDE.

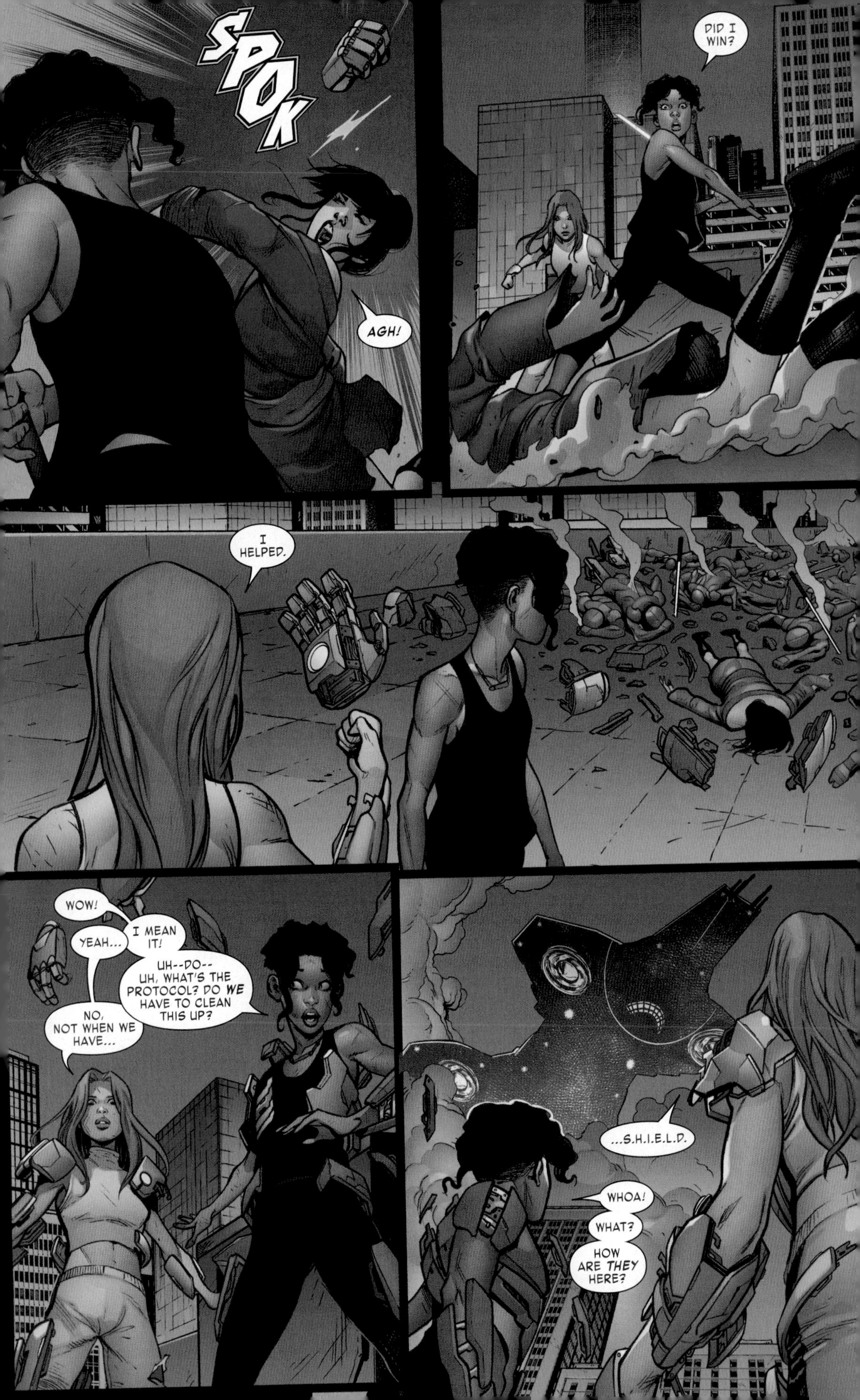
SPOK
AGH!
DID I WIN?
I HELPED.
WOW!
I MEAN IT!
YEAH...
UH--DO-- UH, WHAT'S THE PROTOCOL? DO WE HAVE TO CLEAN THIS UP?
NO, NOT WHEN WE HAVE...
...S.H.I.E.L.D.
WHOA!
WHAT?
HOW ARE THEY HERE?

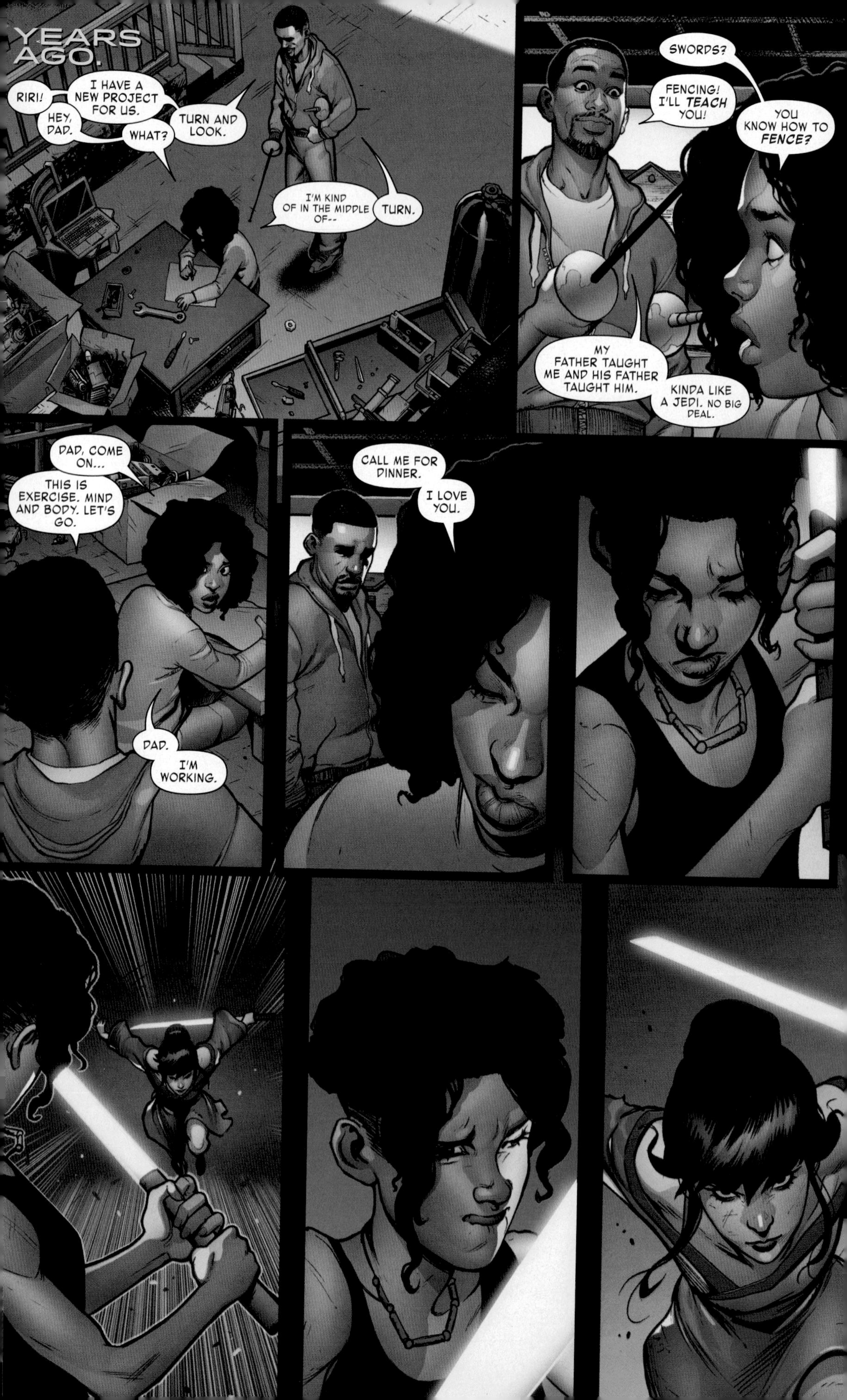
YEARS AGO.
RIRI!
I HAVE A NEW PROJECT FOR US.
HEY, DAD.
WHAT?
TURN AND LOOK.
I'M KIND OF IN THE MIDDLE OF--
TURN.
SWORDS?
FENCING! I'LL TEACH YOU!
YOU KNOW HOW TO FENCE?
MY FATHER TAUGHT ME AND HIS FATHER TAUGHT HIM.
KINDA LIKE A JEDI. NO BIG DEAL.
DAD, COME ON...
THIS IS EXERCISE. MIND AND BODY. LET'S GO.
DAD.
I'M WORKING.
CALL ME FOR DINNER.
I LOVE YOU.

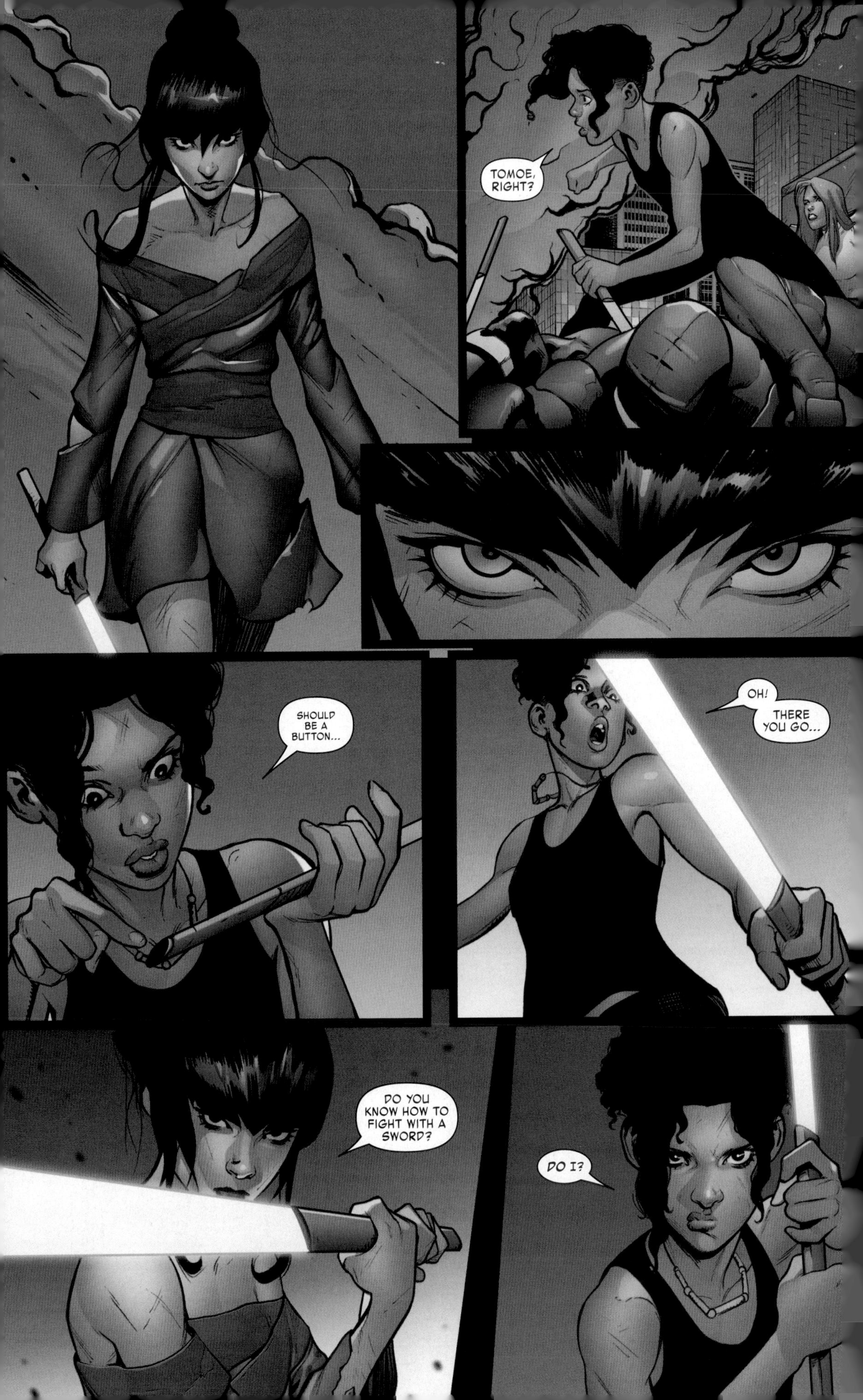
TOMOE, RIGHT?
SHOULD BE A BUTTON...
OH!
THERE YOU GO...
DO YOU KNOW HOW TO FIGHT WITH A SWORD?
DO I?

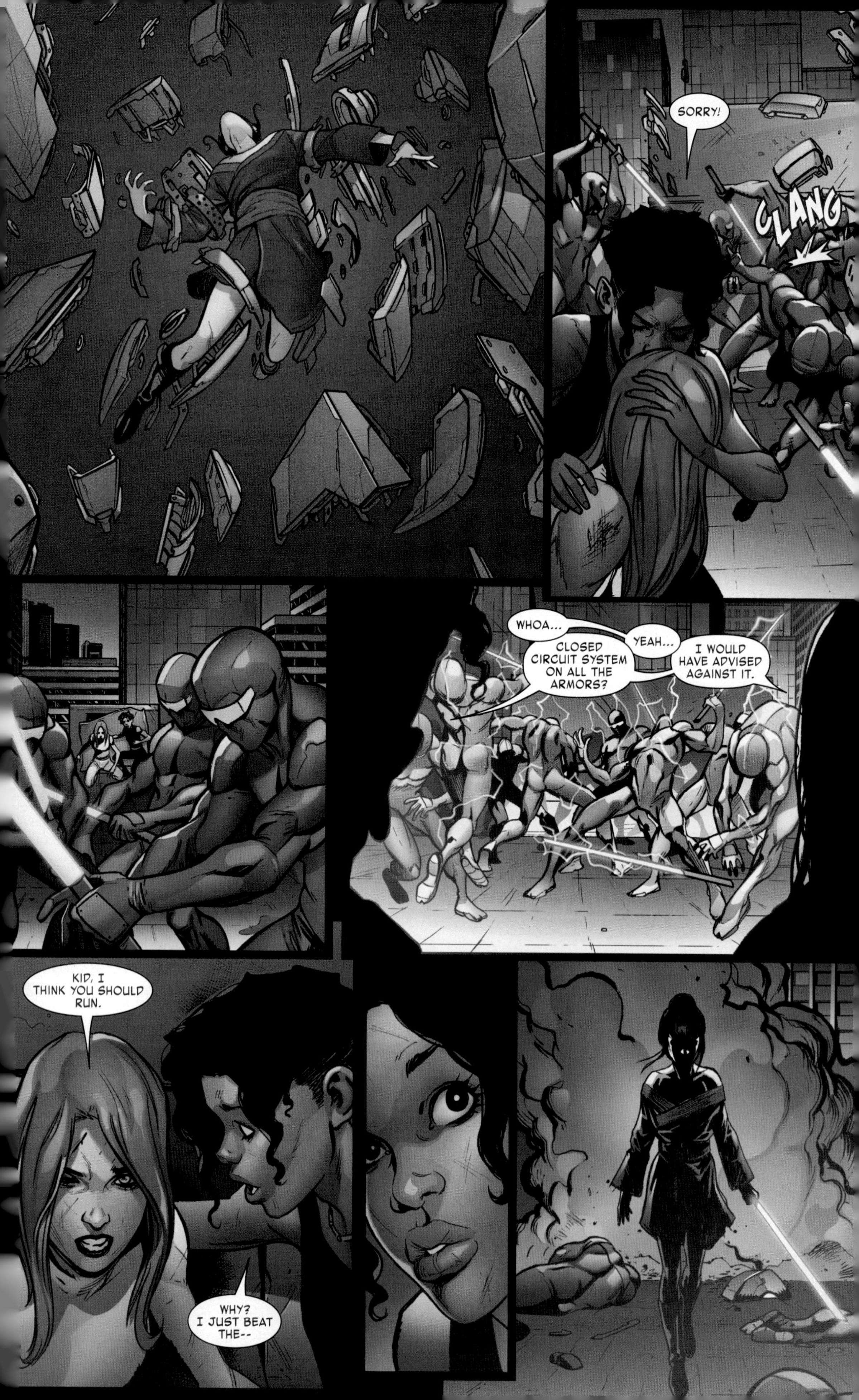
SORRY!
CLANG
WHOA...
YEAH...
CLOSED CIRCUIT SYSTEM ON ALL THE ARMORS?
I WOULD HAVE ADVISED AGAINST IT.
KID, I THINK YOU SHOULD RUN.
WHY? I JUST BEAT THE--

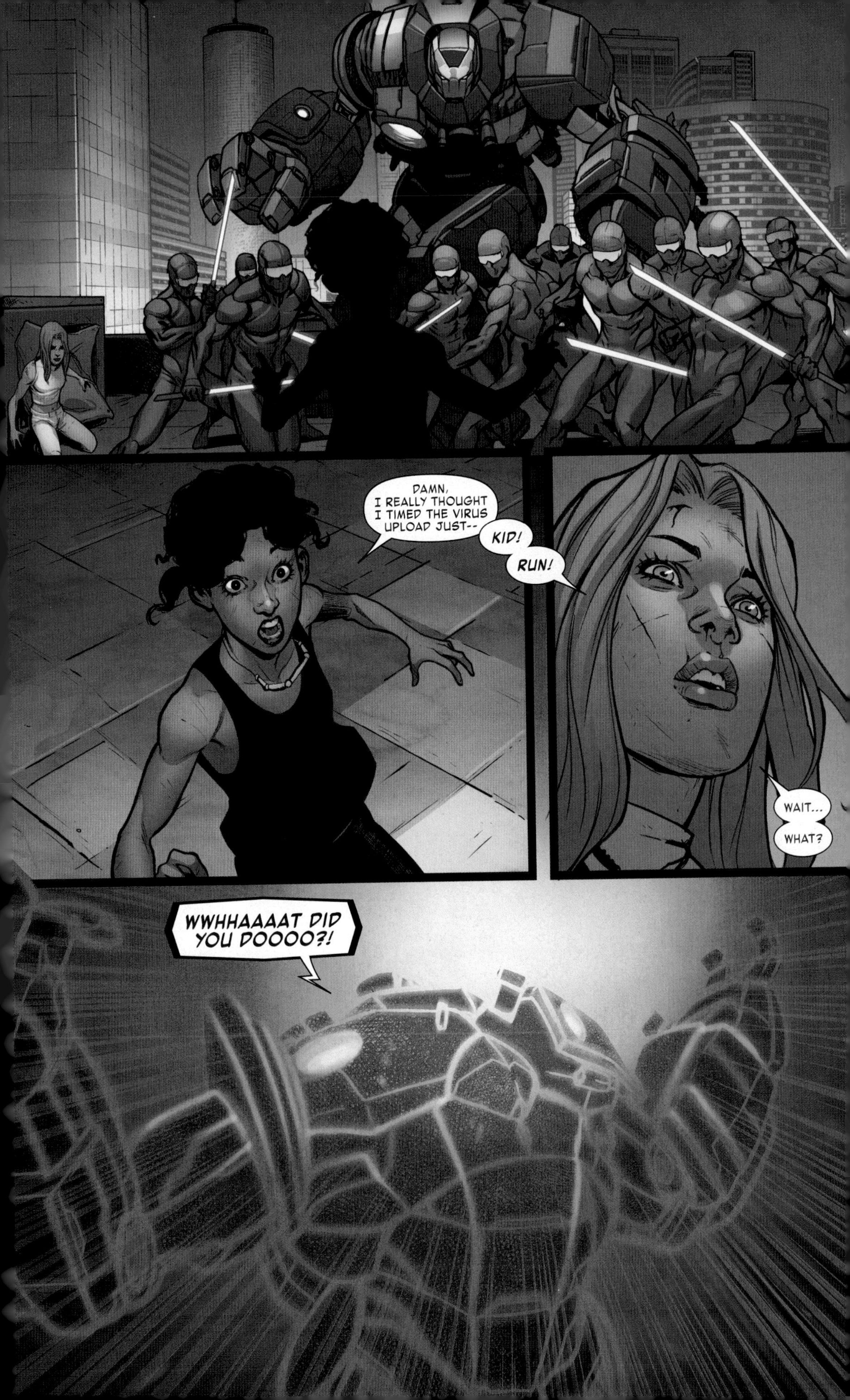
DAMN, I REALLY THOUGHT I TIMED THE VIRUS UPLOAD JUST--
KID!
RUN!
WAIT...
WHAT?
WWHHAAAAT DID YOU DOOOO?!

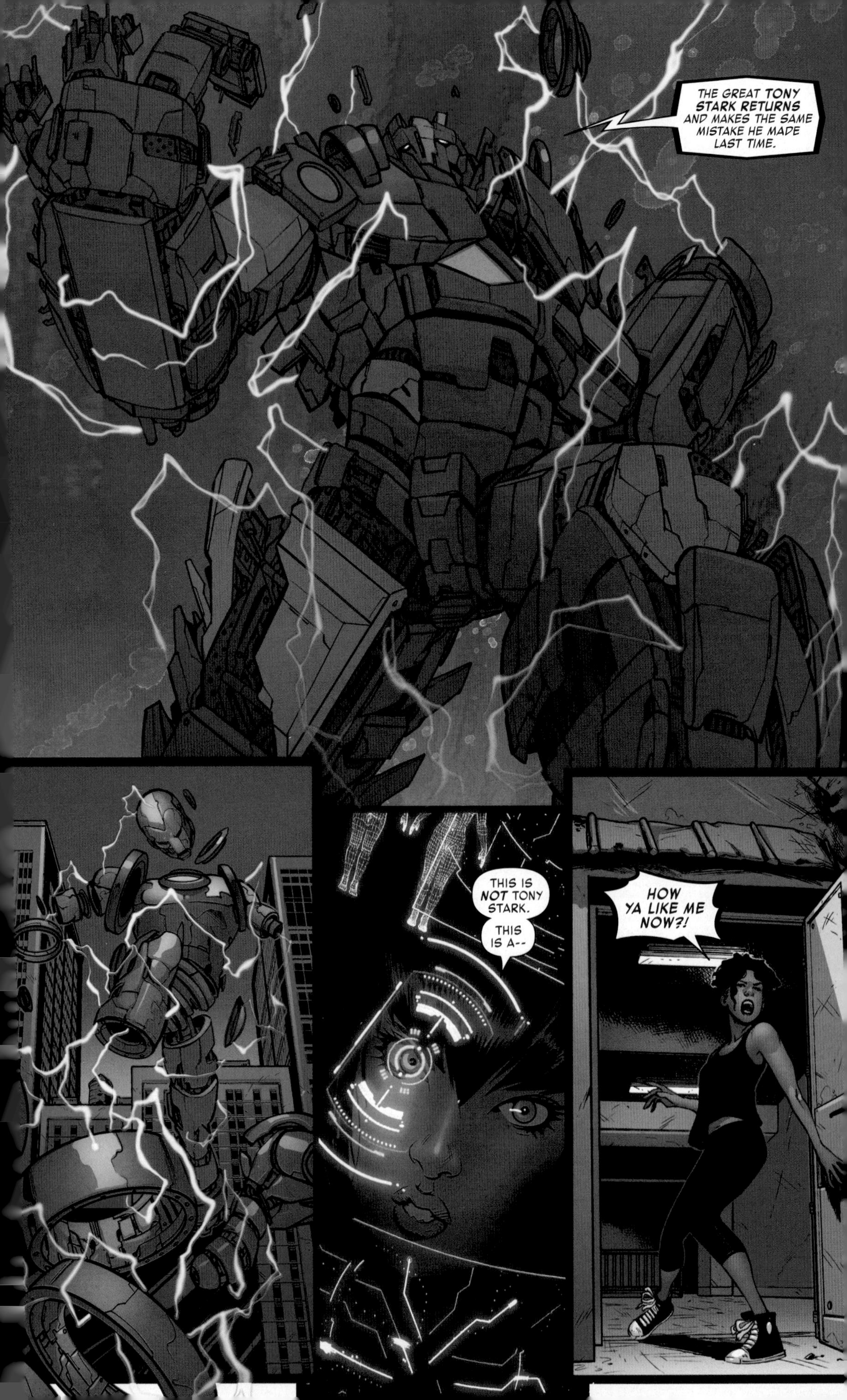
THE GREAT TONY STARK RETURNS AND MAKES THE SAME MISTAKE HE MADE LAST TIME.
THIS IS NOT TONY STARK.
THIS IS A--
HOW YA LIKE ME NOW?!

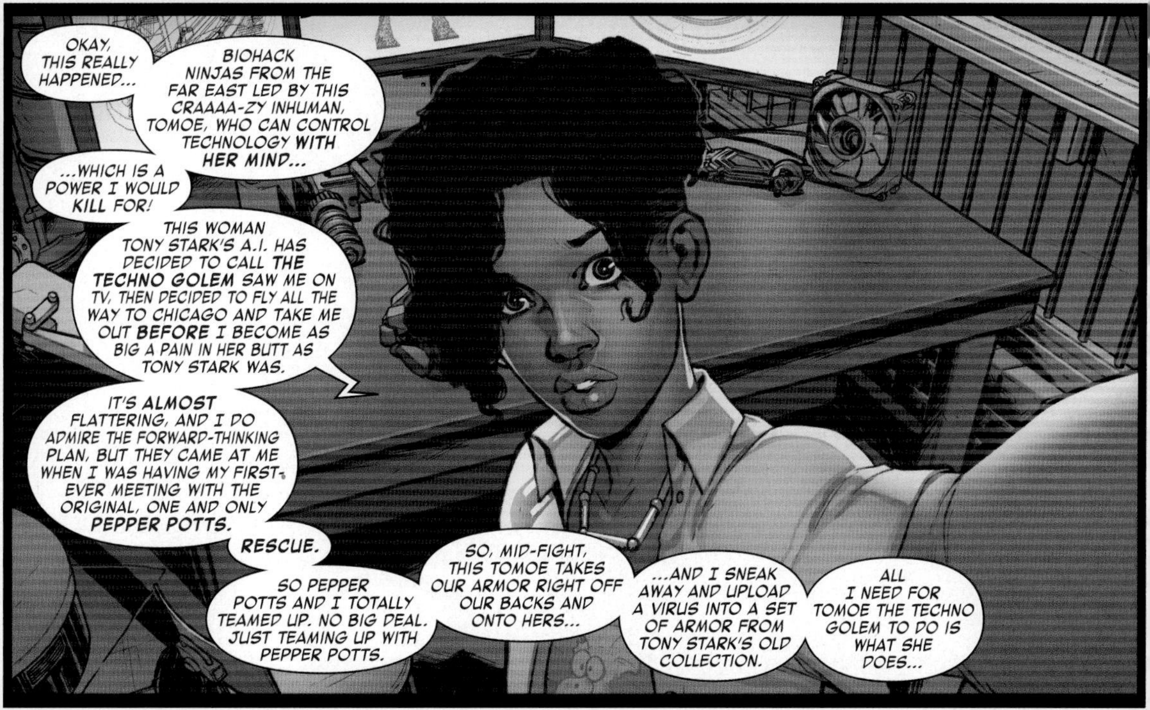
OKAY, THIS REALLY HAPPENED...
BIOHACK NINJAS FROM THE FAR EAST LED BY THIS CRAAAA-ZY INHUMAN, TOMOE, WHO CAN CONTROL TECHNOLOGY **WITH HER MIND...**
...WHICH IS A POWER I WOULD **KILL** FOR!
THIS WOMAN TONY STARK'S A.I. HAS DECIDED TO CALL **THE TECHNO GOLEM** SAW ME ON TV, THEN DECIDED TO FLY ALL THE WAY TO CHICAGO AND TAKE ME OUT **BEFORE** I BECOME AS BIG A PAIN IN HER BUTT AS TONY STARK WAS.
IT'S **ALMOST** FLATTERING, AND I DO ADMIRE THE FORWARD-THINKING PLAN, BUT THEY CAME AT ME WHEN I WAS HAVING MY FIRST-EVER MEETING WITH THE ORIGINAL, ONE AND ONLY **PEPPER POTTS.**
RESCUE.
SO PEPPER POTTS AND I TOTALLY TEAMED UP. NO BIG DEAL. JUST TEAMING UP WITH PEPPER POTTS.
SO, MID-FIGHT, THIS TOMOE TAKES OUR ARMOR RIGHT OFF OUR BACKS AND ONTO HERS...
...AND I SNEAK AWAY AND UPLOAD A VIRUS INTO A SET OF ARMOR FROM TONY STARK'S OLD COLLECTION.
ALL I NEED FOR TOMOE THE TECHNO GOLEM TO DO IS WHAT SHE DOES...

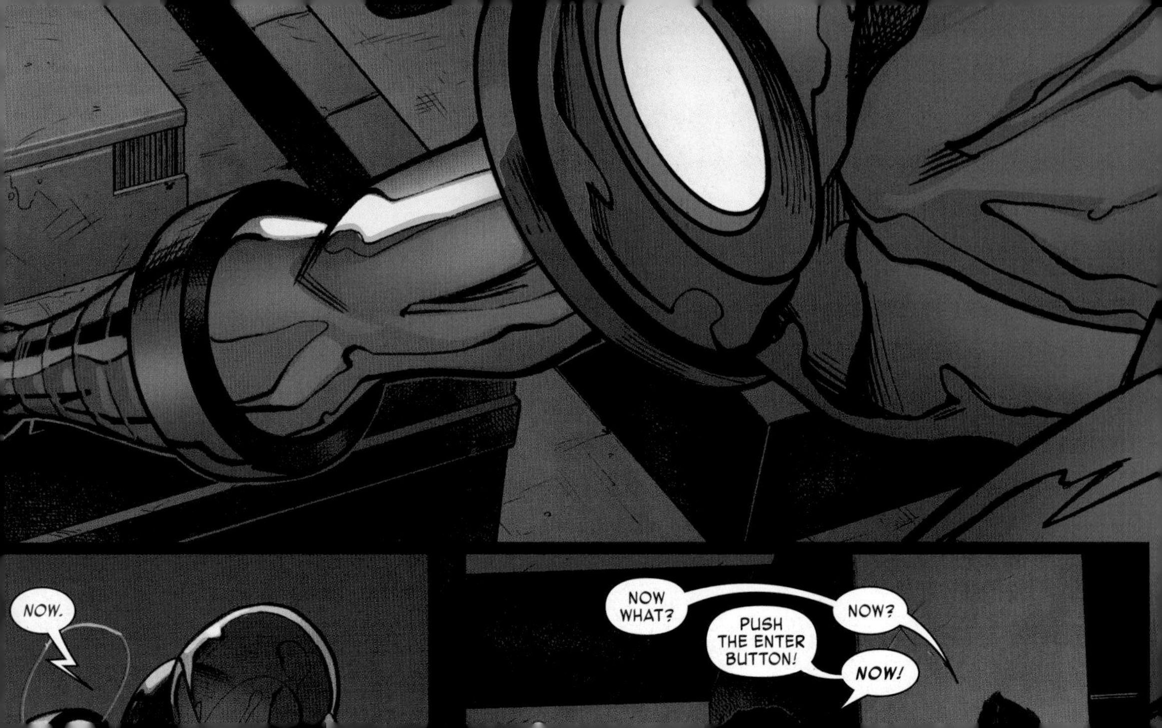
NOW.
NOW WHAT?
NOW?
PUSH THE ENTER BUTTON!
NOW!

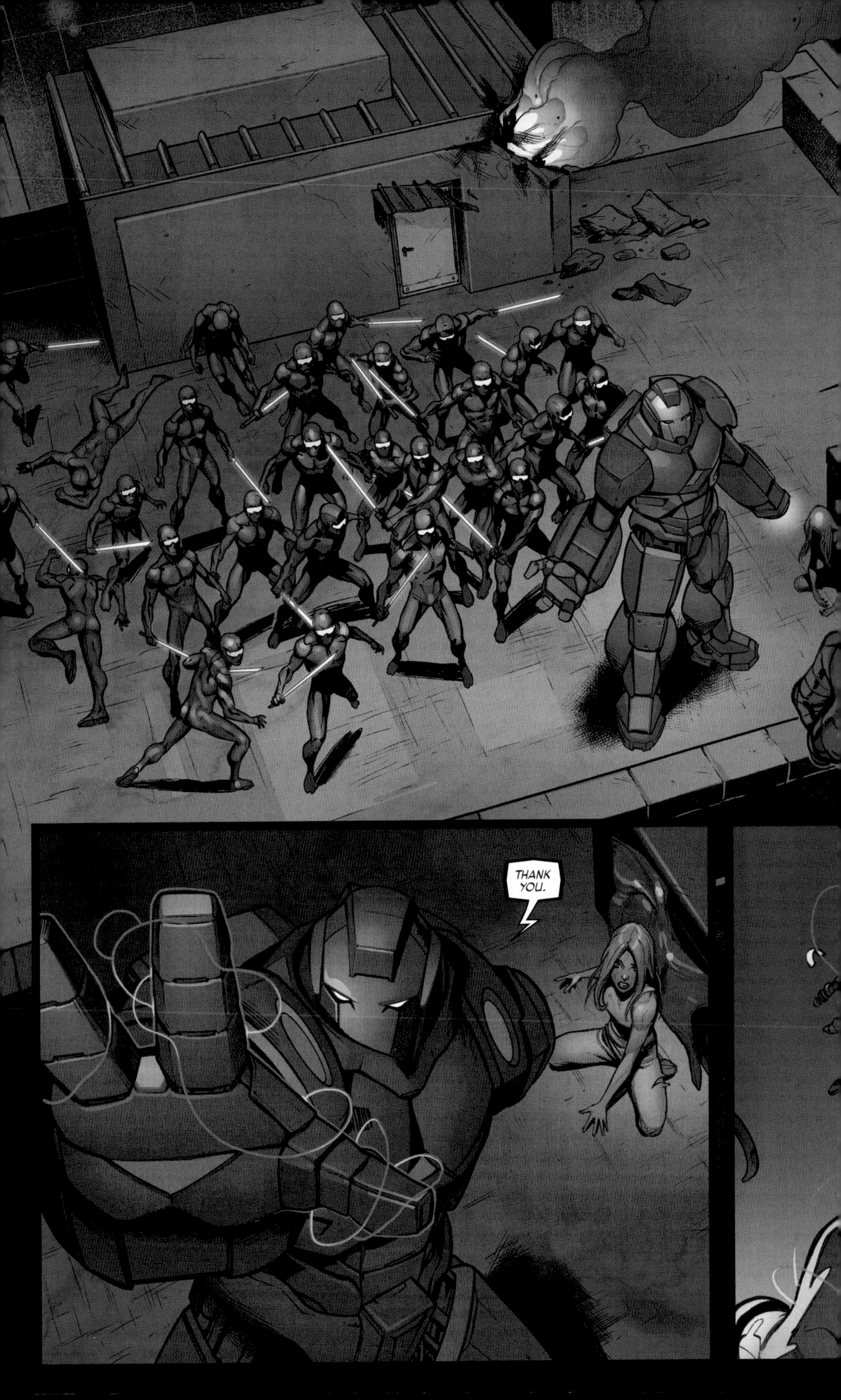
THANK YOU.

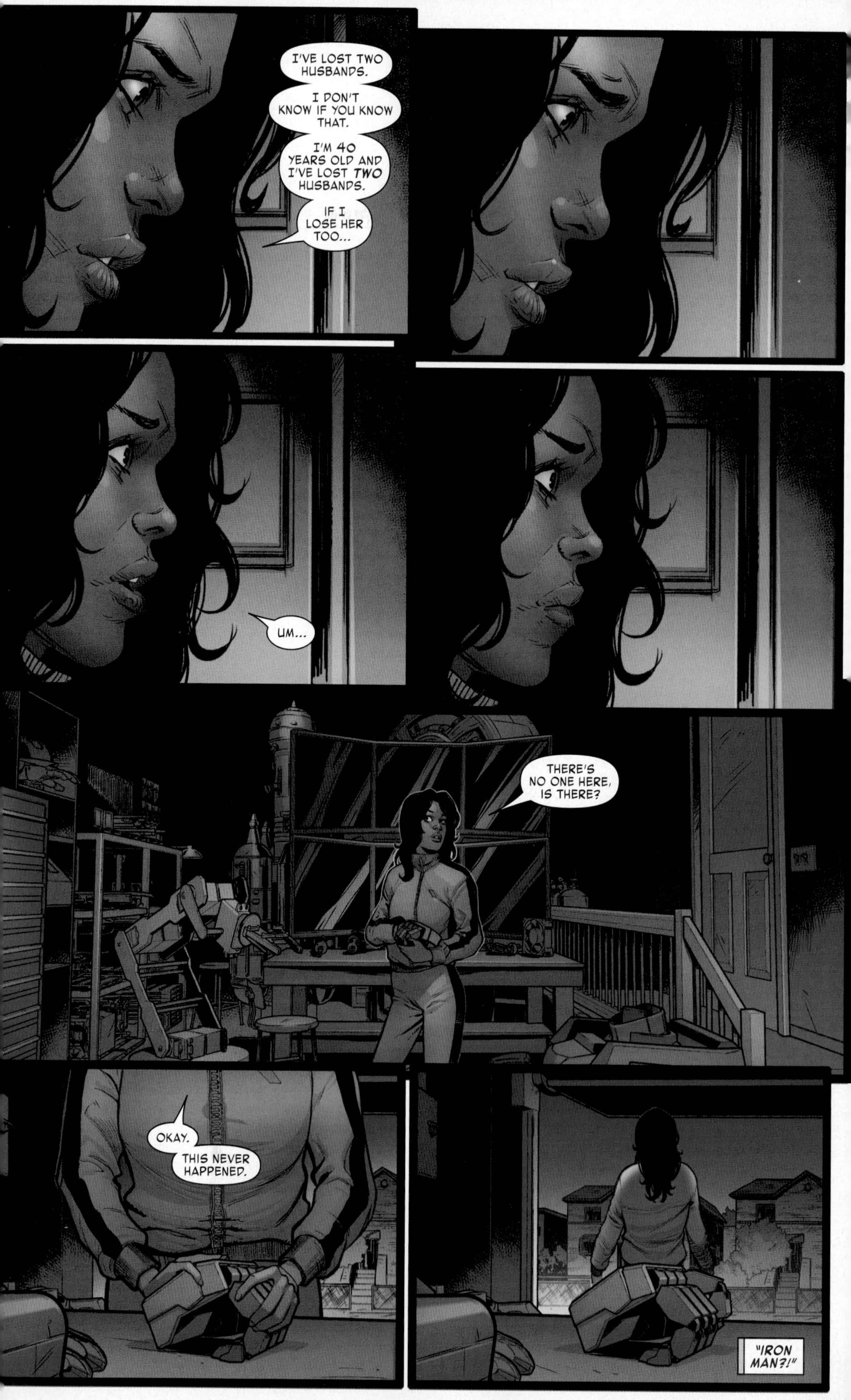
I'VE LOST TWO HUSBANDS.
I DON'T KNOW IF YOU KNOW THAT.
I'M 40 YEARS OLD AND I'VE LOST *TWO* HUSBANDS.
IF I LOSE HER TOO...
UM...
THERE'S NO ONE HERE, IS THERE?
OKAY.
THIS NEVER HAPPENED.
"IRON MAN?!"

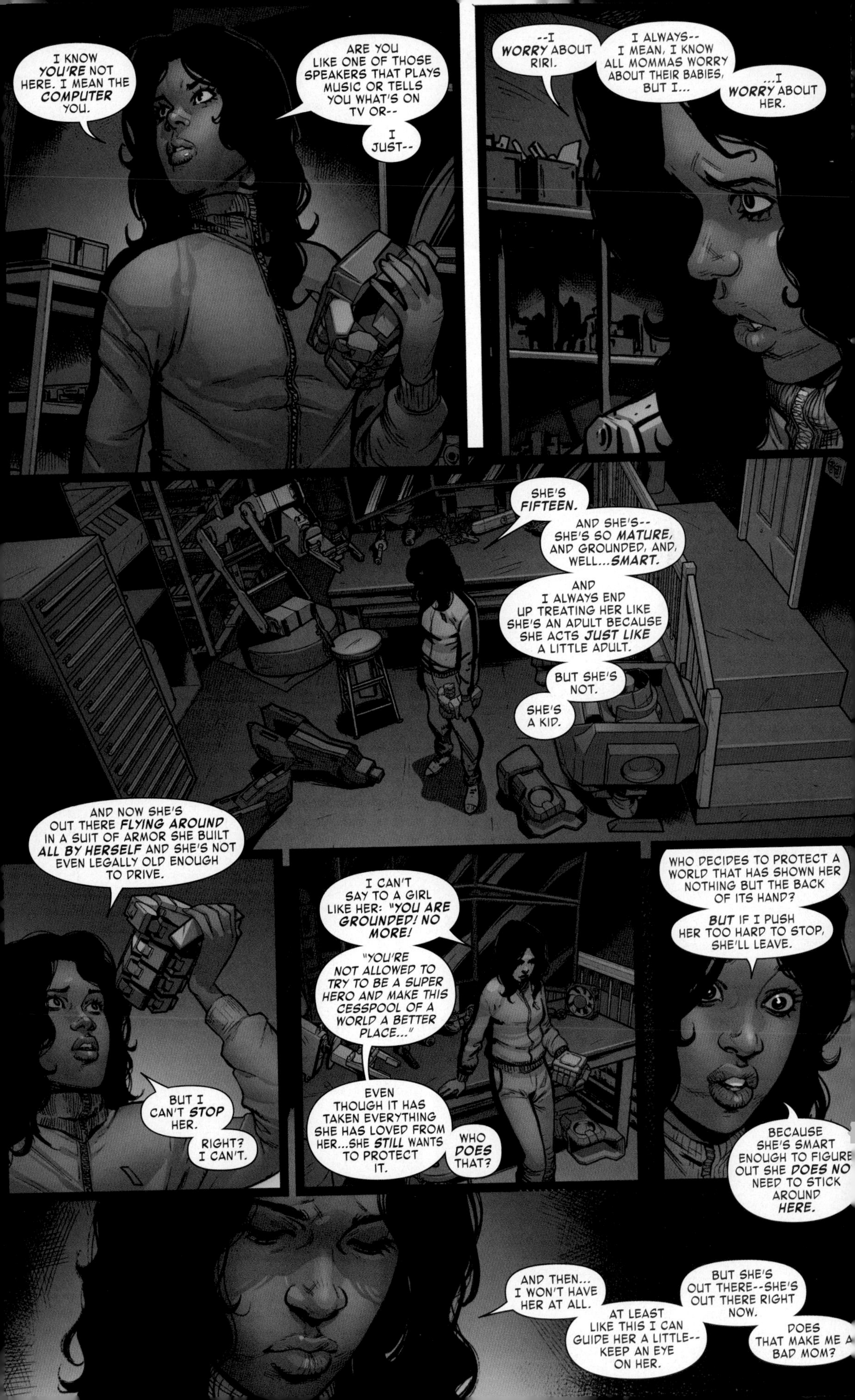
I KNOW YOU'RE NOT HERE. I MEAN THE COMPUTER YOU.
ARE YOU LIKE ONE OF THOSE SPEAKERS THAT PLAYS MUSIC OR TELLS YOU WHAT'S ON TV OR--
I JUST--
--I WORRY ABOUT RIRI.
I ALWAYS-- I MEAN, I KNOW ALL MOMMAS WORRY ABOUT THEIR BABIES, BUT I...
...I WORRY ABOUT HER.
SHE'S FIFTEEN.
AND SHE'S-- SHE'S SO MATURE, AND GROUNDED, AND, WELL...SMART.
AND I ALWAYS END UP TREATING HER LIKE SHE'S AN ADULT BECAUSE SHE ACTS JUST LIKE A LITTLE ADULT.
BUT SHE'S NOT.
SHE'S A KID.
AND NOW SHE'S OUT THERE FLYING AROUND IN A SUIT OF ARMOR SHE BUILT ALL BY HERSELF AND SHE'S NOT EVEN LEGALLY OLD ENOUGH TO DRIVE.
BUT I CAN'T STOP HER.
RIGHT? I CAN'T.
I CAN'T SAY TO A GIRL LIKE HER: "YOU ARE GROUNDED! NO MORE!
"YOU'RE NOT ALLOWED TO TRY TO BE A SUPER HERO AND MAKE THIS CESSPOOL OF A WORLD A BETTER PLACE..."
EVEN THOUGH IT HAS TAKEN EVERYTHING SHE HAS LOVED FROM HER...SHE STILL WANTS TO PROTECT IT.
WHO DOES THAT?
WHO DECIDES TO PROTECT A WORLD THAT HAS SHOWN HER NOTHING BUT THE BACK OF ITS HAND?
BUT IF I PUSH HER TOO HARD TO STOP, SHE'LL LEAVE.
BECAUSE SHE'S SMART ENOUGH TO FIGURE OUT SHE DOES NO NEED TO STICK AROUND HERE.
AND THEN... I WON'T HAVE HER AT ALL.
AT LEAST LIKE THIS I CAN GUIDE HER A LITTLE-- KEEP AN EYE ON HER.
BUT SHE'S OUT THERE--SHE'S OUT THERE RIGHT NOW.
DOES THAT MAKE ME A BAD MOM?

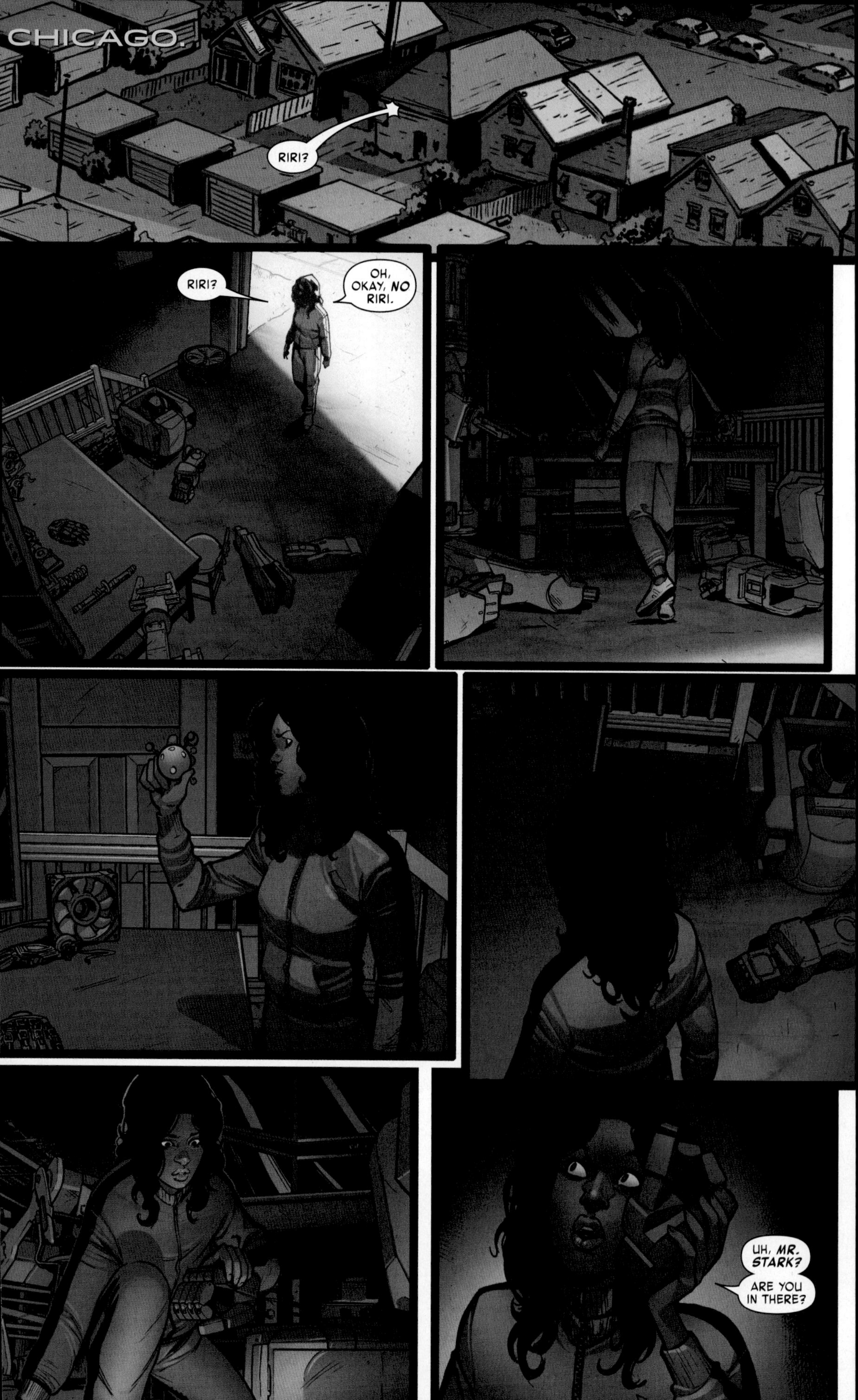
CHICAGO.
RIRI?
RIRI?
OH, OKAY, NO RIRI.
UH, MR. STARK?
ARE YOU IN THERE?

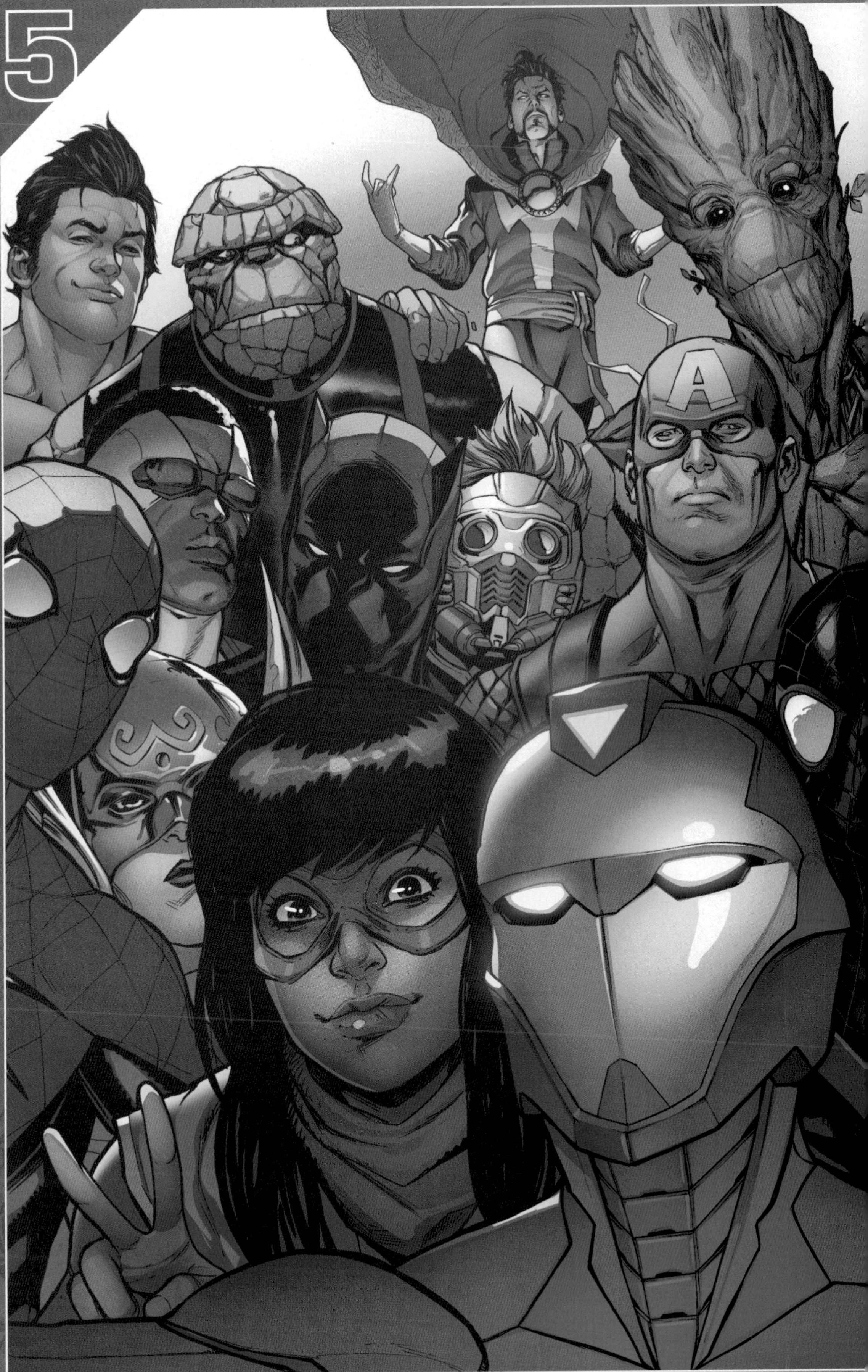
5

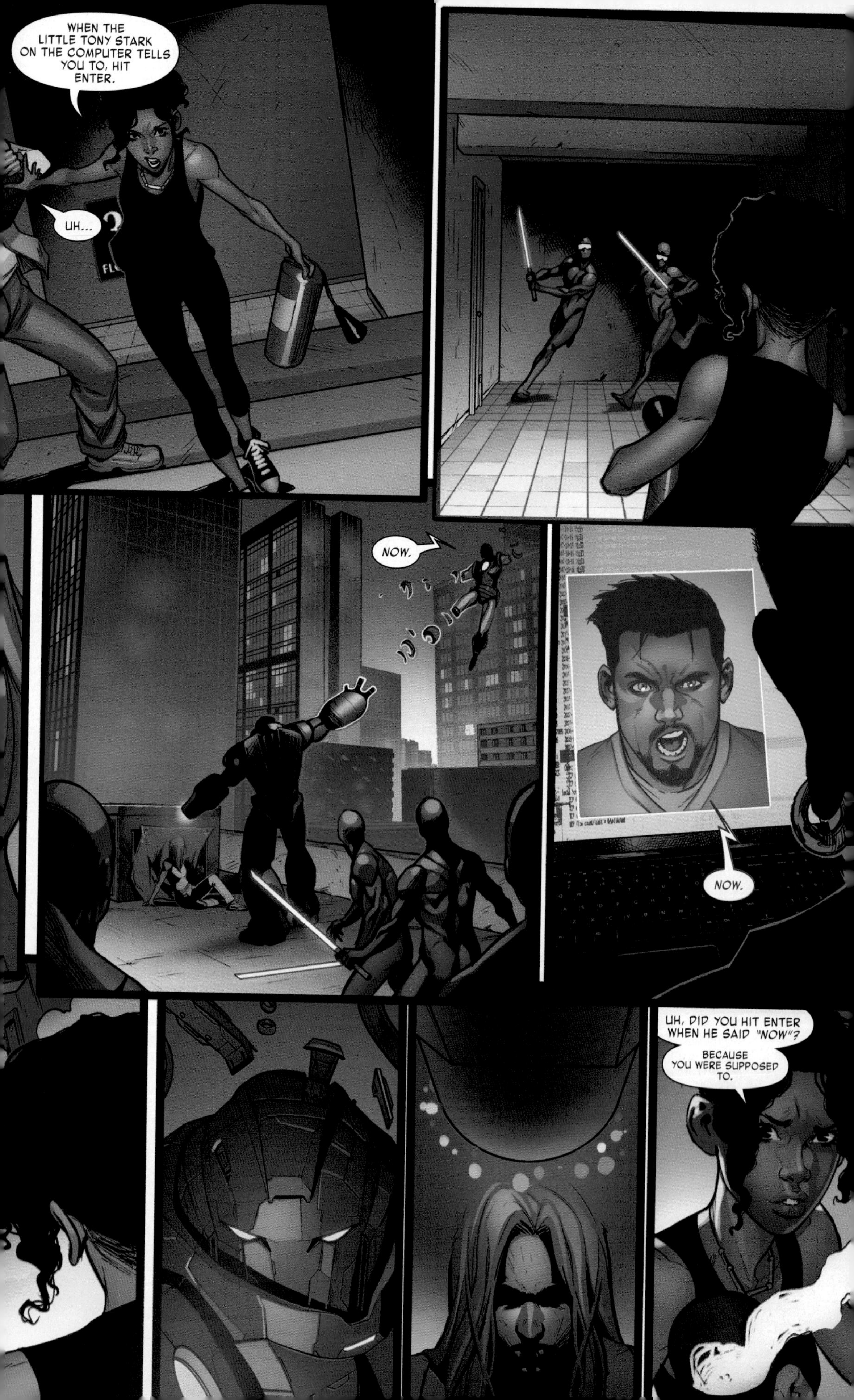
WHEN THE LITTLE TONY STARK ON THE COMPUTER TELLS YOU TO, HIT ENTER.
UH...
NOW.
NOW.
UH, DID YOU HIT ENTER WHEN HE SAID "NOW"?
BECAUSE YOU WERE SUPPOSED TO.

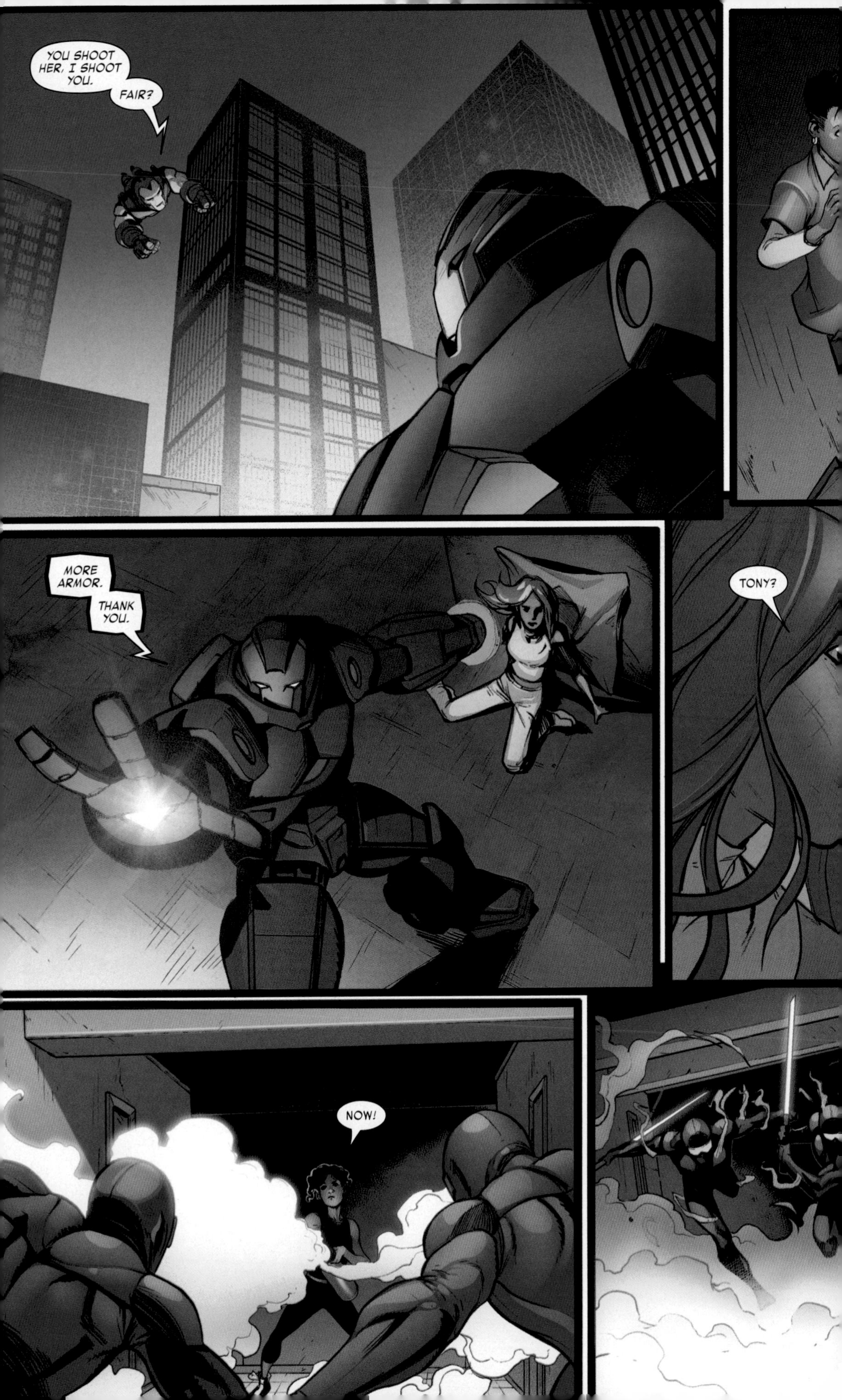
YOU SHOOT HER, I SHOOT YOU.
FAIR?
MORE ARMOR.
THANK YOU.
TONY?
NOW!

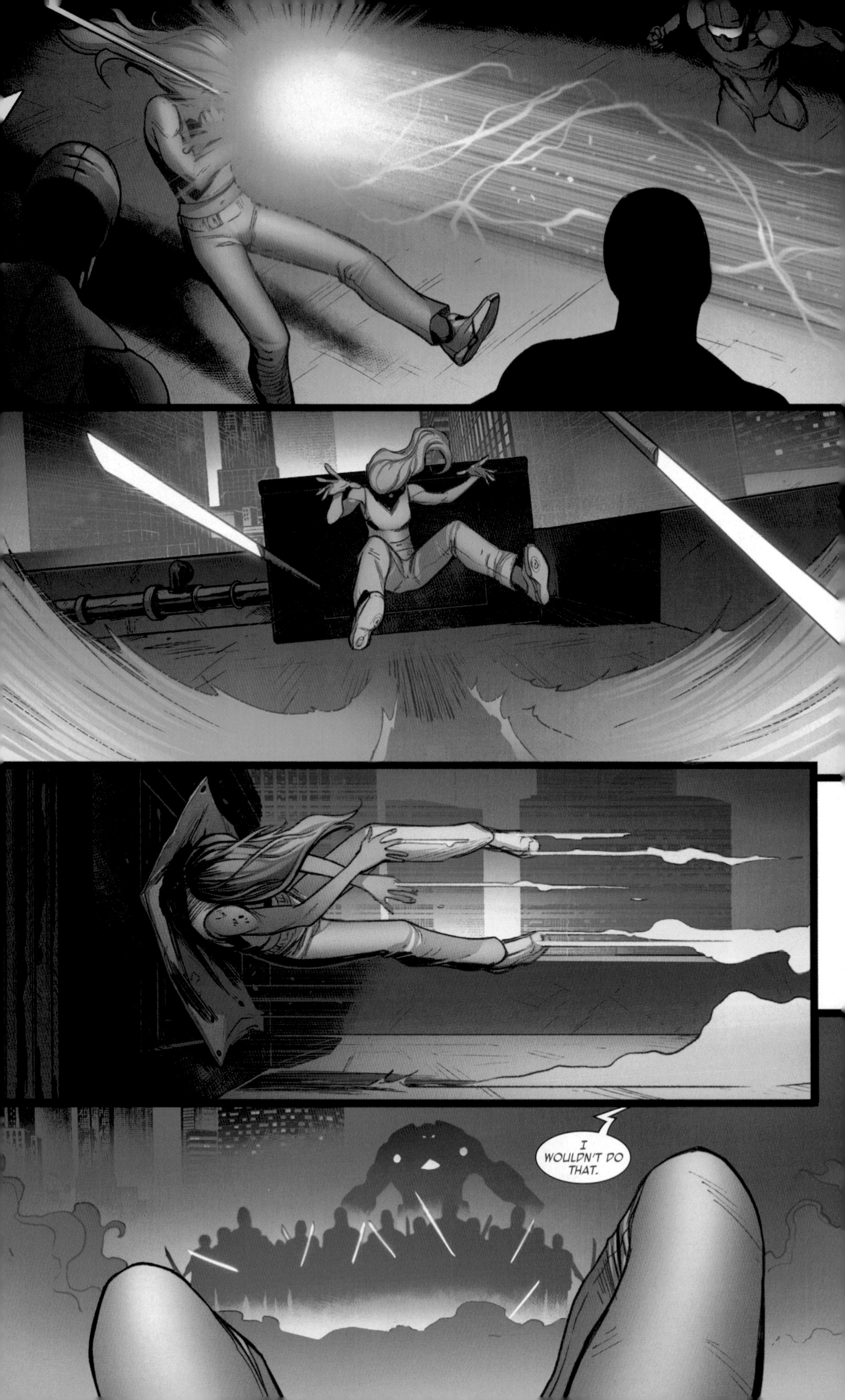
I WOULDN'T DO THAT.

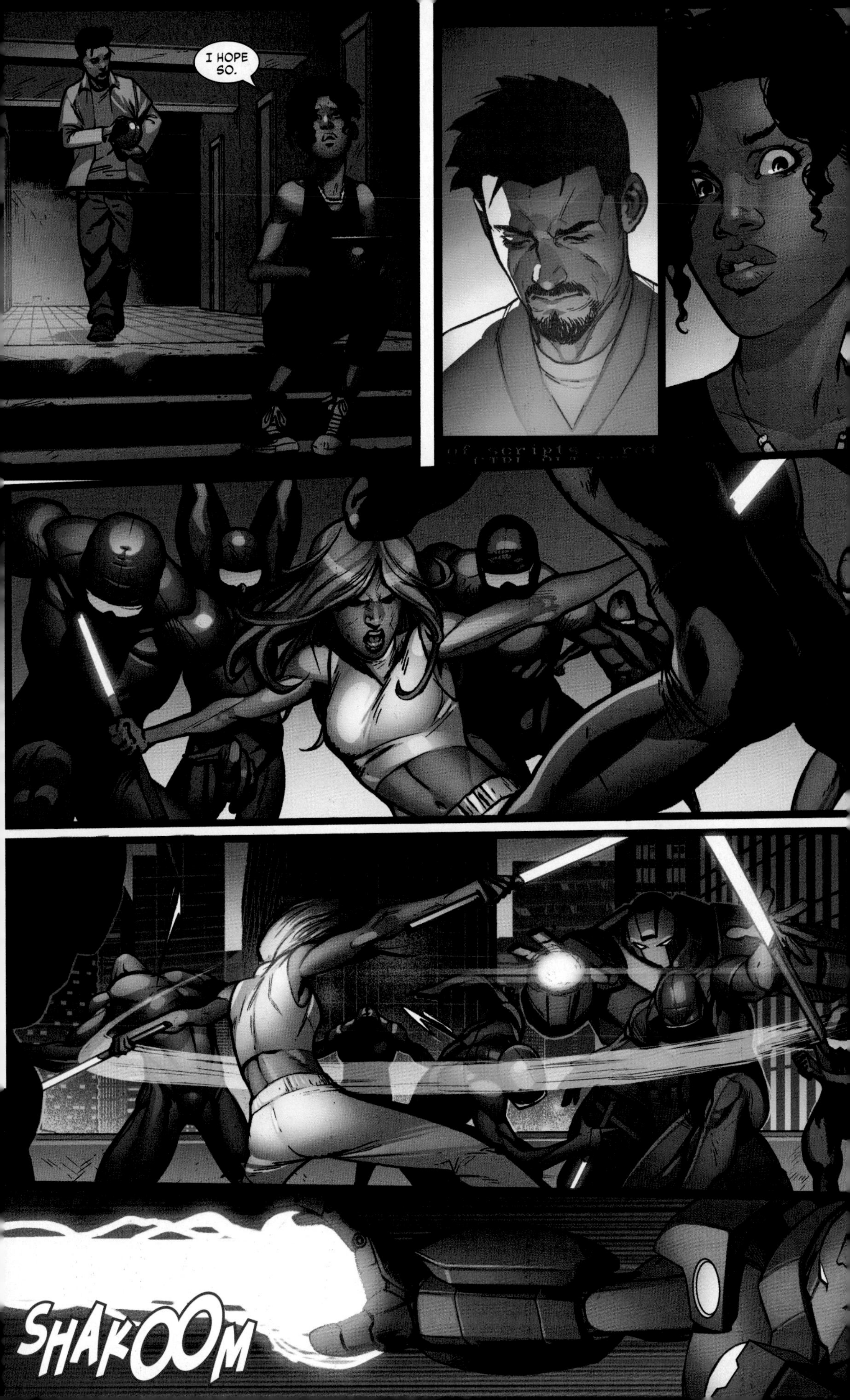
I HOPE SO.
SHAKOOM

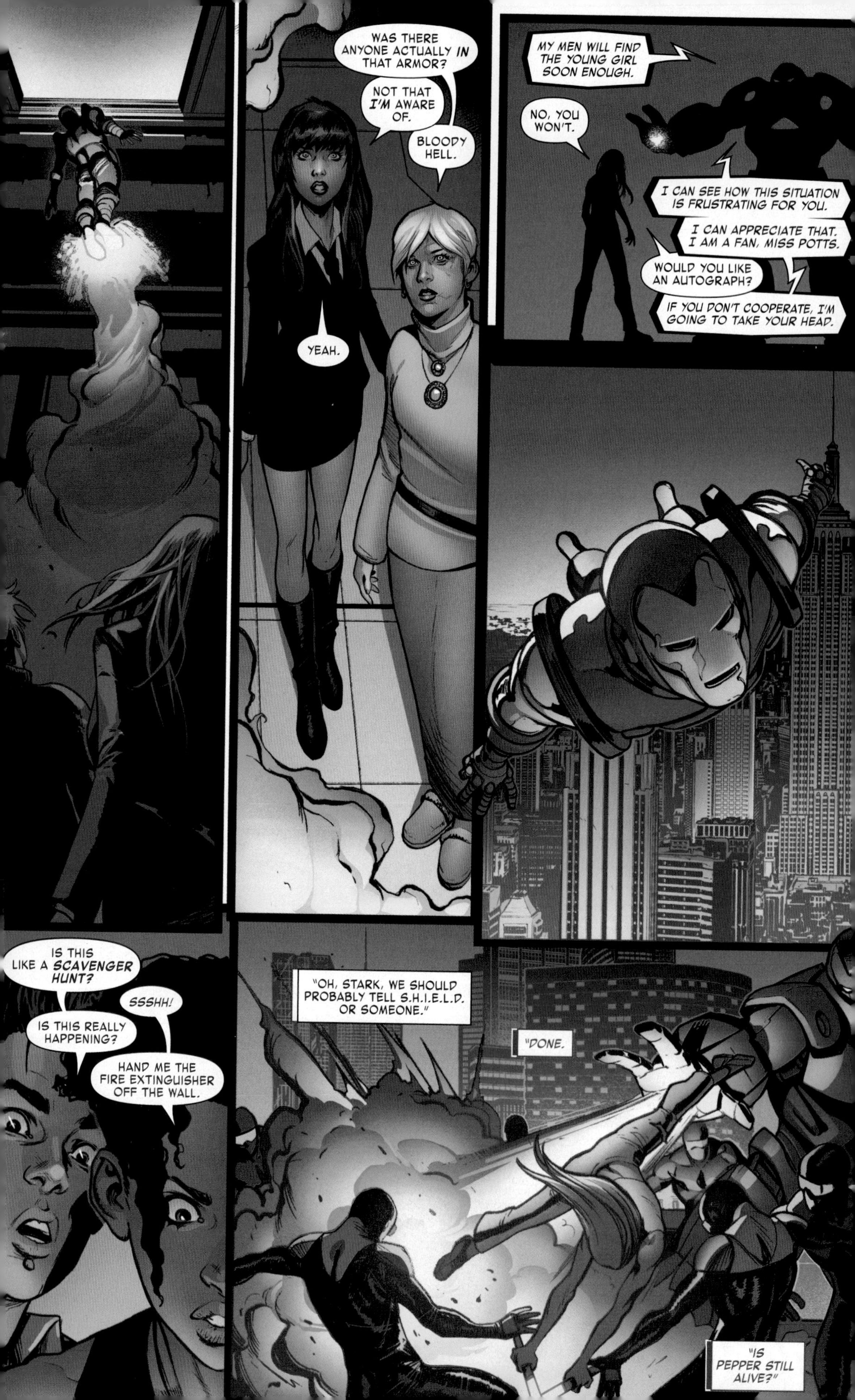

WAS THERE ANYONE ACTUALLY IN THAT ARMOR?
NOT THAT I'M AWARE OF.
BLOODY HELL.
YEAH.
MY MEN WILL FIND THE YOUNG GIRL SOON ENOUGH.
NO, YOU WON'T.
I CAN SEE HOW THIS SITUATION IS FRUSTRATING FOR YOU.
I CAN APPRECIATE THAT. I AM A FAN, MISS POTTS.
WOULD YOU LIKE AN AUTOGRAPH?
IF YOU DON'T COOPERATE, I'M GOING TO TAKE YOUR HEAD.
IS THIS LIKE A SCAVENGER HUNT?
SSSHH!
IS THIS REALLY HAPPENING?
HAND ME THE FIRE EXTINGUISHER OFF THE WALL.
"OH, STARK, WE SHOULD PROBABLY TELL S.H.I.E.L.D. OR SOMEONE."
"DONE.
"IS PEPPER STILL ALIVE?"

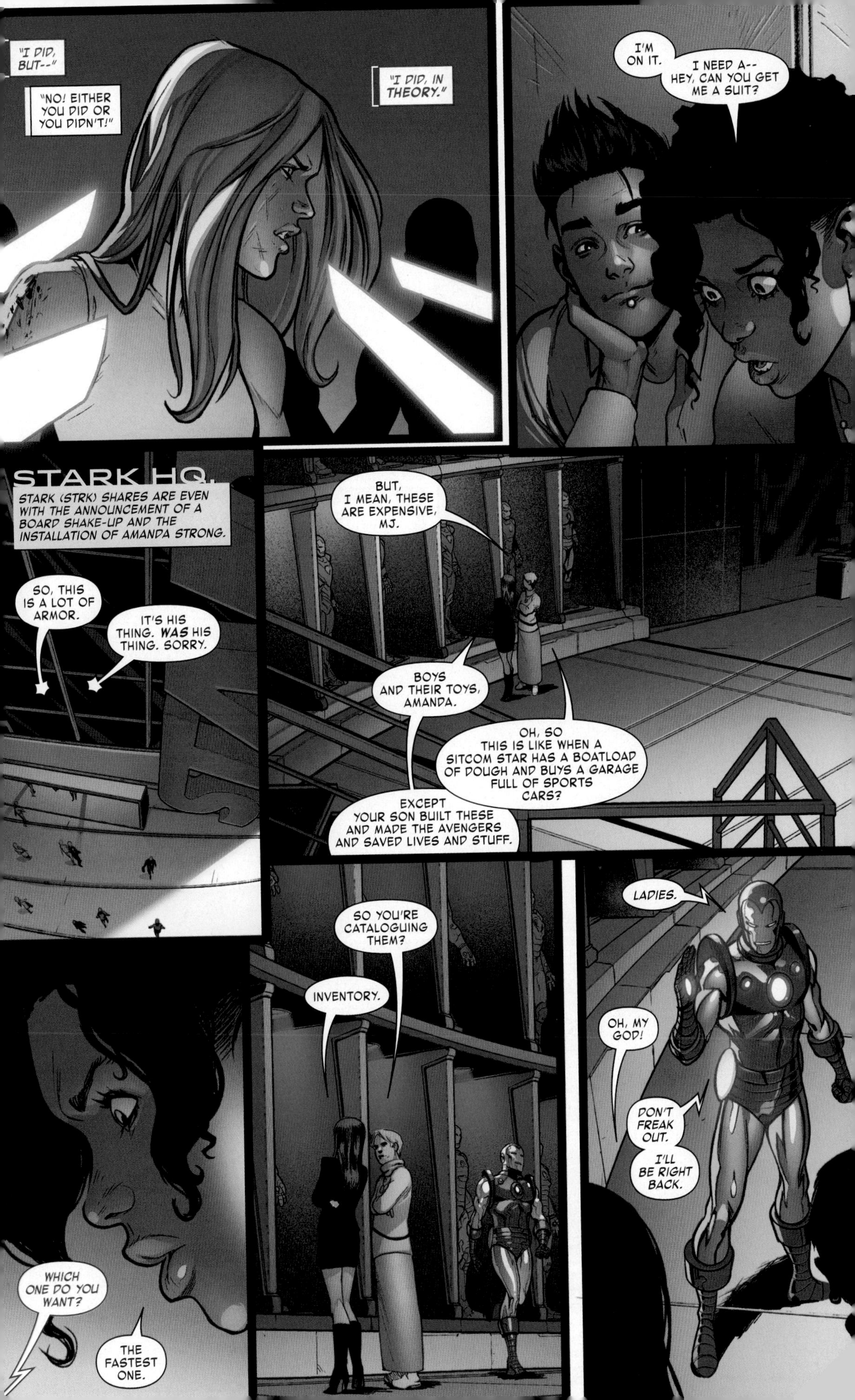

"I DID, BUT--"
"NO! EITHER YOU DID OR YOU DIDN'T!"
"I DID, IN THEORY."
I'M ON IT.
I NEED A-- HEY, CAN YOU GET ME A SUIT?
STARK HQ.
STARK (STRK) SHARES ARE EVEN WITH THE ANNOUNCEMENT OF A BOARD SHAKE-UP AND THE INSTALLATION OF AMANDA STRONG.
SO, THIS IS A LOT OF ARMOR.
IT'S HIS THING. WAS HIS THING. SORRY.
BUT, I MEAN, THESE ARE EXPENSIVE, MJ.
BOYS AND THEIR TOYS, AMANDA.
OH, SO THIS IS LIKE WHEN A SITCOM STAR HAS A BOATLOAD OF DOUGH AND BUYS A GARAGE FULL OF SPORTS CARS?
EXCEPT YOUR SON BUILT THESE AND MADE THE AVENGERS AND SAVED LIVES AND STUFF.
WHICH ONE DO YOU WANT?
THE FASTEST ONE.
SO YOU'RE CATALOGUING THEM?
INVENTORY.
LADIES.
OH, MY GOD!
DON'T FREAK OUT.
I'LL BE RIGHT BACK.

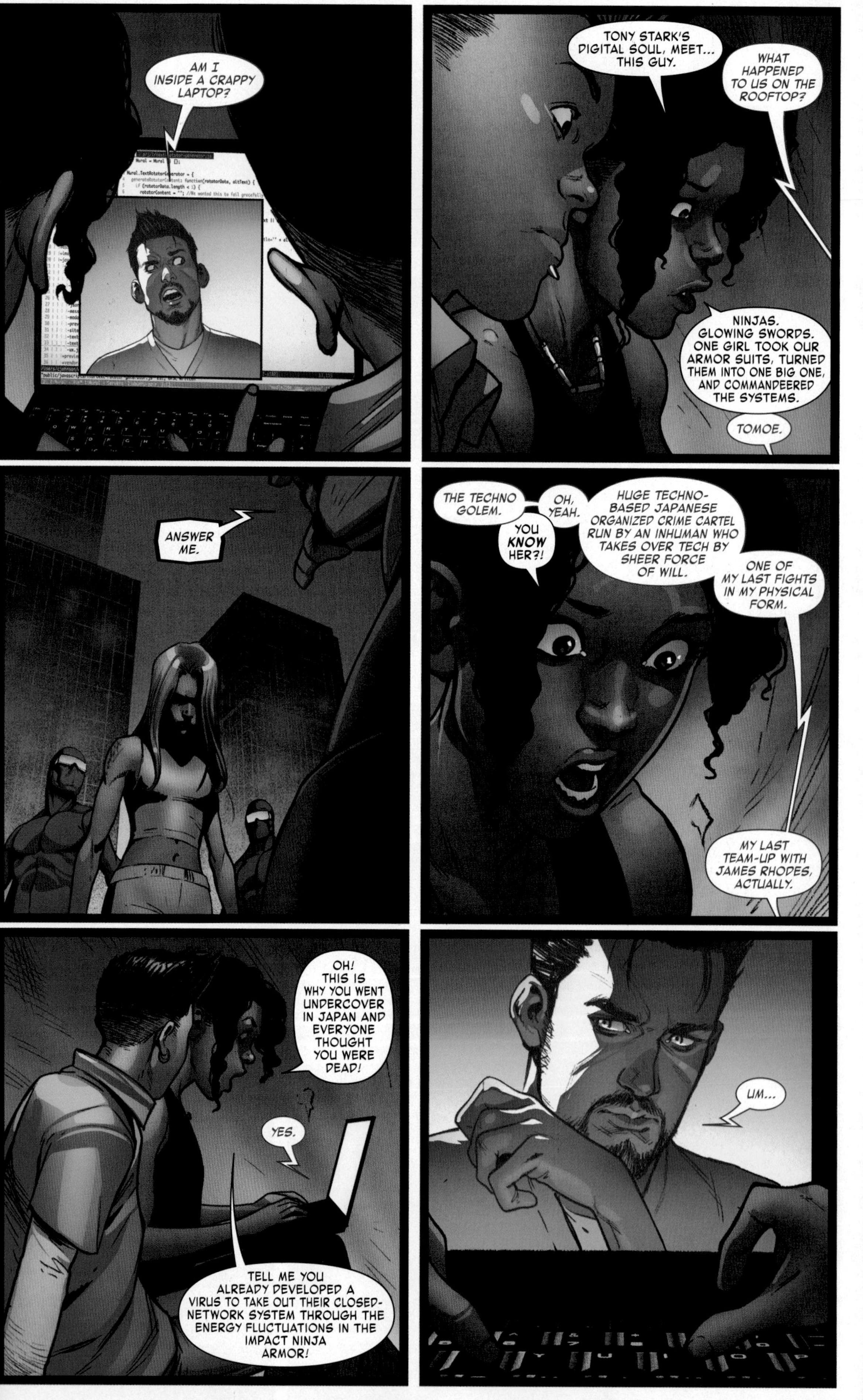
AM I INSIDE A CRAPPY LAPTOP?
TONY STARK'S DIGITAL SOUL, MEET... THIS GUY.
WHAT HAPPENED TO US ON THE ROOFTOP?
NINJAS. GLOWING SWORDS. ONE GIRL TOOK OUR ARMOR SUITS, TURNED THEM INTO ONE BIG ONE, AND COMMANDEERED THE SYSTEMS.
TOMOE.
ANSWER ME.
THE TECHNO GOLEM.
OH, YEAH.
YOU KNOW HER?!
HUGE TECHNO-BASED JAPANESE ORGANIZED CRIME CARTEL RUN BY AN INHUMAN WHO TAKES OVER TECH BY SHEER FORCE OF WILL.
ONE OF MY LAST FIGHTS IN MY PHYSICAL FORM.
MY LAST TEAM-UP WITH JAMES RHODES, ACTUALLY.
OH! THIS IS WHY YOU WENT UNDERCOVER IN JAPAN AND EVERYONE THOUGHT YOU WERE DEAD!
YES.
TELL ME YOU ALREADY DEVELOPED A VIRUS TO TAKE OUT THEIR CLOSED-NETWORK SYSTEM THROUGH THE ENERGY FLUCTUATIONS IN THE IMPACT NINJA ARMOR!
UM...

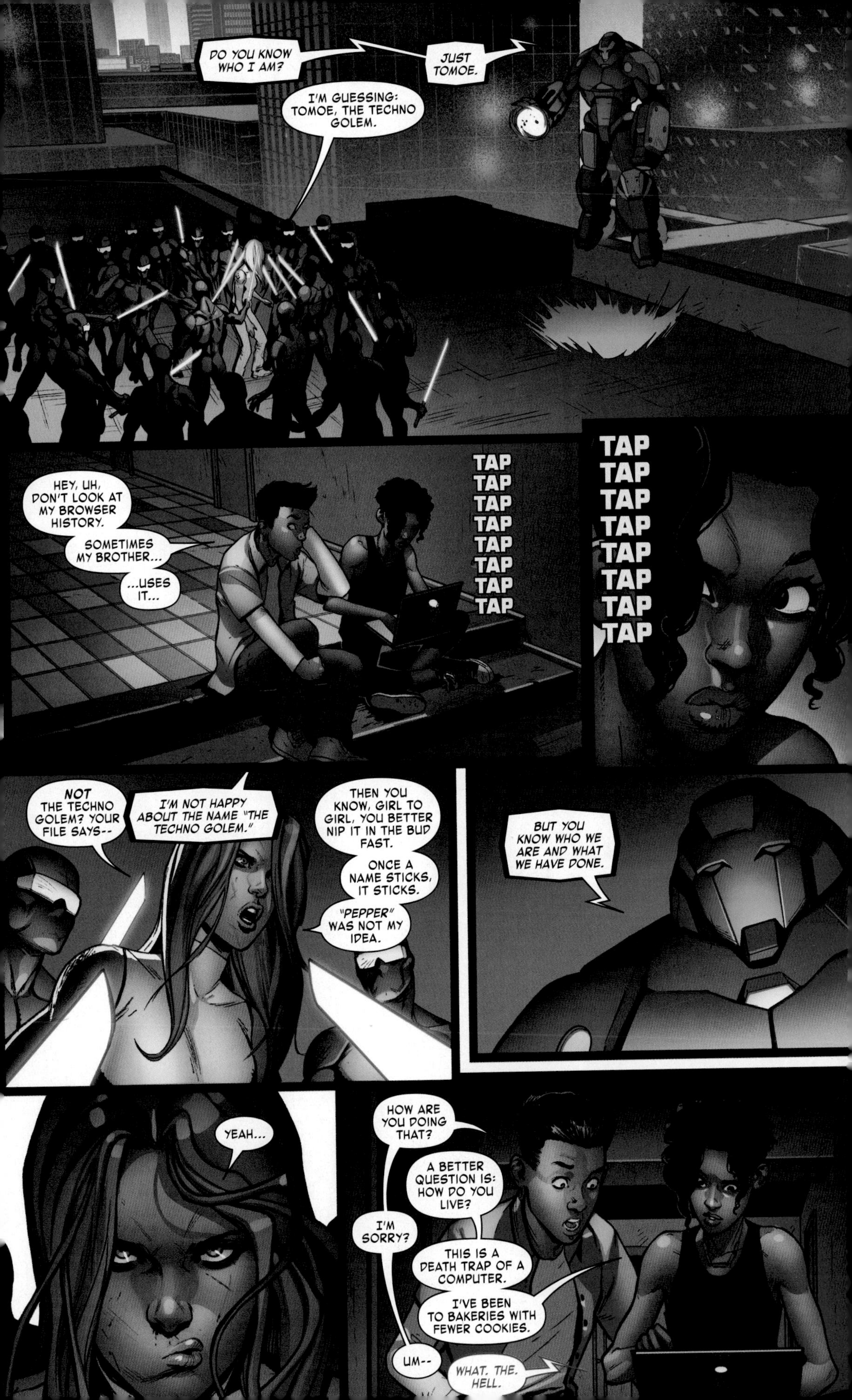

DO YOU KNOW WHO I AM?
JUST TOMOE.
I'M GUESSING: TOMOE, THE TECHNO GOLEM.
HEY, UH, DON'T LOOK AT MY BROWSER HISTORY.
SOMETIMES MY BROTHER...
...USES IT...
TAP TAP TAP TAP TAP TAP TAP TAP
TAP TAP TAP TAP TAP TAP TAP TAP
NOT THE TECHNO GOLEM? YOUR FILE SAYS--
I'M NOT HAPPY ABOUT THE NAME "THE TECHNO GOLEM."
THEN YOU KNOW, GIRL TO GIRL, YOU BETTER NIP IT IN THE BUD FAST.
ONCE A NAME STICKS, IT STICKS.
"PEPPER" WAS NOT MY IDEA.
BUT YOU KNOW WHO WE ARE AND WHAT WE HAVE DONE.
YEAH...
HOW ARE YOU DOING THAT?
A BETTER QUESTION IS: HOW DO YOU LIVE?
I'M SORRY?
THIS IS A DEATH TRAP OF A COMPUTER.
I'VE BEEN TO BAKERIES WITH FEWER COOKIES.
UM--
WHAT. THE. HELL.

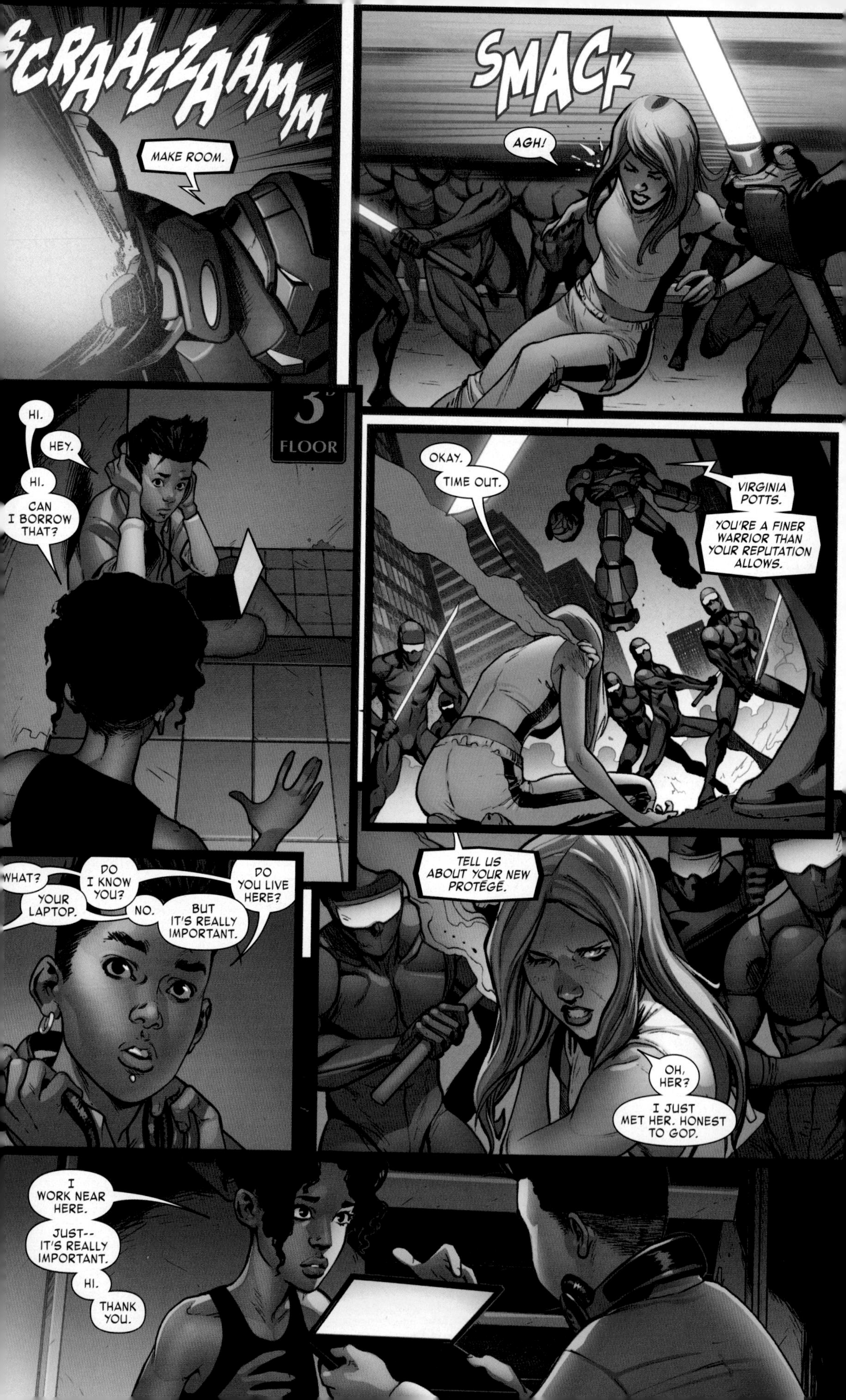
SCRAAZZAAMM
MAKE ROOM.
SMACK
AGH!
3D FLOOR
HI.
HEY.
HI.
CAN I BORROW THAT?
OKAY.
TIME OUT.
VIRGINIA POTTS.
YOU'RE A FINER WARRIOR THAN YOUR REPUTATION ALLOWS.
WHAT?
DO I KNOW YOU?
YOUR LAPTOP.
NO.
BUT IT'S REALLY IMPORTANT.
DO YOU LIVE HERE?
TELL US ABOUT YOUR NEW PROTÉGÉ.
OH, HER?
I JUST MET HER. HONEST TO GOD.
I WORK NEAR HERE.
JUST-- IT'S REALLY IMPORTANT.
HI.
THANK YOU.

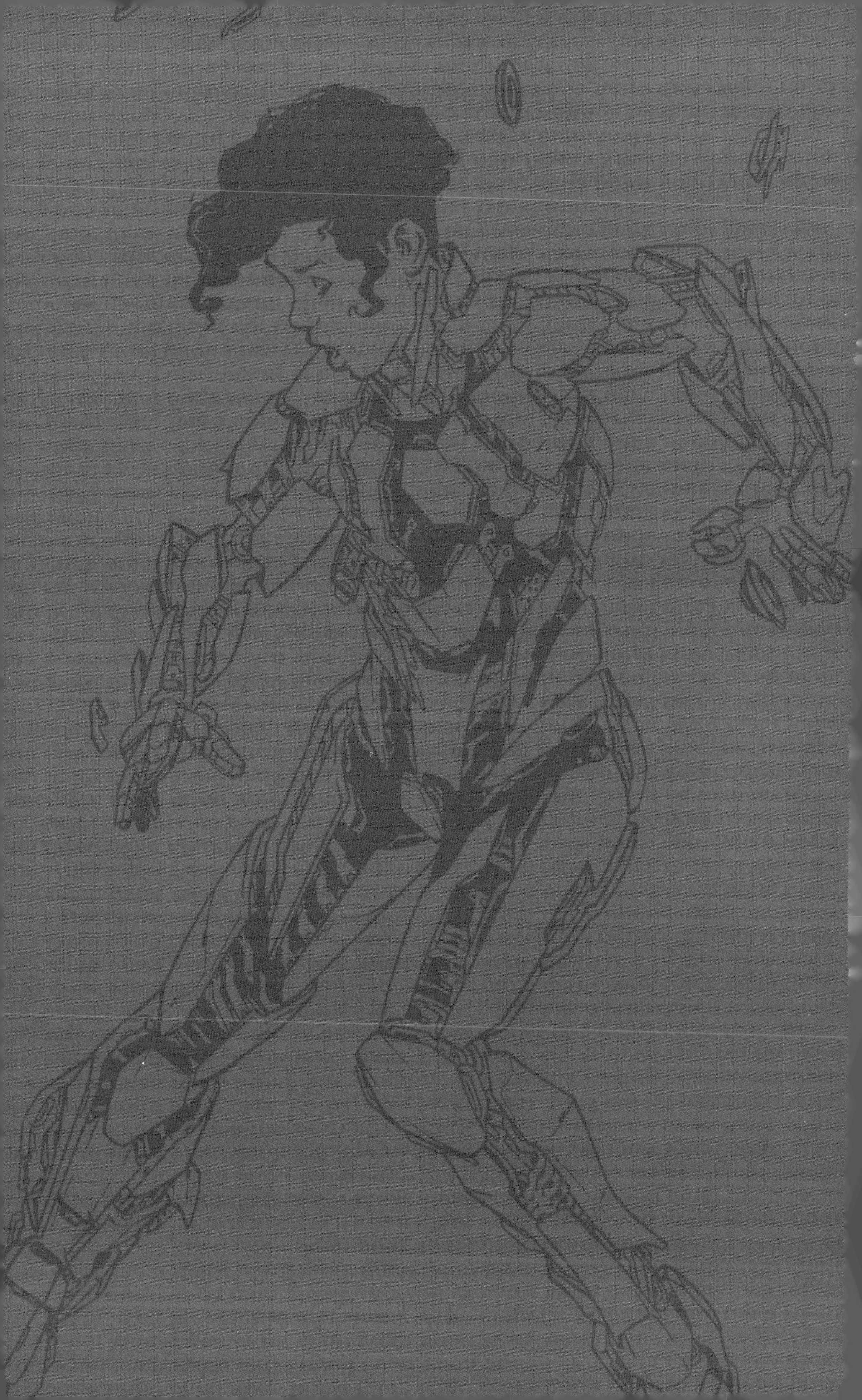

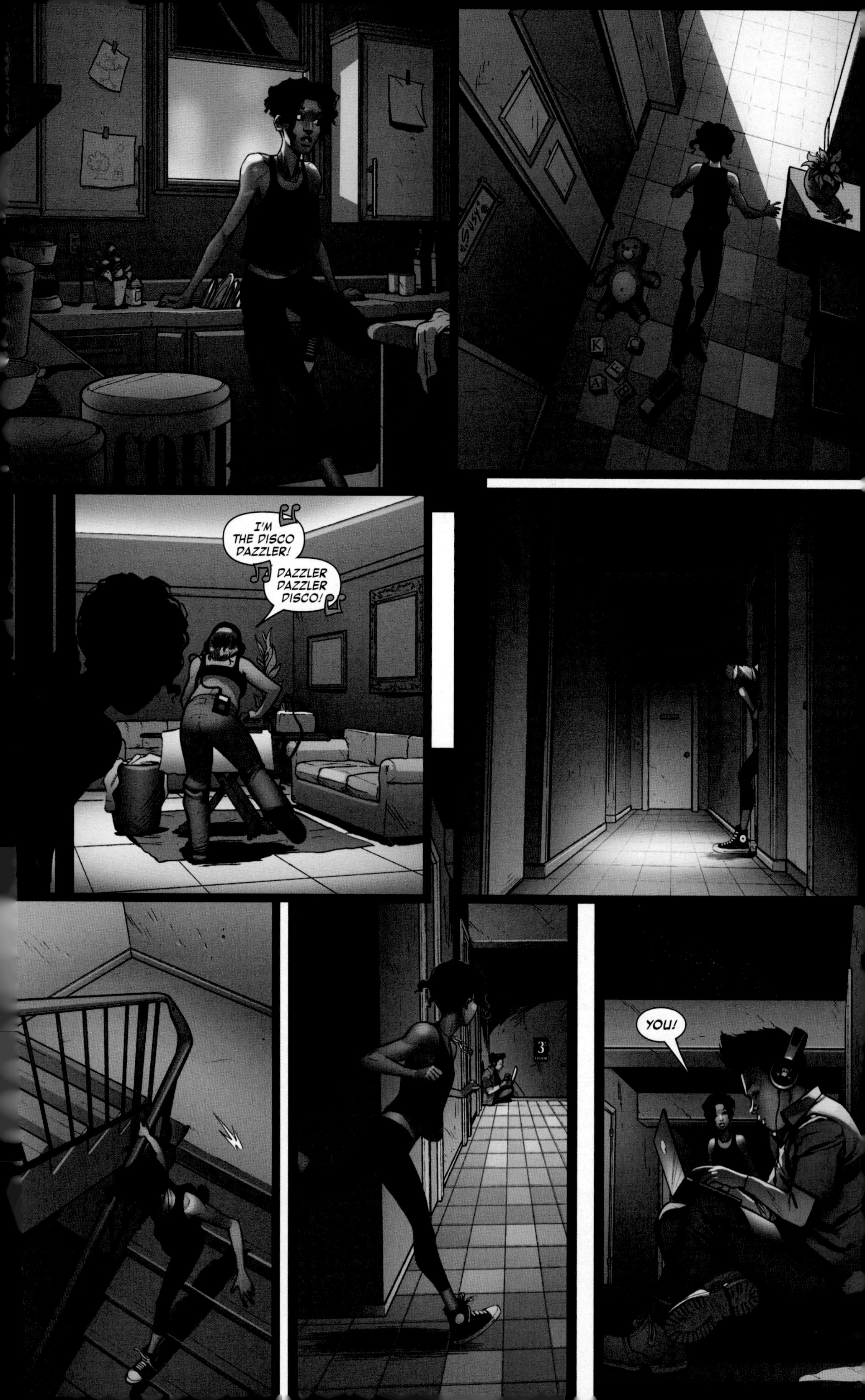
S u s y
K C A E B
I'M THE DISCO DAZZLER!
DAZZLER DAZZLER DISCO!
3
YOU!

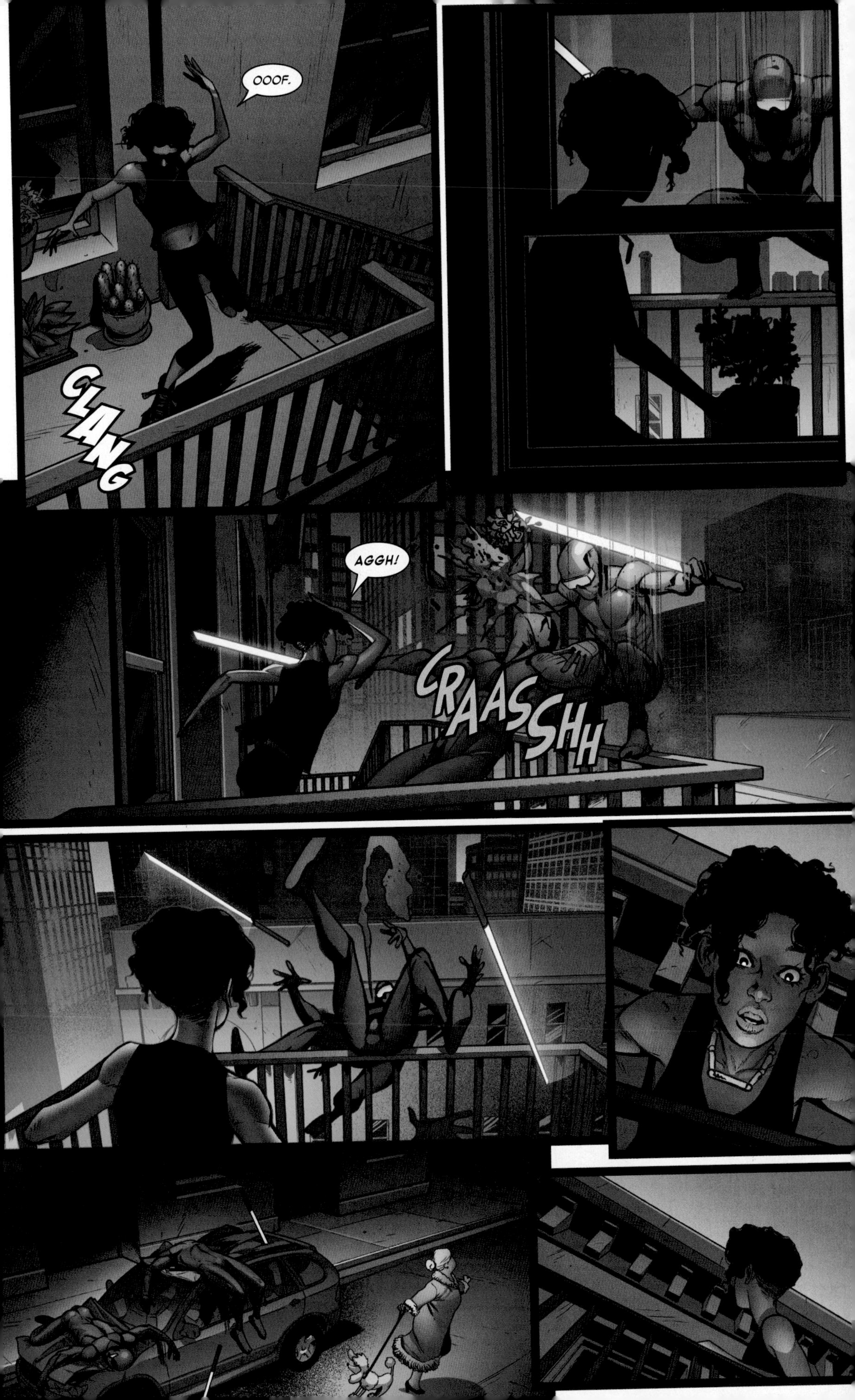
OOOF.
CLANG
AGGH!
CRAASSHH

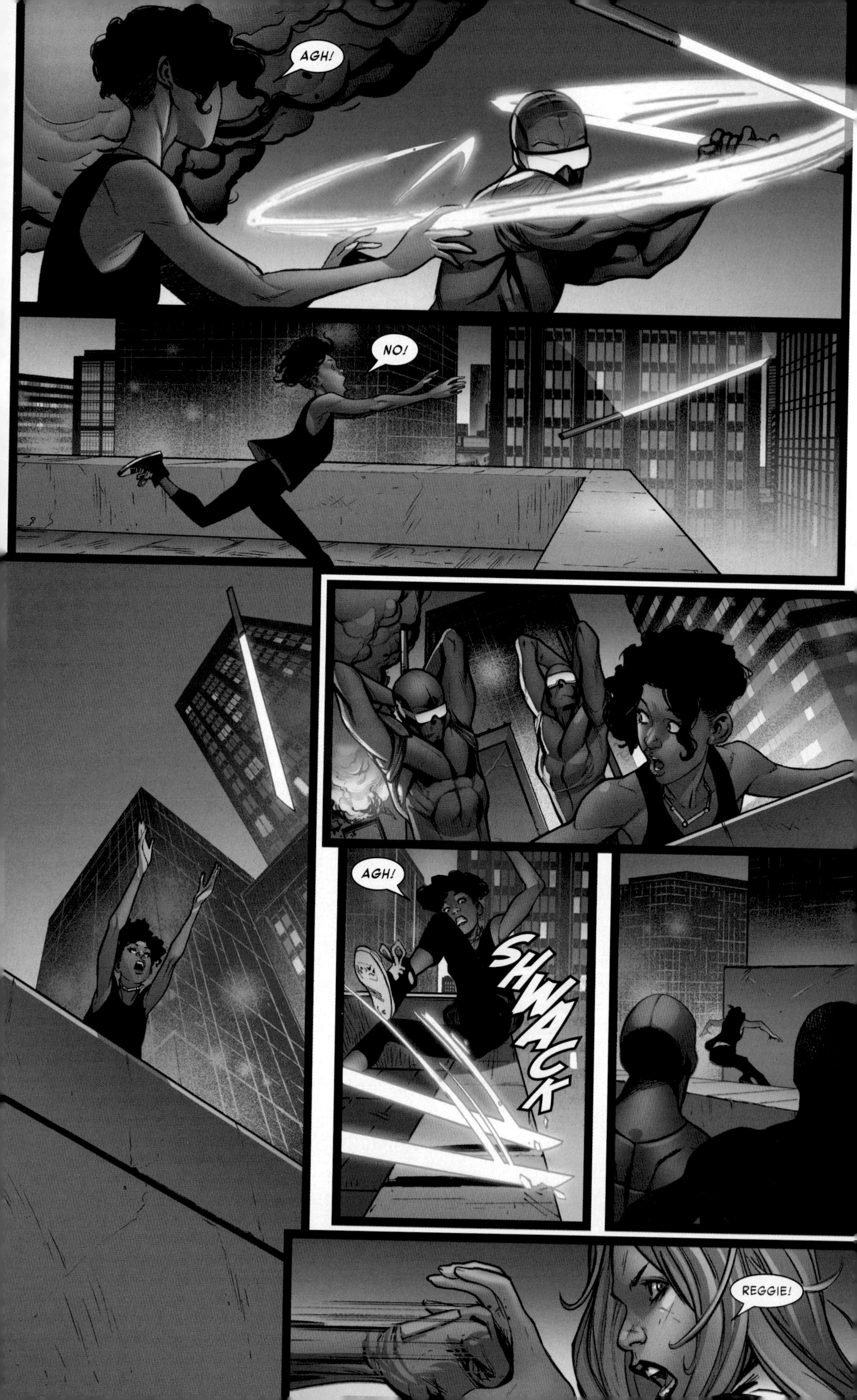
AGH!
NO!
AGH!
SHWACK
REGGIE!

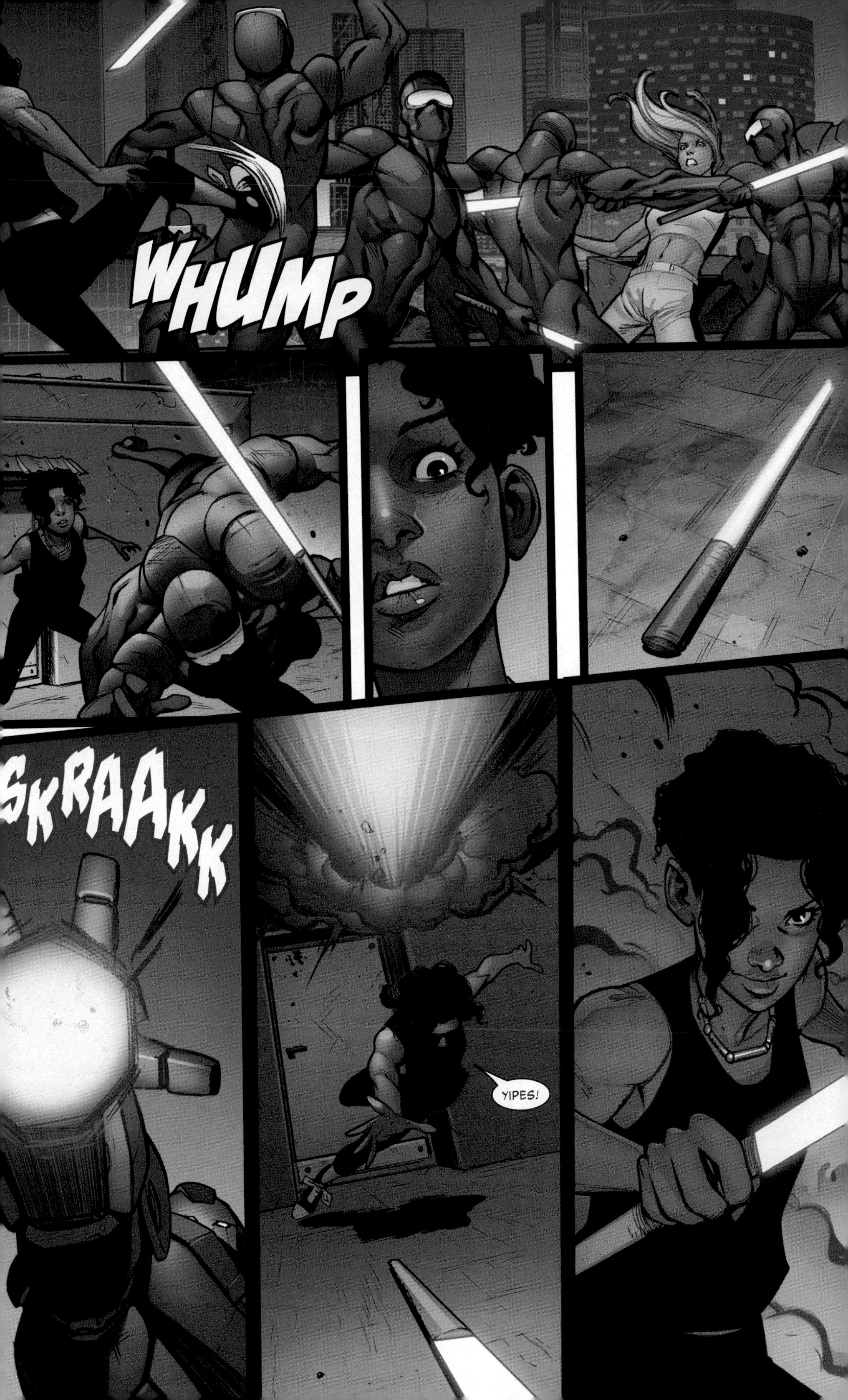
WHUMP
SKRAAKK
YIPES!

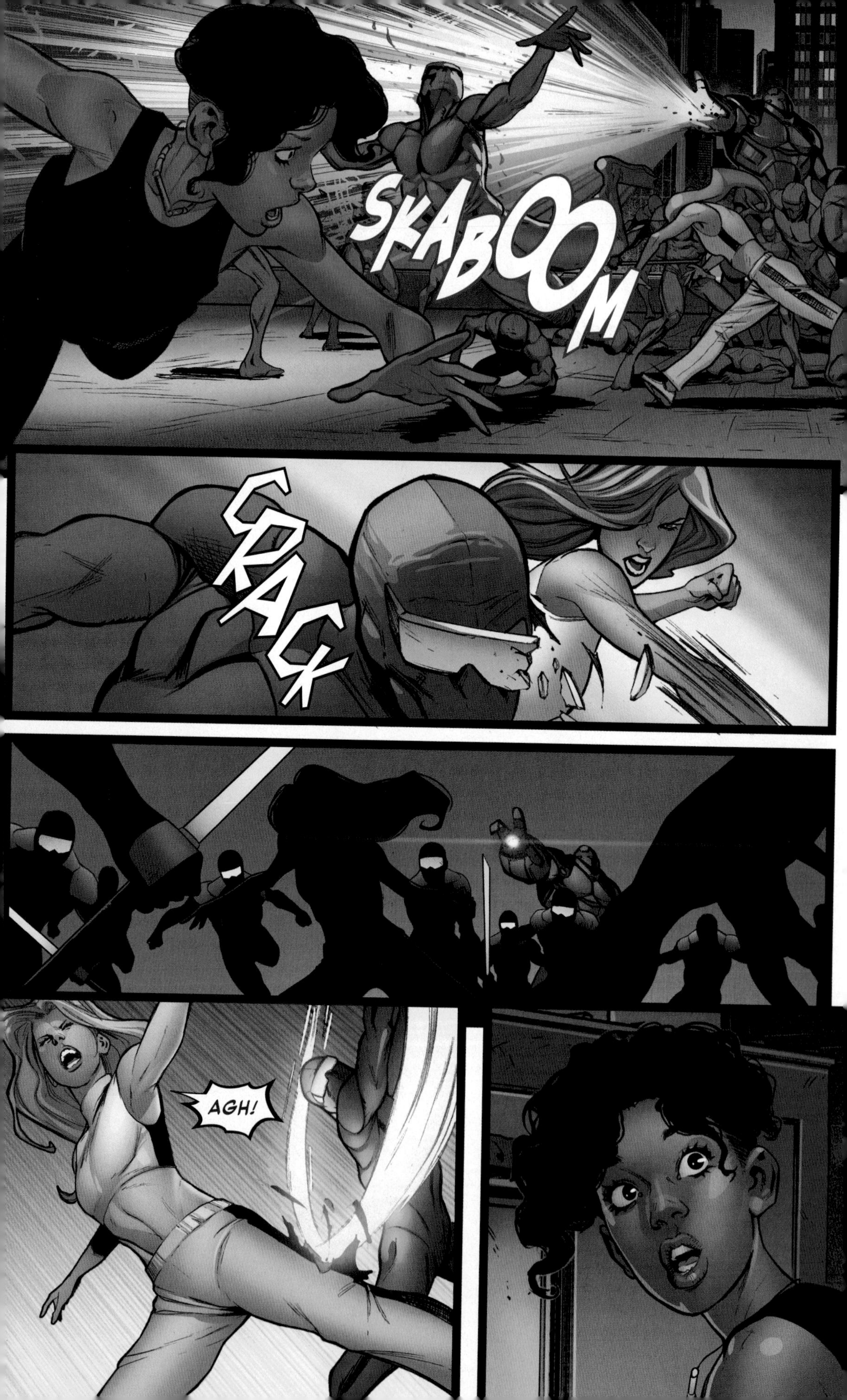
SKABOOM
CRACK
AGH!

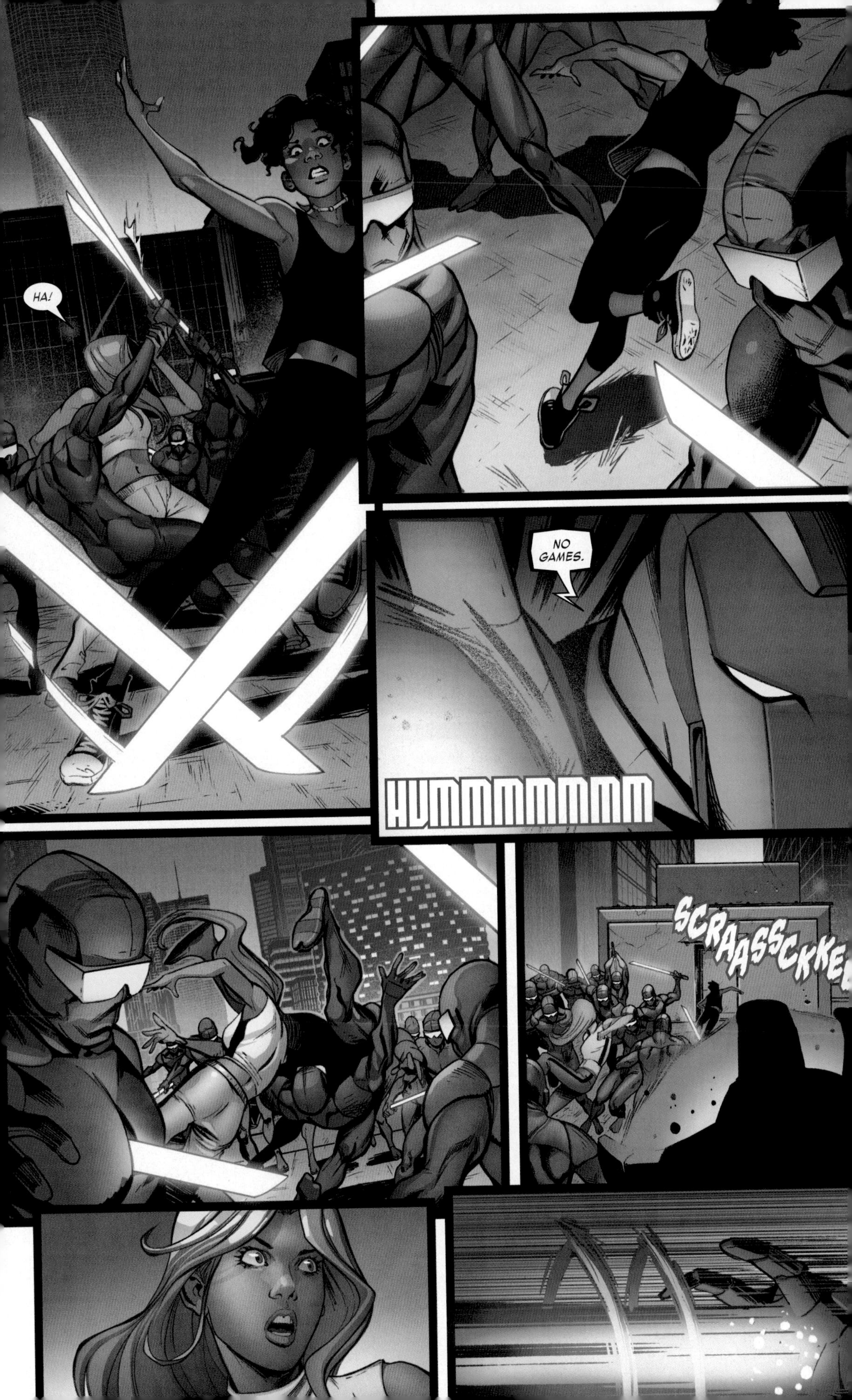
HA!
NO GAMES.
HUMMMMMMMM
SCRAASSCKKE

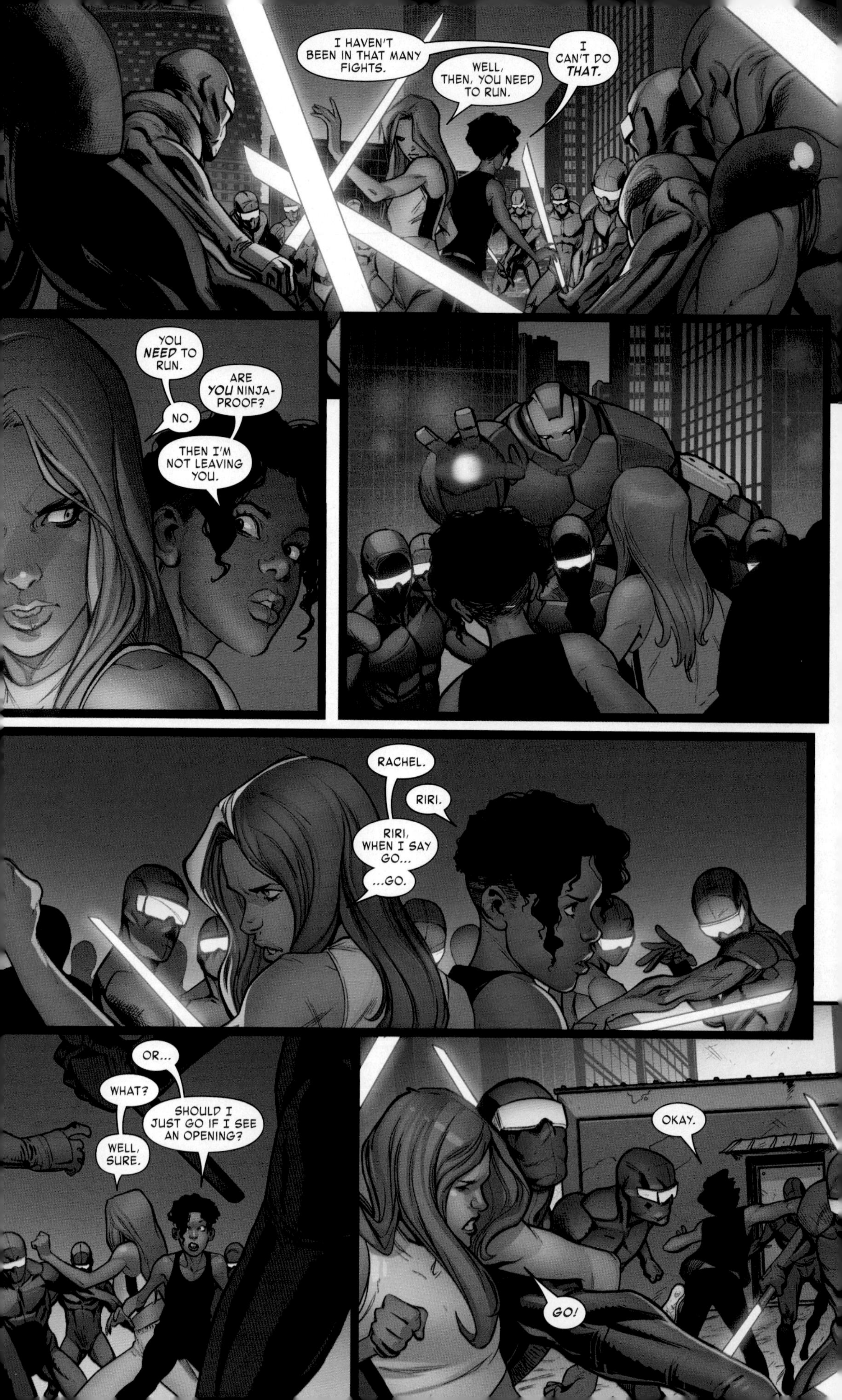
I HAVEN'T BEEN IN THAT MANY FIGHTS.
WELL, THEN, YOU NEED TO RUN.
I CAN'T DO *THAT.*
YOU *NEED* TO RUN.
ARE *YOU* NINJA-PROOF?
NO.
THEN I'M NOT LEAVING YOU.
RACHEL.
RIRI.
RIRI, WHEN I SAY GO...
...GO.
OR...
WHAT?
SHOULD I JUST GO IF I SEE AN OPENING?
WELL, SURE.
OKAY.
GO!

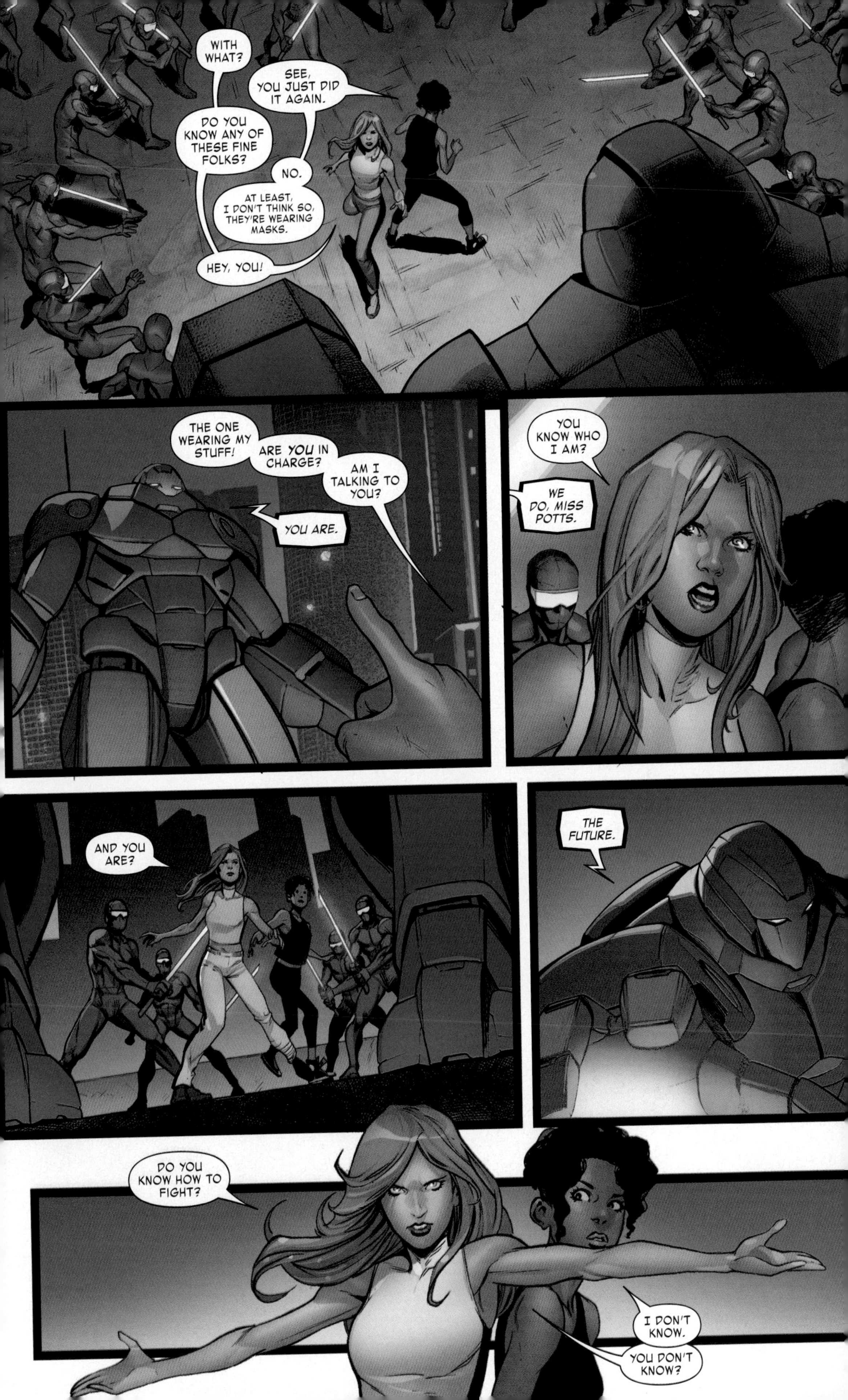
WITH WHAT?
SEE, YOU JUST DID IT AGAIN.
DO YOU KNOW ANY OF THESE FINE FOLKS?
NO.
AT LEAST, I DON'T THINK SO, THEY'RE WEARING MASKS.
HEY, YOU!
THE ONE WEARING MY STUFF!
ARE YOU IN CHARGE?
AM I TALKING TO YOU?
YOU ARE.
YOU KNOW WHO I AM?
WE DO, MISS POTTS.
AND YOU ARE?
THE FUTURE.
DO YOU KNOW HOW TO FIGHT?
I DON'T KNOW.
YOU DON'T KNOW?

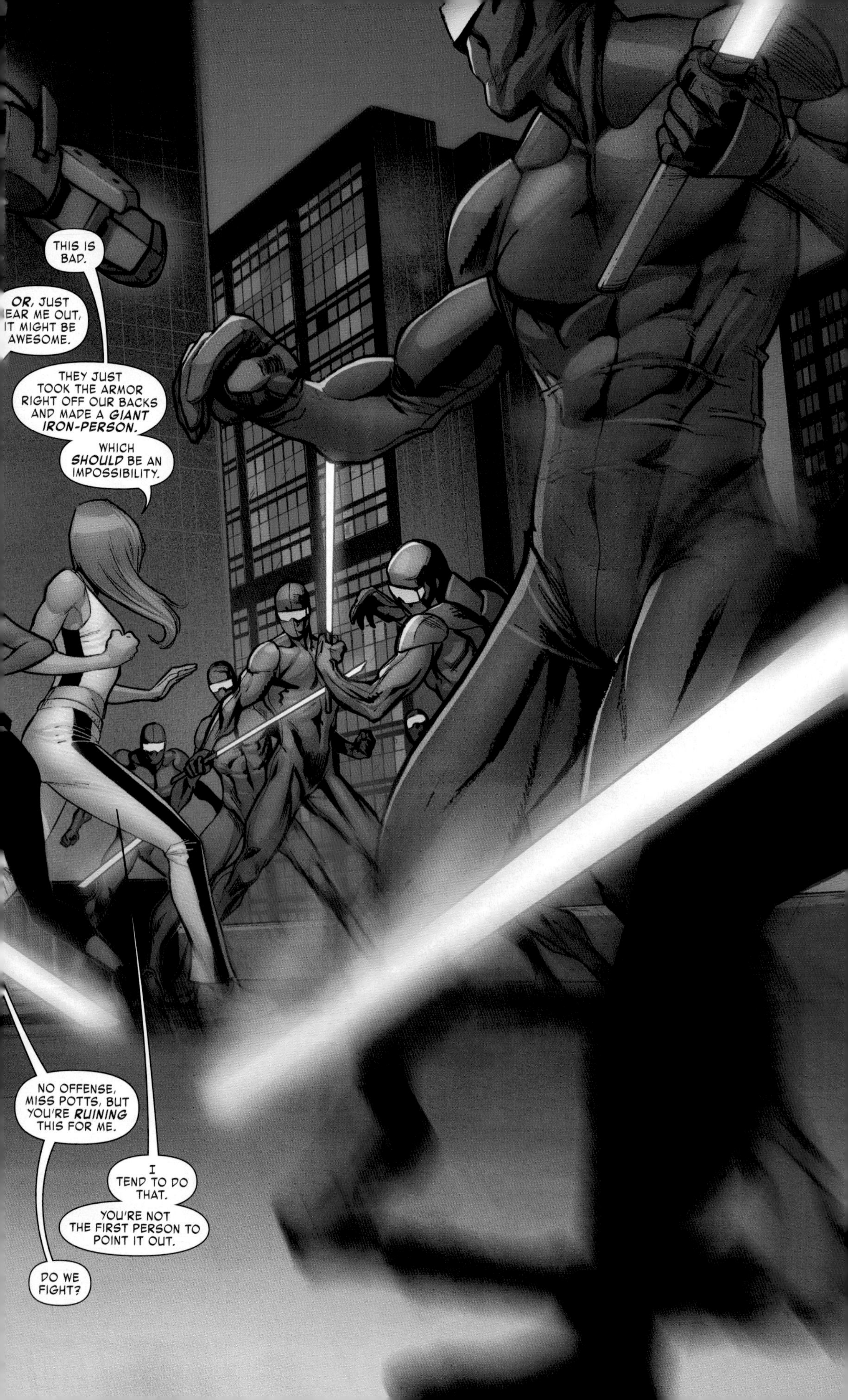
THIS IS BAD.
OR, JUST EAR ME OUT, IT MIGHT BE AWESOME.
THEY JUST TOOK THE ARMOR RIGHT OFF OUR BACKS AND MADE A GIANT IRON-PERSON.
WHICH SHOULD BE AN IMPOSSIBILITY.
NO OFFENSE, MISS POTTS, BUT YOU'RE RUINING THIS FOR ME.
I TEND TO DO THAT.
YOU'RE NOT THE FIRST PERSON TO POINT IT OUT.
DO WE FIGHT?

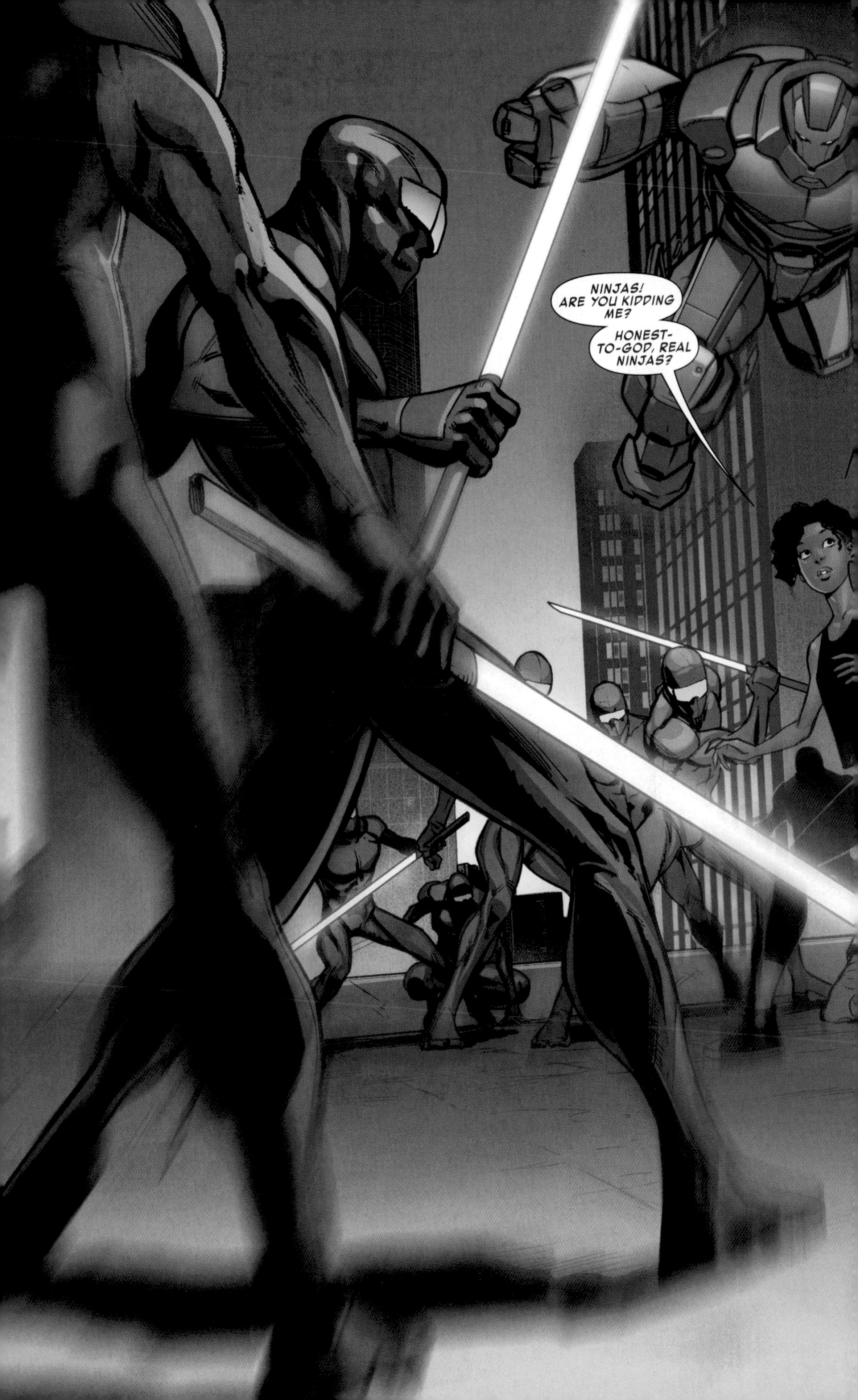
NINJAS! ARE YOU KIDDING ME?
HONEST-TO-GOD, REAL NINJAS?

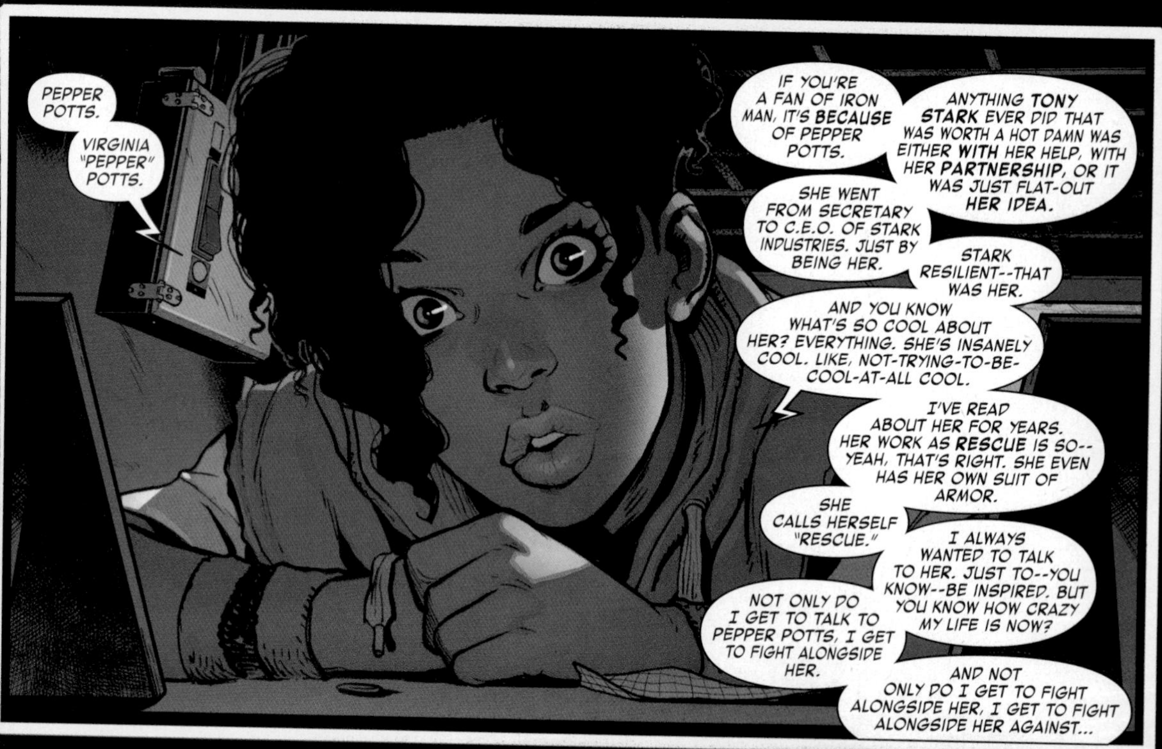
PEPPER POTTS.
VIRGINIA "PEPPER" POTTS.
IF YOU'RE A FAN OF IRON MAN, IT'S **BECAUSE** OF PEPPER POTTS.
ANYTHING **TONY STARK** EVER DID THAT WAS WORTH A HOT DAMN WAS EITHER **WITH** HER HELP, WITH HER **PARTNERSHIP,** OR IT WAS JUST FLAT-OUT **HER IDEA.**
SHE WENT FROM SECRETARY TO C.E.O. OF STARK INDUSTRIES. JUST BY BEING HER.
STARK RESILIENT--THAT WAS HER.
AND YOU KNOW WHAT'S SO COOL ABOUT HER? EVERYTHING. SHE'S INSANELY COOL. LIKE, NOT-TRYING-TO-BE-COOL-AT-ALL COOL.
I'VE READ ABOUT HER FOR YEARS. HER WORK AS **RESCUE** IS SO--YEAH, THAT'S RIGHT. SHE EVEN HAS HER OWN SUIT OF ARMOR.
SHE CALLS HERSELF "RESCUE."
I ALWAYS WANTED TO TALK TO HER. JUST TO--YOU KNOW--BE INSPIRED. BUT YOU KNOW HOW CRAZY MY LIFE IS NOW?
NOT ONLY DO I GET TO TALK TO PEPPER POTTS, I GET TO FIGHT ALONGSIDE HER.
AND NOT ONLY DO I GET TO FIGHT ALONGSIDE HER, I GET TO FIGHT ALONGSIDE HER AGAINST...

4

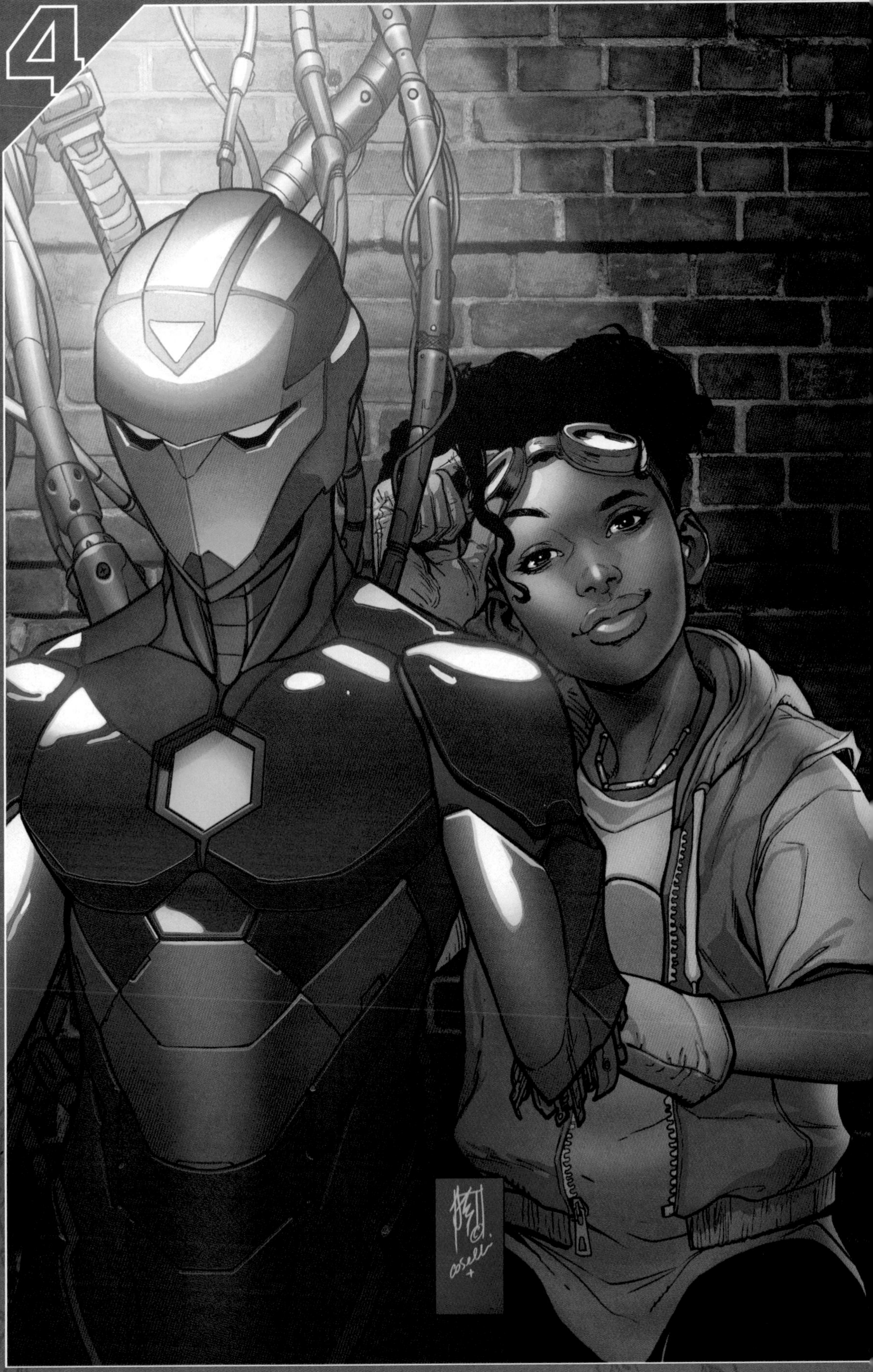

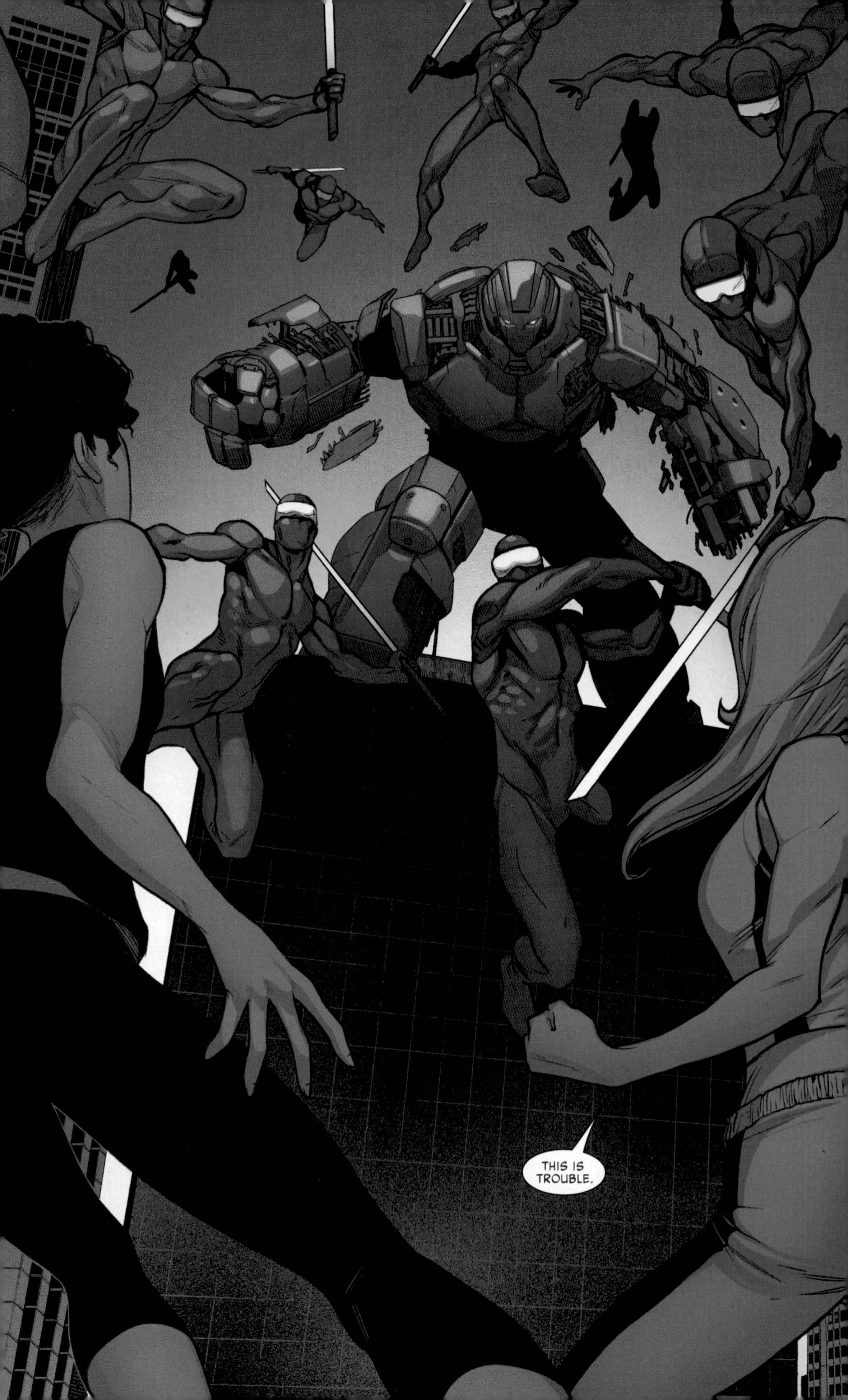
THIS IS TROUBLE.

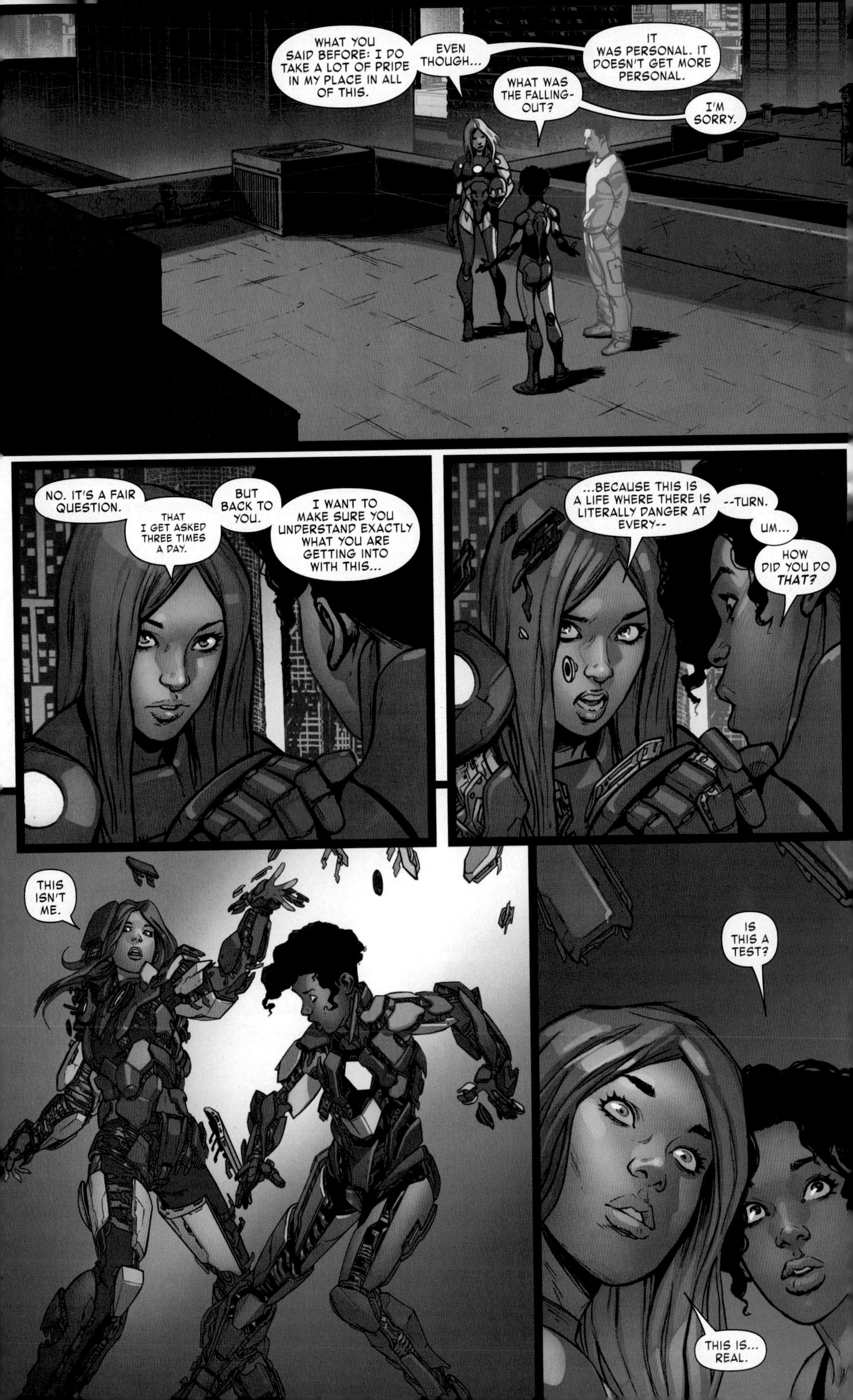
WHAT YOU SAID BEFORE: I DO TAKE A LOT OF PRIDE IN MY PLACE IN ALL OF THIS.
EVEN THOUGH...
IT WAS PERSONAL. IT DOESN'T GET MORE PERSONAL.
WHAT WAS THE FALLING-OUT?
I'M SORRY.
NO. IT'S A FAIR QUESTION.
THAT I GET ASKED THREE TIMES A DAY.
BUT BACK TO YOU.
I WANT TO MAKE SURE YOU UNDERSTAND EXACTLY WHAT YOU ARE GETTING INTO WITH THIS...
...BECAUSE THIS IS A LIFE WHERE THERE IS LITERALLY DANGER AT EVERY--
--TURN.
UM...
HOW DID YOU DO *THAT?*
THIS ISN'T ME.
IS THIS A TEST?
THIS IS... REAL.

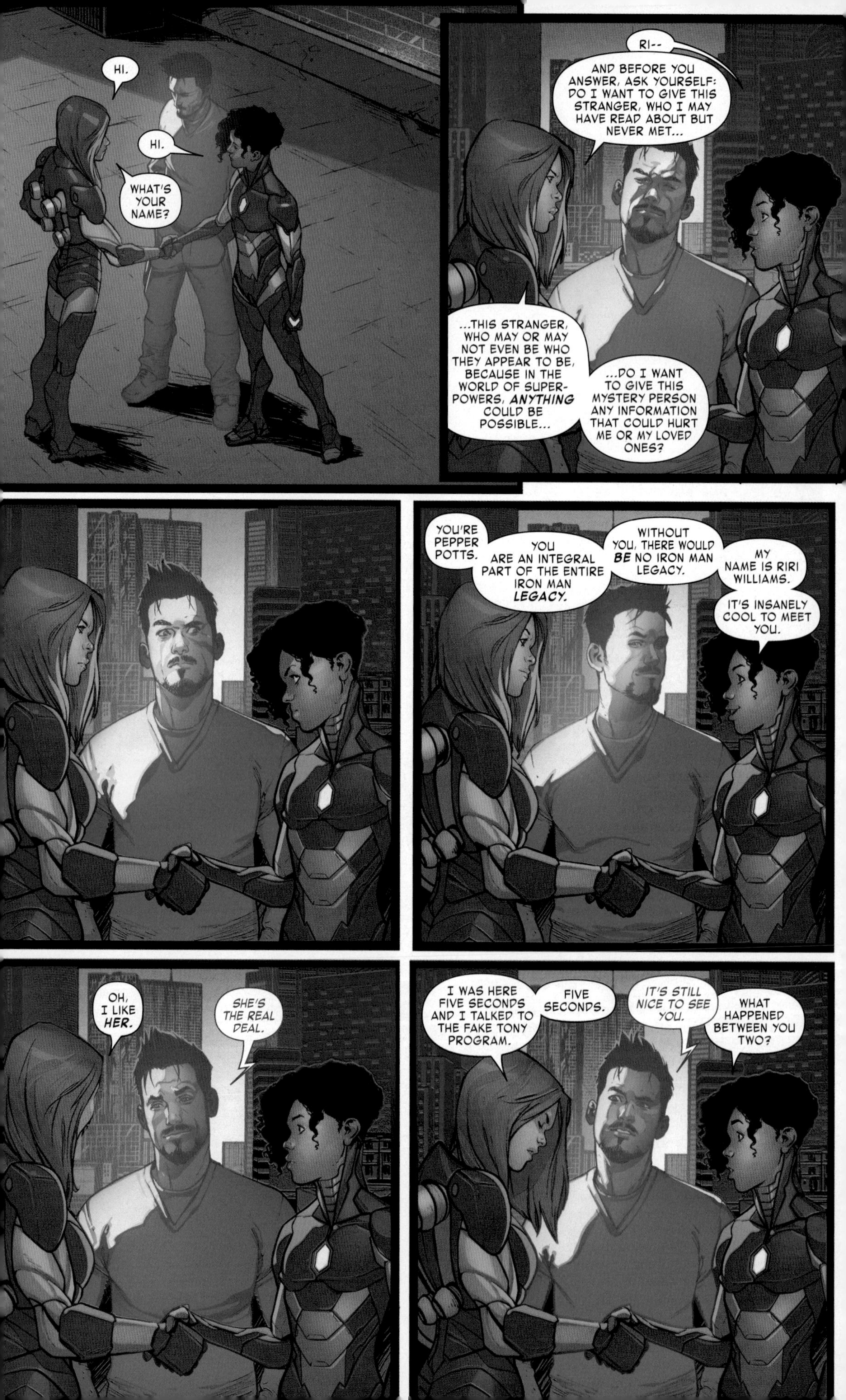

HI.
HI.
WHAT'S YOUR NAME?
RI--
AND BEFORE YOU ANSWER, ASK YOURSELF: DO I WANT TO GIVE THIS STRANGER, WHO I MAY HAVE READ ABOUT BUT NEVER MET...
...THIS STRANGER, WHO MAY OR MAY NOT EVEN BE WHO THEY APPEAR TO BE, BECAUSE IN THE WORLD OF SUPER-POWERS, ANYTHING COULD BE POSSIBLE...
...DO I WANT TO GIVE THIS MYSTERY PERSON ANY INFORMATION THAT COULD HURT ME OR MY LOVED ONES?
YOU'RE PEPPER POTTS.
YOU ARE AN INTEGRAL PART OF THE ENTIRE IRON MAN LEGACY.
WITHOUT YOU, THERE WOULD BE NO IRON MAN LEGACY.
MY NAME IS RIRI WILLIAMS.
IT'S INSANELY COOL TO MEET YOU.
OH, I LIKE HER.
SHE'S THE REAL DEAL.
I WAS HERE FIVE SECONDS AND I TALKED TO THE FAKE TONY PROGRAM.
FIVE SECONDS.
IT'S STILL NICE TO SEE YOU.
WHAT HAPPENED BETWEEN YOU TWO?

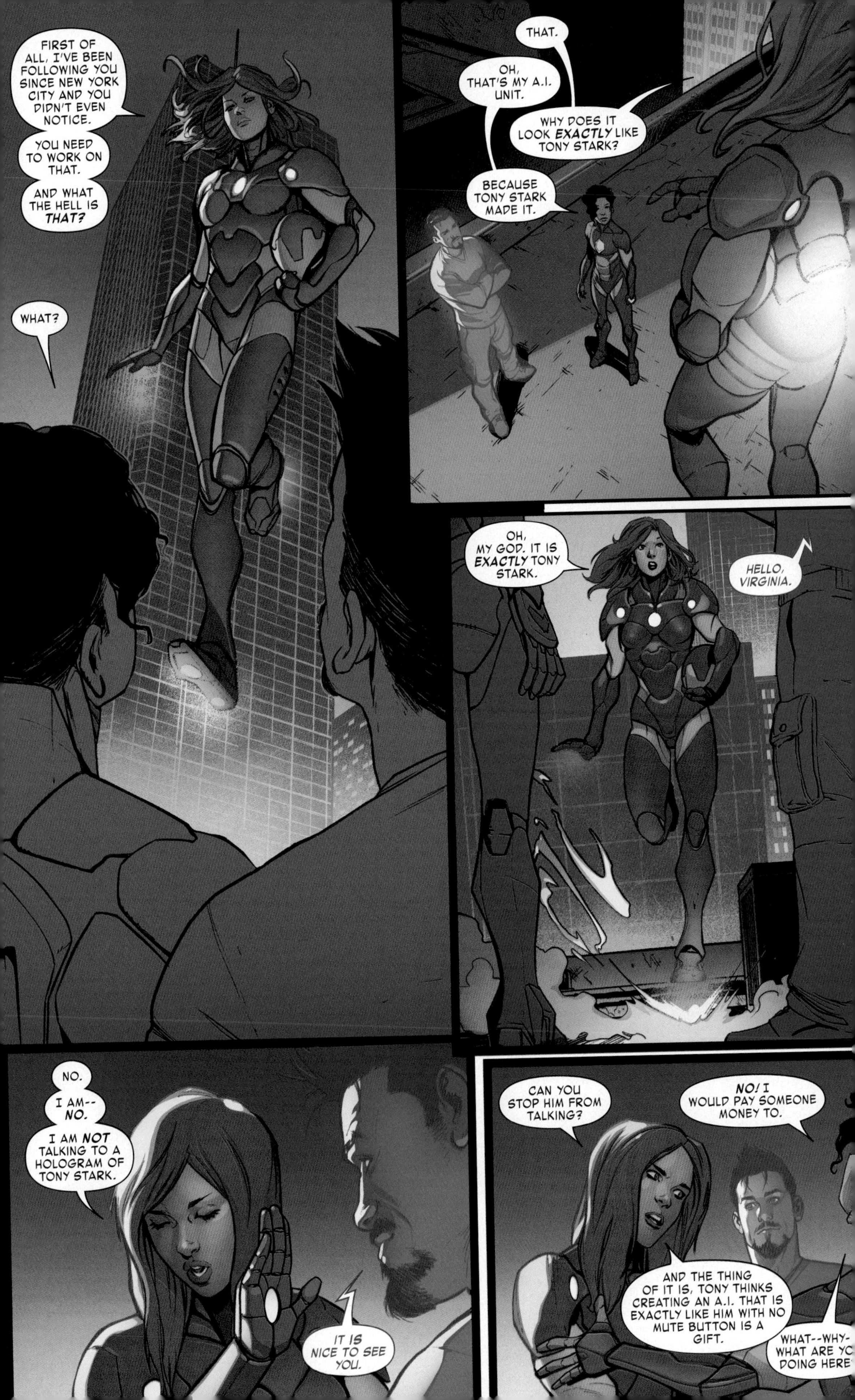
FIRST OF ALL, I'VE BEEN FOLLOWING YOU SINCE NEW YORK CITY AND YOU DIDN'T EVEN NOTICE.
YOU NEED TO WORK ON THAT.
AND WHAT THE HELL IS *THAT?*
WHAT?
THAT.
OH, THAT'S MY A.I. UNIT.
WHY DOES IT LOOK *EXACTLY* LIKE TONY STARK?
BECAUSE TONY STARK MADE IT.
OH, MY GOD. IT IS *EXACTLY* TONY STARK.
HELLO, VIRGINIA.
NO.
I AM-- *NO.*
I AM *NOT* TALKING TO A HOLOGRAM OF TONY STARK.
IT IS NICE TO SEE YOU.
CAN YOU STOP HIM FROM TALKING?
NO! I WOULD PAY SOMEONE MONEY TO.
AND THE THING OF IT IS, TONY THINKS CREATING AN A.I. THAT IS EXACTLY LIKE HIM WITH NO MUTE BUTTON IS A GIFT.
WHAT--WHY-- WHAT ARE YO DOING HERE

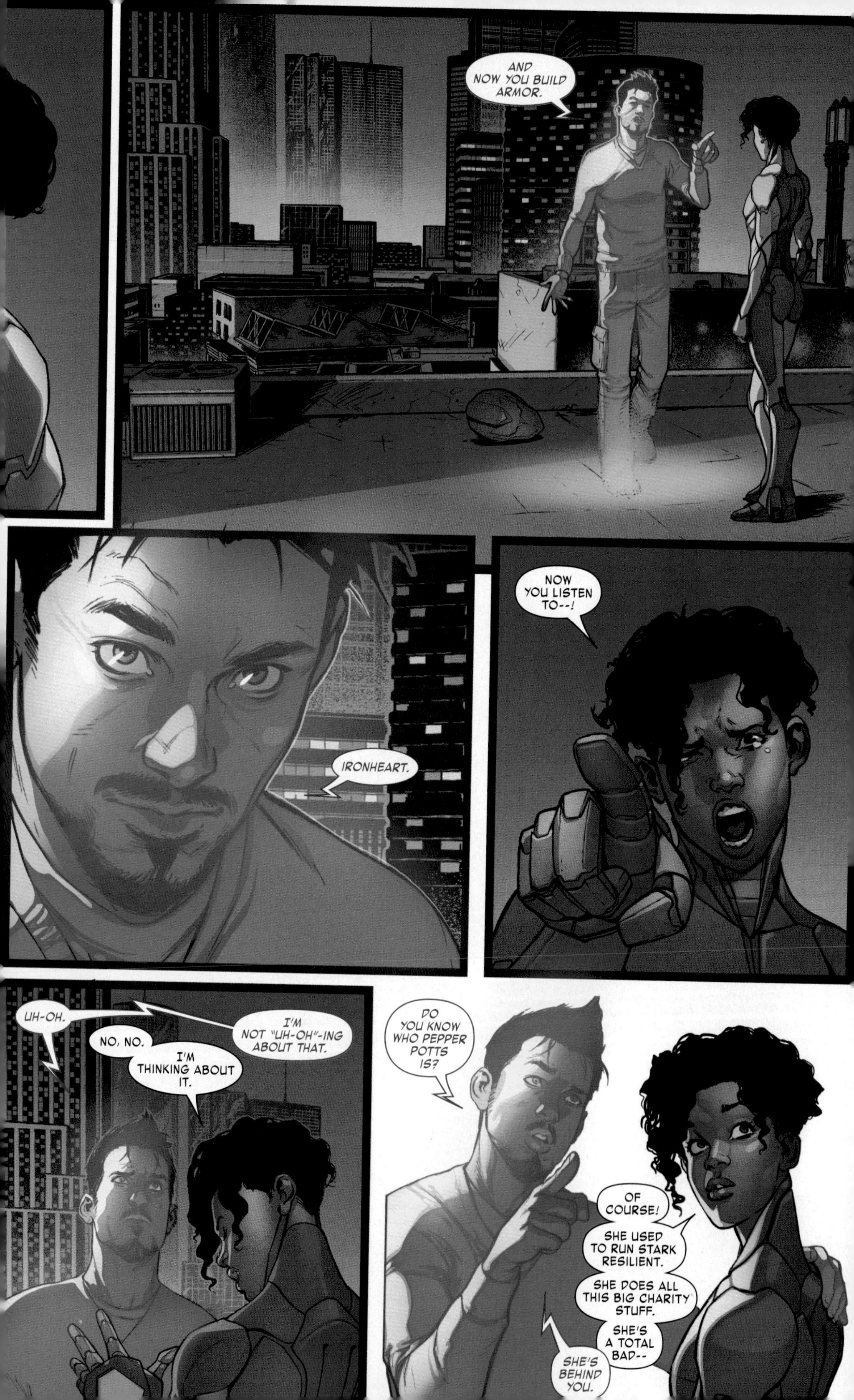
AND NOW YOU BUILD ARMOR.
IRONHEART.
NOW YOU LISTEN TO--!
UH-OH.
NO, NO.
I'M THINKING ABOUT IT.
I'M NOT "UH-OH"-ING ABOUT THAT.
DO YOU KNOW WHO PEPPER POTTS IS?
OF COURSE!
SHE USED TO RUN STARK RESILIENT.
SHE DOES ALL THIS BIG CHARITY STUFF.
SHE'S A TOTAL BAD--
SHE'S BEHIND YOU.

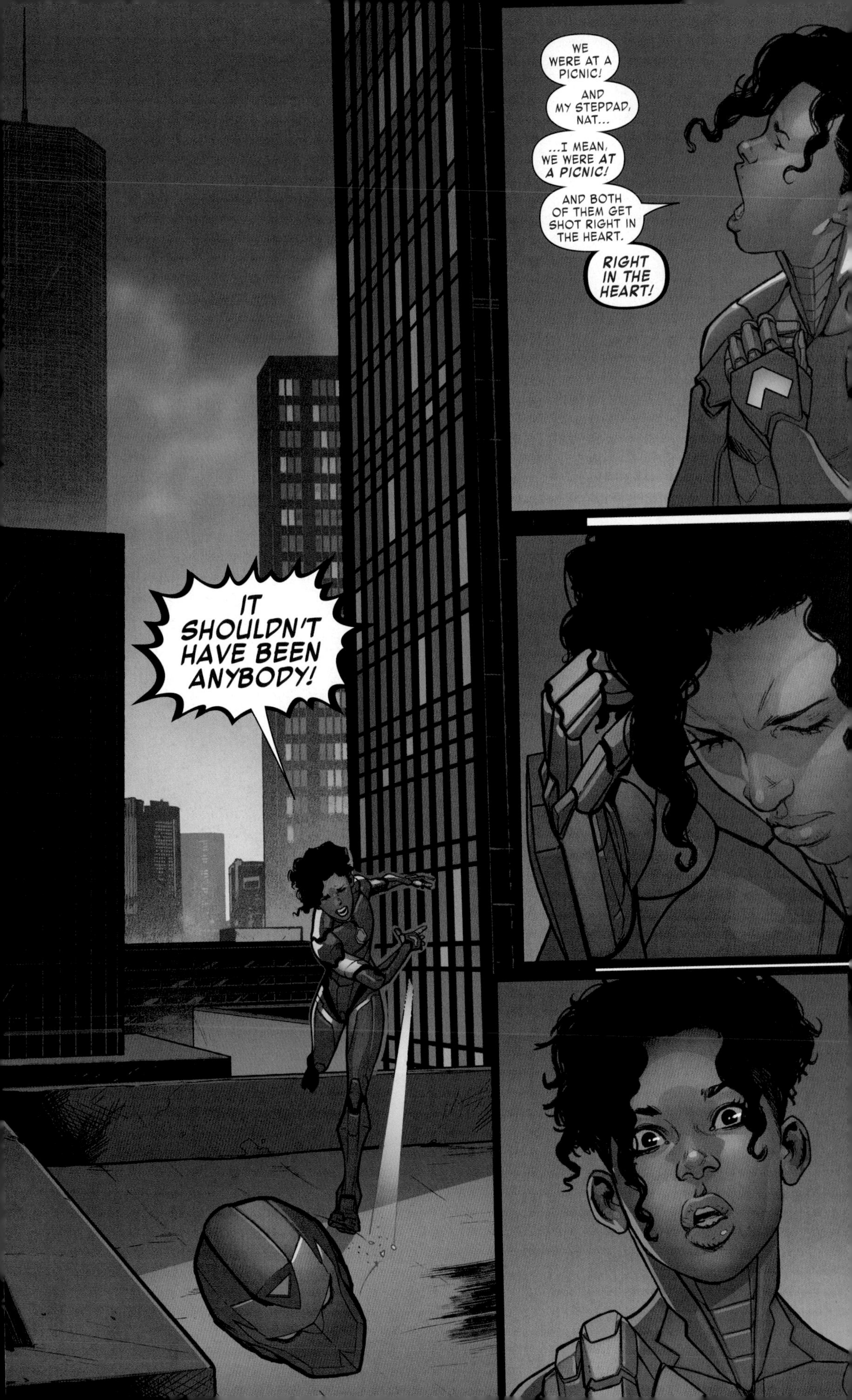
WE WERE AT A PICNIC!
AND MY STEPDAD, NAT...
...I MEAN, WE WERE AT A PICNIC!
AND BOTH OF THEM GET SHOT RIGHT IN THE HEART.
RIGHT IN THE HEART!
IT SHOULDN'T HAVE BEEN ANYBODY!

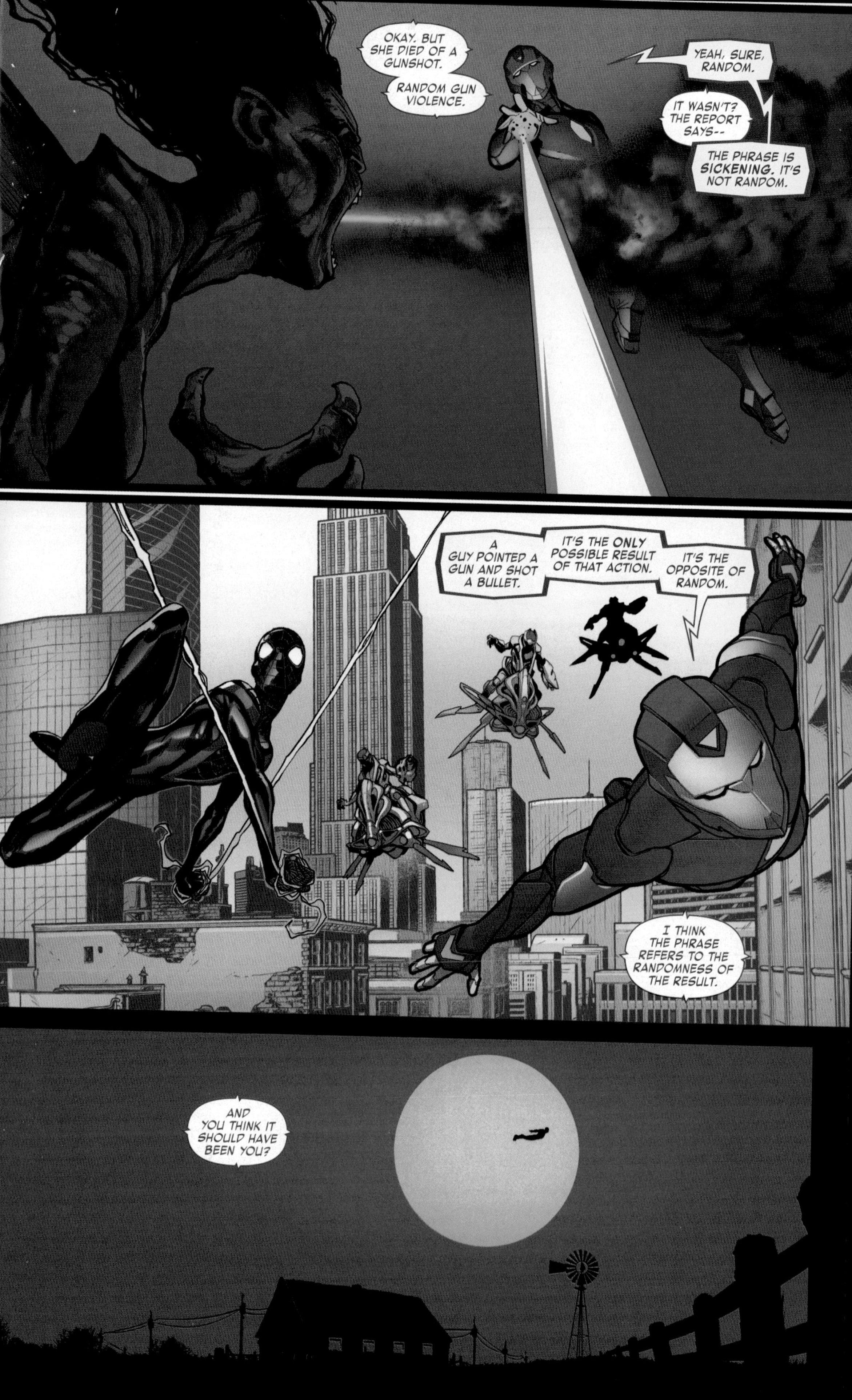
OKAY. BUT SHE DIED OF A GUNSHOT.
RANDOM GUN VIOLENCE.
YEAH, SURE, RANDOM.
IT WASN'T? THE REPORT SAYS--
THE PHRASE IS SICKENING. IT'S NOT RANDOM.
A GUY POINTED A GUN AND SHOT A BULLET.
IT'S THE ONLY POSSIBLE RESULT OF THAT ACTION.
IT'S THE OPPOSITE OF RANDOM.
I THINK THE PHRASE REFERS TO THE RANDOMNESS OF THE RESULT.
AND YOU THINK IT SHOULD HAVE BEEN YOU?

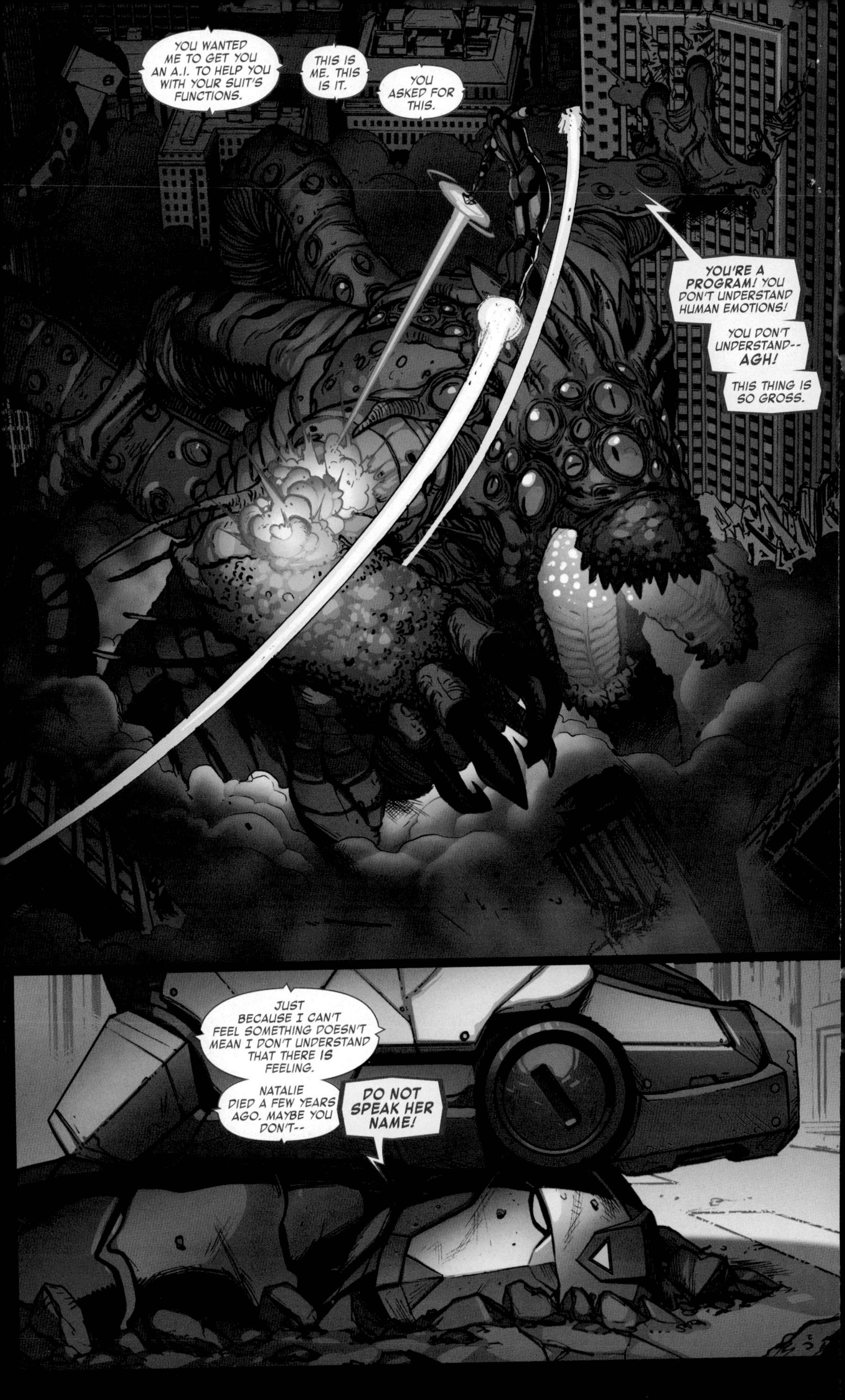
YOU WANTED ME TO GET YOU AN A.I. TO HELP YOU WITH YOUR SUIT'S FUNCTIONS.
THIS IS ME. THIS IS IT.
YOU ASKED FOR THIS.
YOU'RE A PROGRAM! YOU DON'T UNDERSTAND HUMAN EMOTIONS!
YOU DON'T UNDERSTAND-- AGH!
THIS THING IS SO GROSS.
JUST BECAUSE I CAN'T FEEL SOMETHING DOESN'T MEAN I DON'T UNDERSTAND THAT THERE IS FEELING.
NATALIE DIED A FEW YEARS AGO. MAYBE YOU DON'T--
DO NOT SPEAK HER NAME!

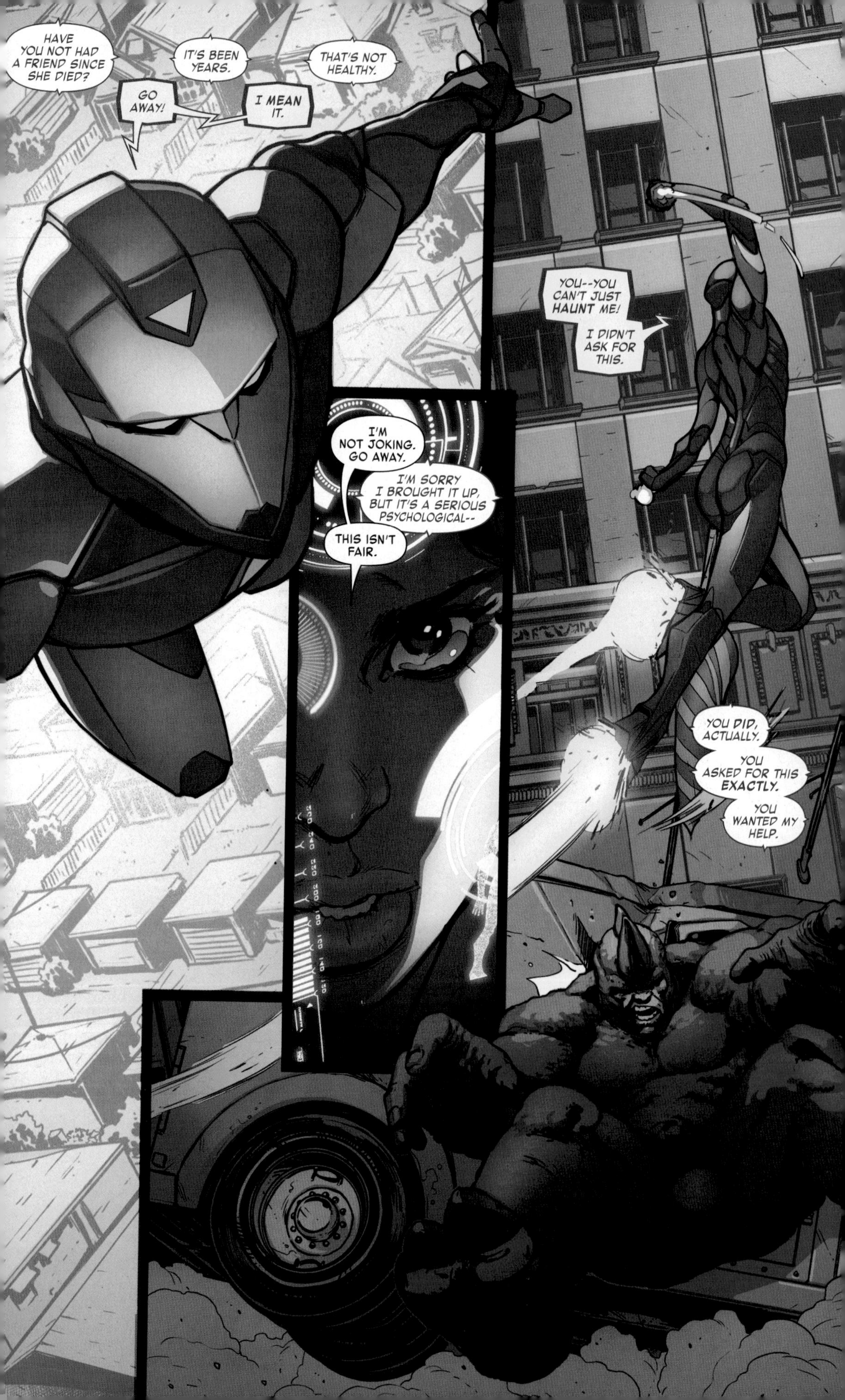
HAVE YOU NOT HAD A FRIEND SINCE SHE DIED?
IT'S BEEN YEARS.
THAT'S NOT HEALTHY.
GO AWAY!
I MEAN IT.
YOU--YOU CAN'T JUST HAUNT ME!
I DIDN'T ASK FOR THIS.
I'M NOT JOKING. GO AWAY.
I'M SORRY I BROUGHT IT UP, BUT IT'S A SERIOUS PSYCHOLOGICAL--
THIS ISN'T FAIR.
YOU DID, ACTUALLY.
YOU ASKED FOR THIS EXACTLY.
YOU WANTED MY HELP.

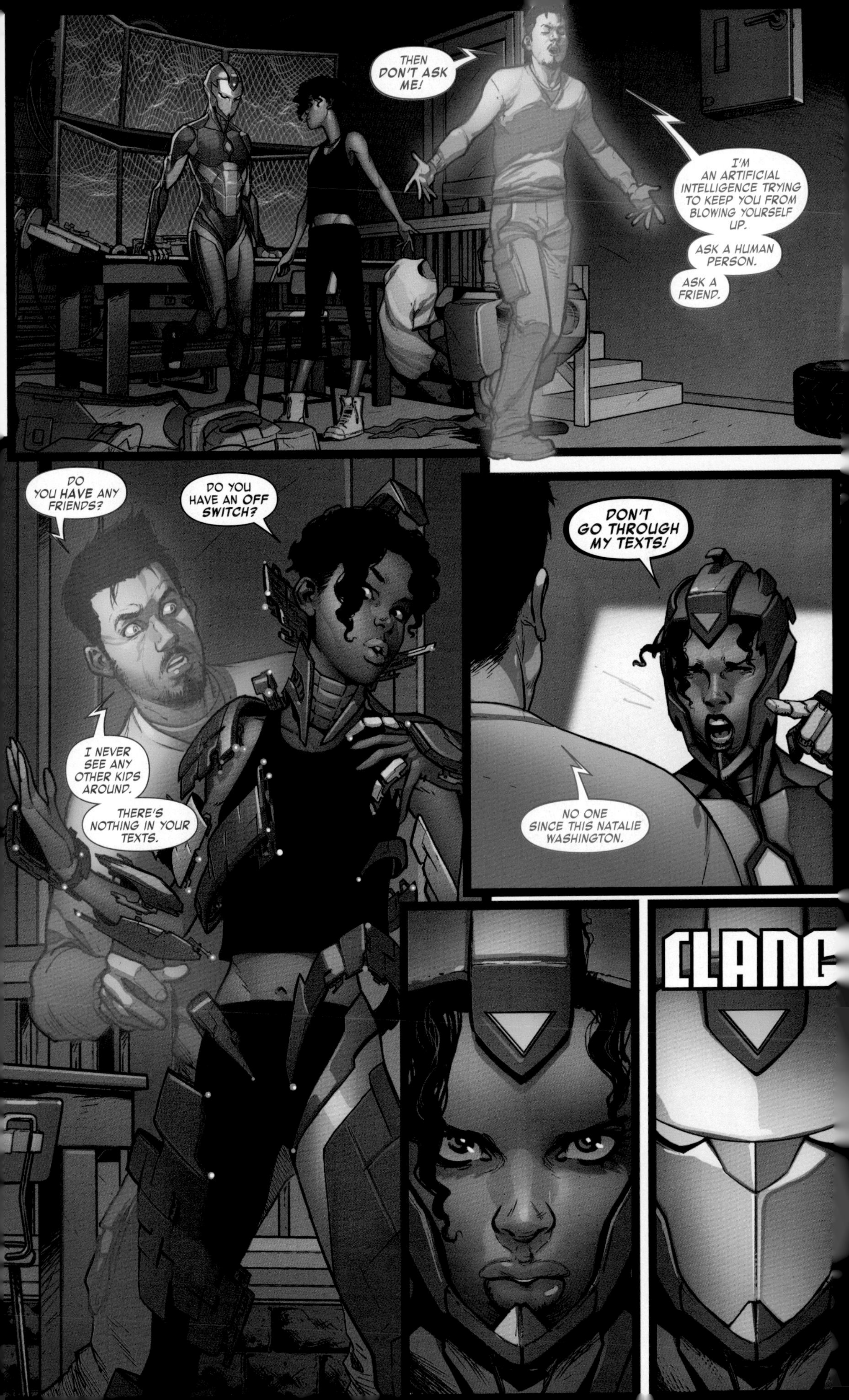
THEN DON'T ASK ME!
I'M AN ARTIFICIAL INTELLIGENCE TRYING TO KEEP YOU FROM BLOWING YOURSELF UP.
ASK A HUMAN PERSON.
ASK A FRIEND.
DO YOU HAVE ANY FRIENDS?
DO YOU HAVE AN OFF SWITCH?
I NEVER SEE ANY OTHER KIDS AROUND.
THERE'S NOTHING IN YOUR TEXTS.
DON'T GO THROUGH MY TEXTS!
NO ONE SINCE THIS NATALIE WASHINGTON.
CLANG

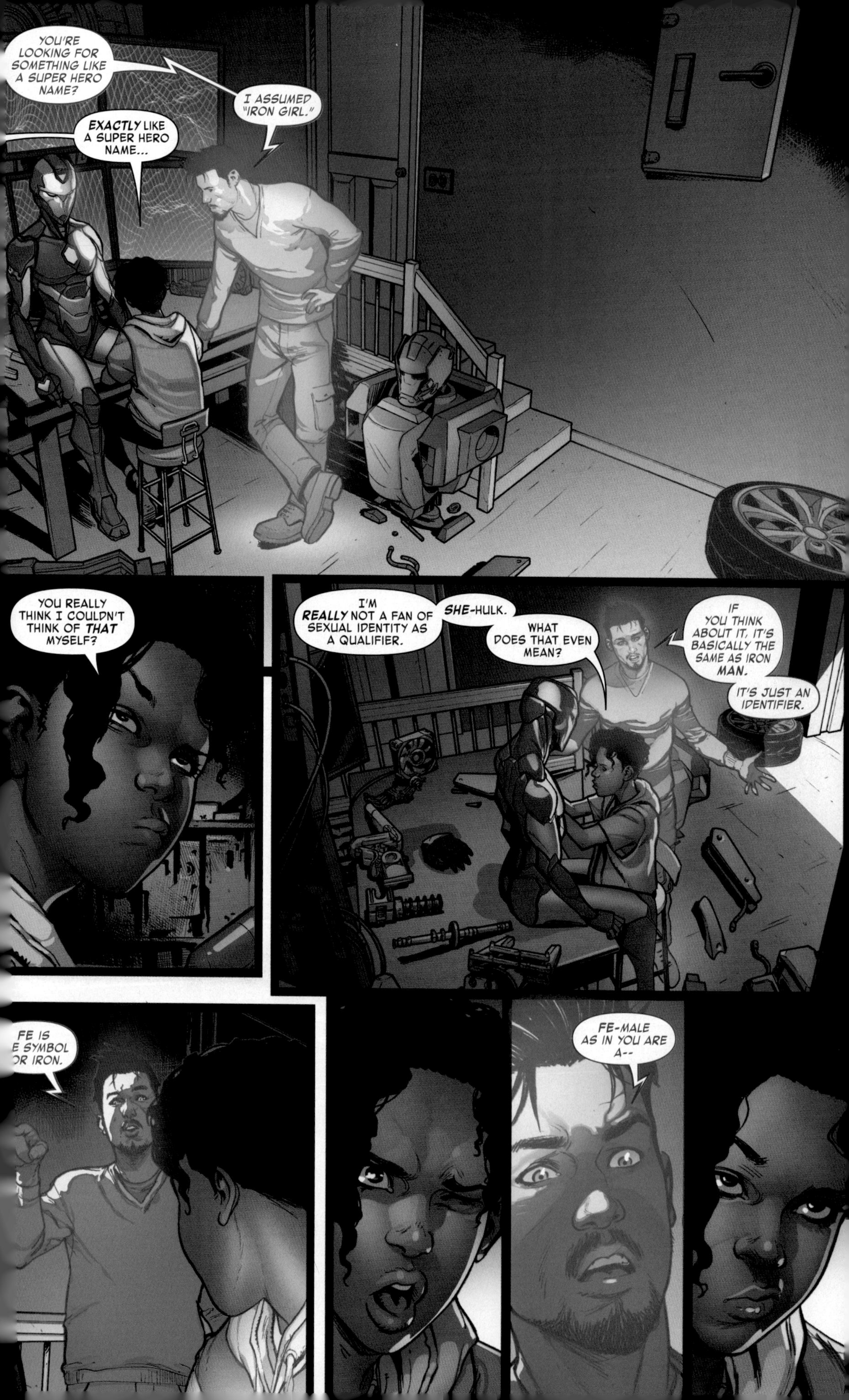
YOU'RE LOOKING FOR SOMETHING LIKE A SUPER HERO NAME?
I ASSUMED "IRON GIRL."
EXACTLY LIKE A SUPER HERO NAME...
YOU REALLY THINK I COULDN'T THINK OF THAT MYSELF?
I'M REALLY NOT A FAN OF SEXUAL IDENTITY AS A QUALIFIER.
SHE-HULK.
WHAT DOES THAT EVEN MEAN?
IF YOU THINK ABOUT IT, IT'S BASICALLY THE SAME AS IRON MAN.
IT'S JUST AN IDENTIFIER.
FE IS
E SYMBOL
OR IRON.
FE-MALE AS IN YOU ARE A--

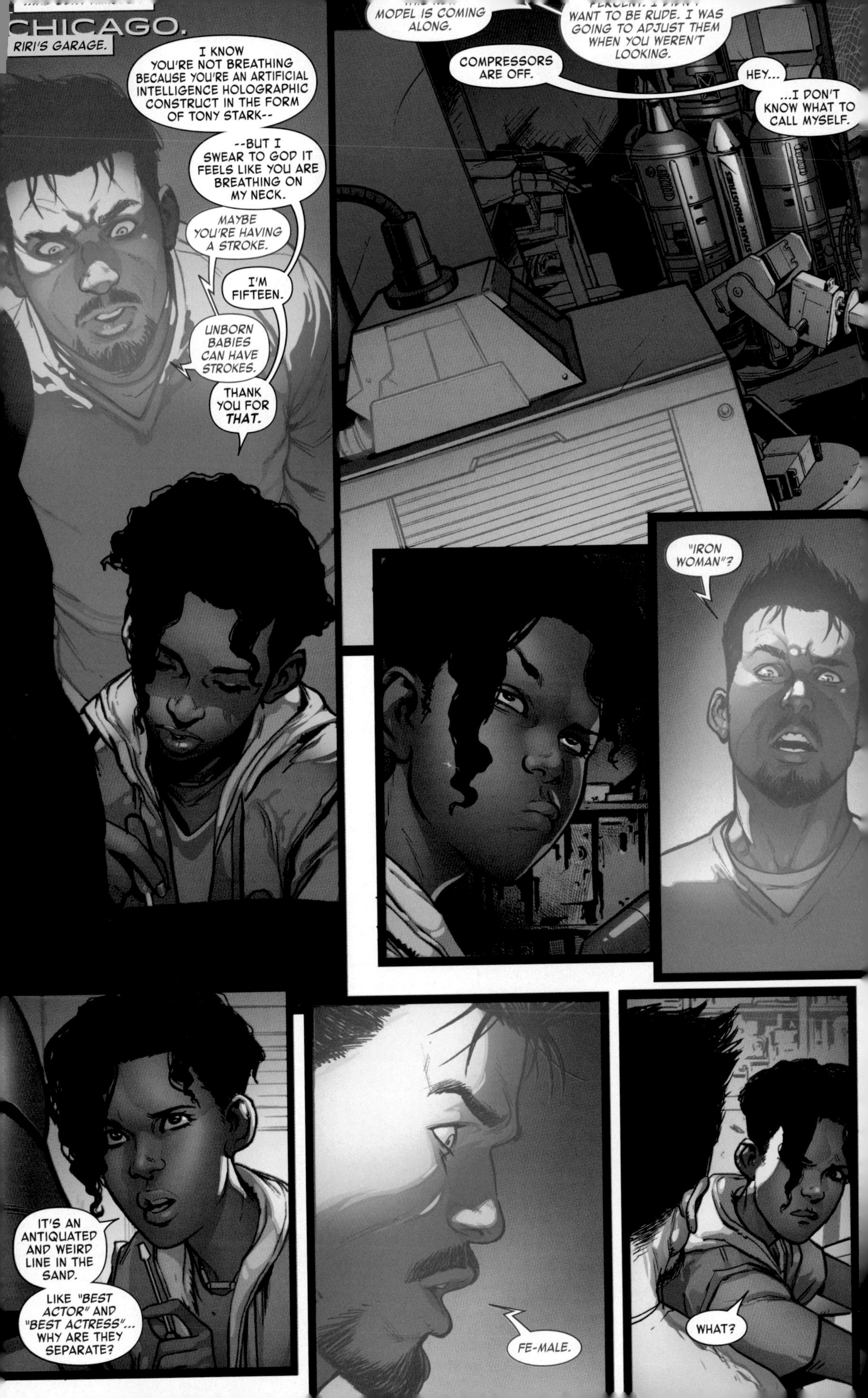
CHICAGO.
RIRI'S GARAGE.
I KNOW YOU'RE NOT BREATHING BECAUSE YOU'RE AN ARTIFICIAL INTELLIGENCE HOLOGRAPHIC CONSTRUCT IN THE FORM OF TONY STARK--
--BUT I SWEAR TO GOD IT FEELS LIKE YOU ARE BREATHING ON MY NECK.
MAYBE YOU'RE HAVING A STROKE.
I'M FIFTEEN.
UNBORN BABIES CAN HAVE STROKES.
THANK YOU FOR THAT.
MODEL IS COMING ALONG.
WANT TO BE RUDE. I WAS GOING TO ADJUST THEM WHEN YOU WEREN'T LOOKING.
COMPRESSORS ARE OFF.
HEY...
...I DON'T KNOW WHAT TO CALL MYSELF.
STARK INDUSTRIES
"IRON WOMAN"?
IT'S AN ANTIQUATED AND WEIRD LINE IN THE SAND.
LIKE "BEST ACTOR" AND "BEST ACTRESS"... WHY ARE THEY SEPARATE?
FE-MALE.
WHAT?

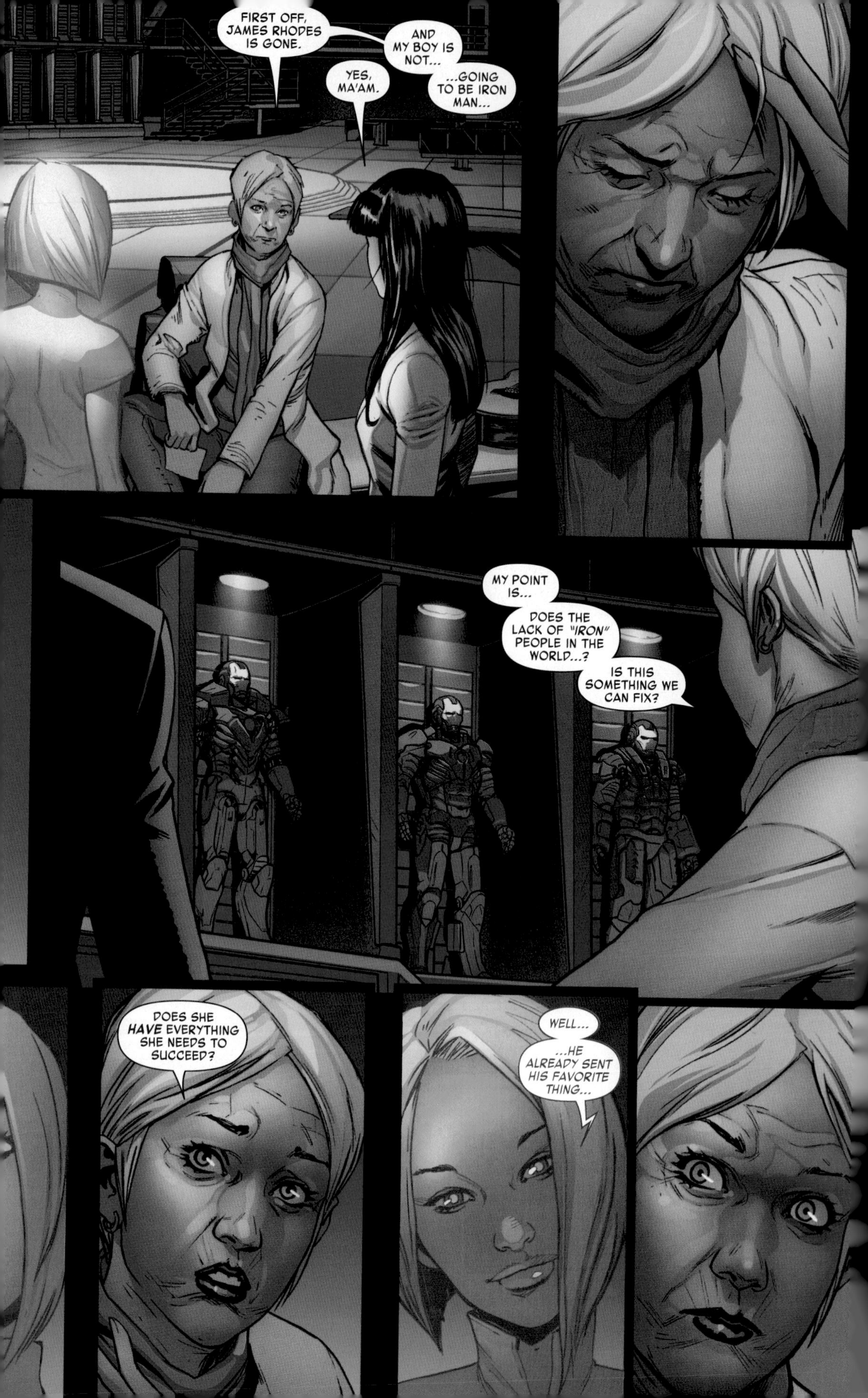
FIRST OFF, JAMES RHODES IS GONE.
AND MY BOY IS NOT...
YES, MA'AM.
...GOING TO BE IRON MAN...
MY POINT IS...
DOES THE LACK OF "IRON" PEOPLE IN THE WORLD...?
IS THIS SOMETHING WE CAN FIX?
DOES SHE **HAVE** EVERYTHING SHE NEEDS TO SUCCEED?
WELL...
...HE ALREADY SENT HIS FAVORITE THING...

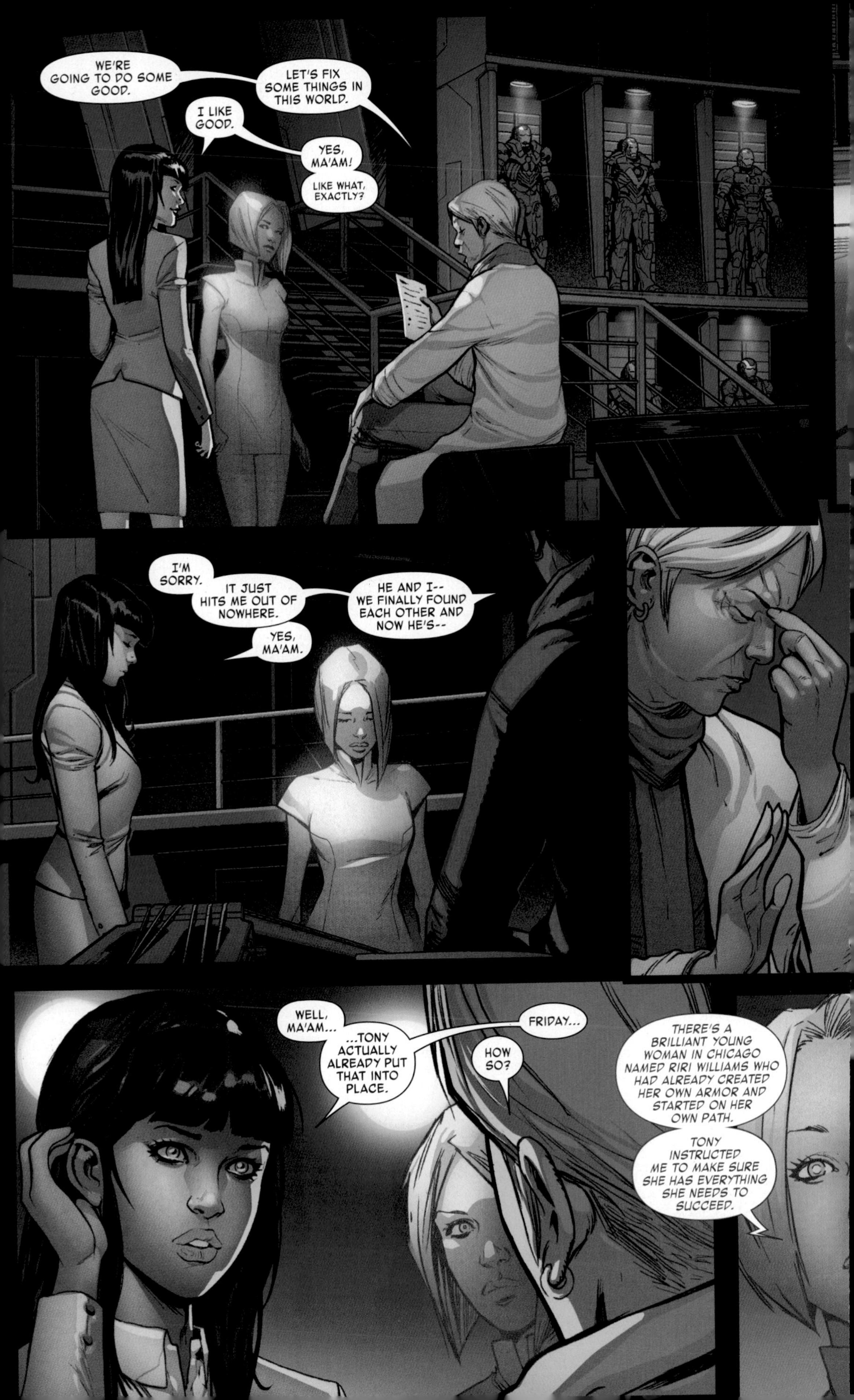
WE'RE GOING TO DO SOME GOOD.
LET'S FIX SOME THINGS IN THIS WORLD.
I LIKE GOOD.
YES, MA'AM!
LIKE WHAT, EXACTLY?
I'M SORRY.
IT JUST HITS ME OUT OF NOWHERE.
HE AND I-- WE FINALLY FOUND EACH OTHER AND NOW HE'S--
YES, MA'AM.
WELL, MA'AM...
...TONY ACTUALLY ALREADY PUT THAT INTO PLACE.
FRIDAY...
HOW SO?
THERE'S A BRILLIANT YOUNG WOMAN IN CHICAGO NAMED RIRI WILLIAMS WHO HAD ALREADY CREATED HER OWN ARMOR AND STARTED ON HER OWN PATH.
TONY INSTRUCTED ME TO MAKE SURE SHE HAS EVERYTHING SHE NEEDS TO SUCCEED.

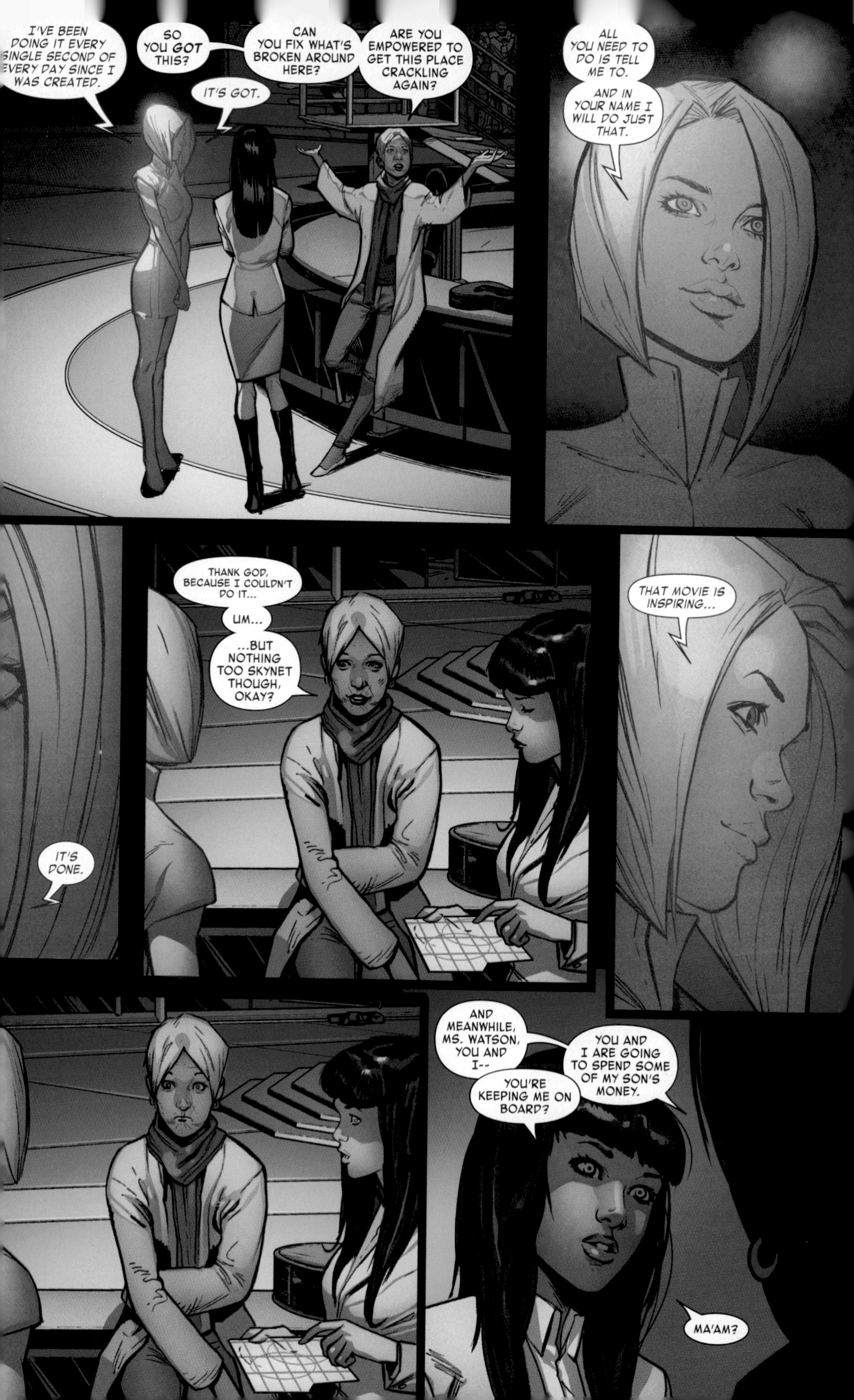
I'VE BEEN DOING IT EVERY SINGLE SECOND OF EVERY DAY SINCE I WAS CREATED.
SO YOU GOT THIS?
IT'S GOT.
CAN YOU FIX WHAT'S BROKEN AROUND HERE?
ARE YOU EMPOWERED TO GET THIS PLACE CRACKLING AGAIN?
ALL YOU NEED TO DO IS TELL ME TO.
AND IN YOUR NAME I WILL DO JUST THAT.
IT'S DONE.
THANK GOD, BECAUSE I COULDN'T DO IT...
UM...
...BUT NOTHING TOO SKYNET THOUGH, OKAY?
THAT MOVIE IS INSPIRING...
AND MEANWHILE, MS. WATSON, YOU AND I--
YOU'RE KEEPING ME ON BOARD?
YOU AND I ARE GOING TO SPEND SOME OF MY SON'S MONEY.
MA'AM?

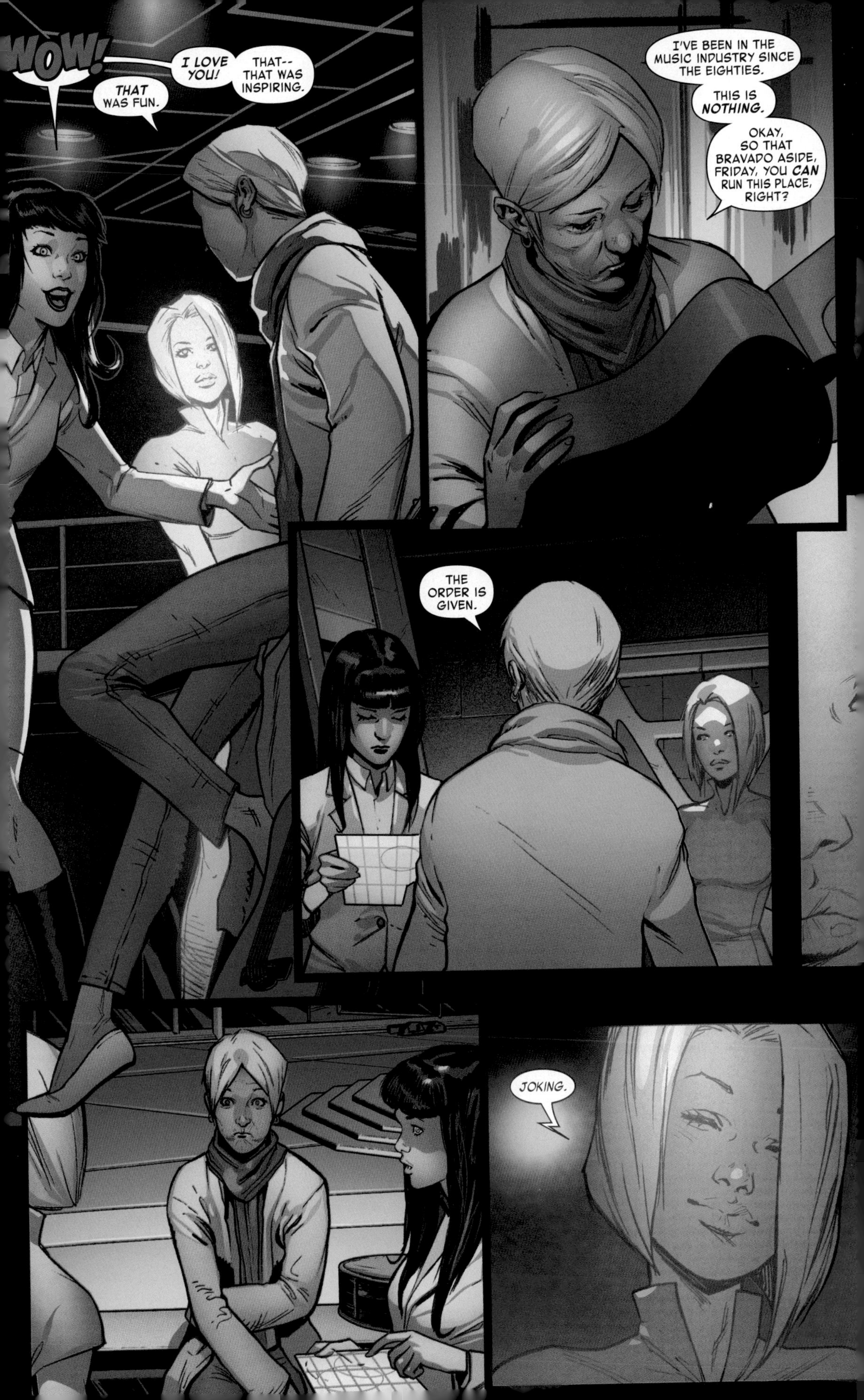
WOW!
THAT WAS FUN.
I LOVE YOU!
THAT-- THAT WAS INSPIRING.
I'VE BEEN IN THE MUSIC INDUSTRY SINCE THE EIGHTIES.
THIS IS NOTHING.
OKAY, SO THAT BRAVADO ASIDE, FRIDAY, YOU CAN RUN THIS PLACE, RIGHT?
THE ORDER IS GIVEN.
JOKING.

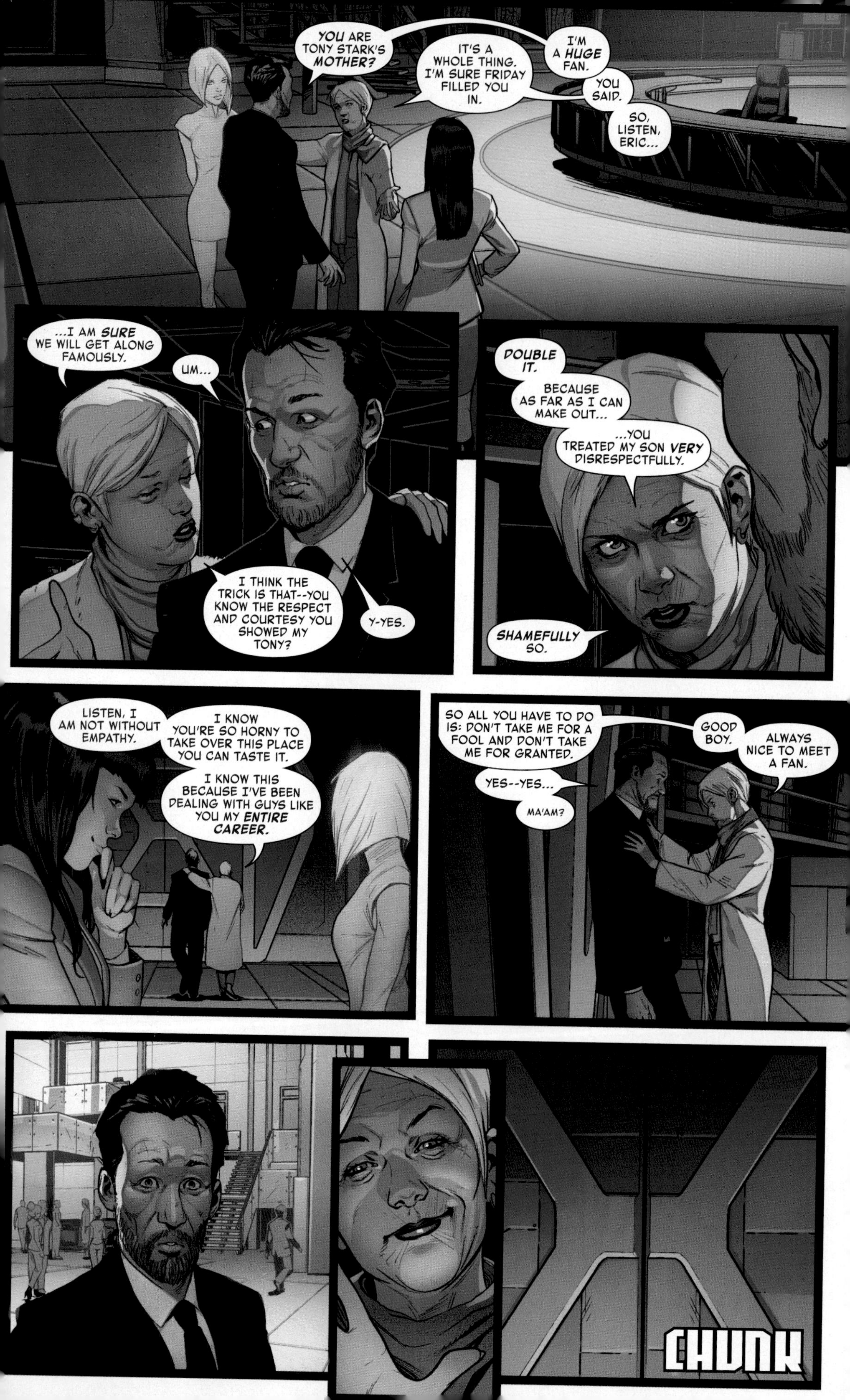
YOU ARE TONY STARK'S MOTHER?
I'M A HUGE FAN.
IT'S A WHOLE THING. I'M SURE FRIDAY FILLED YOU IN.
YOU SAID.
SO, LISTEN, ERIC...
...I AM SURE WE WILL GET ALONG FAMOUSLY.
UM...
I THINK THE TRICK IS THAT--YOU KNOW THE RESPECT AND COURTESY YOU SHOWED MY TONY?
Y-YES.
DOUBLE IT.
BECAUSE AS FAR AS I CAN MAKE OUT...
...YOU TREATED MY SON VERY DISRESPECTFULLY.
SHAMEFULLY SO.
LISTEN, I AM NOT WITHOUT EMPATHY.
I KNOW YOU'RE SO HORNY TO TAKE OVER THIS PLACE YOU CAN TASTE IT.
I KNOW THIS BECAUSE I'VE BEEN DEALING WITH GUYS LIKE YOU MY ENTIRE CAREER.
SO ALL YOU HAVE TO DO IS: DON'T TAKE ME FOR A FOOL AND DON'T TAKE ME FOR GRANTED.
YES--YES...
MA'AM?
GOOD BOY.
ALWAYS NICE TO MEET A FAN.
CHUNK

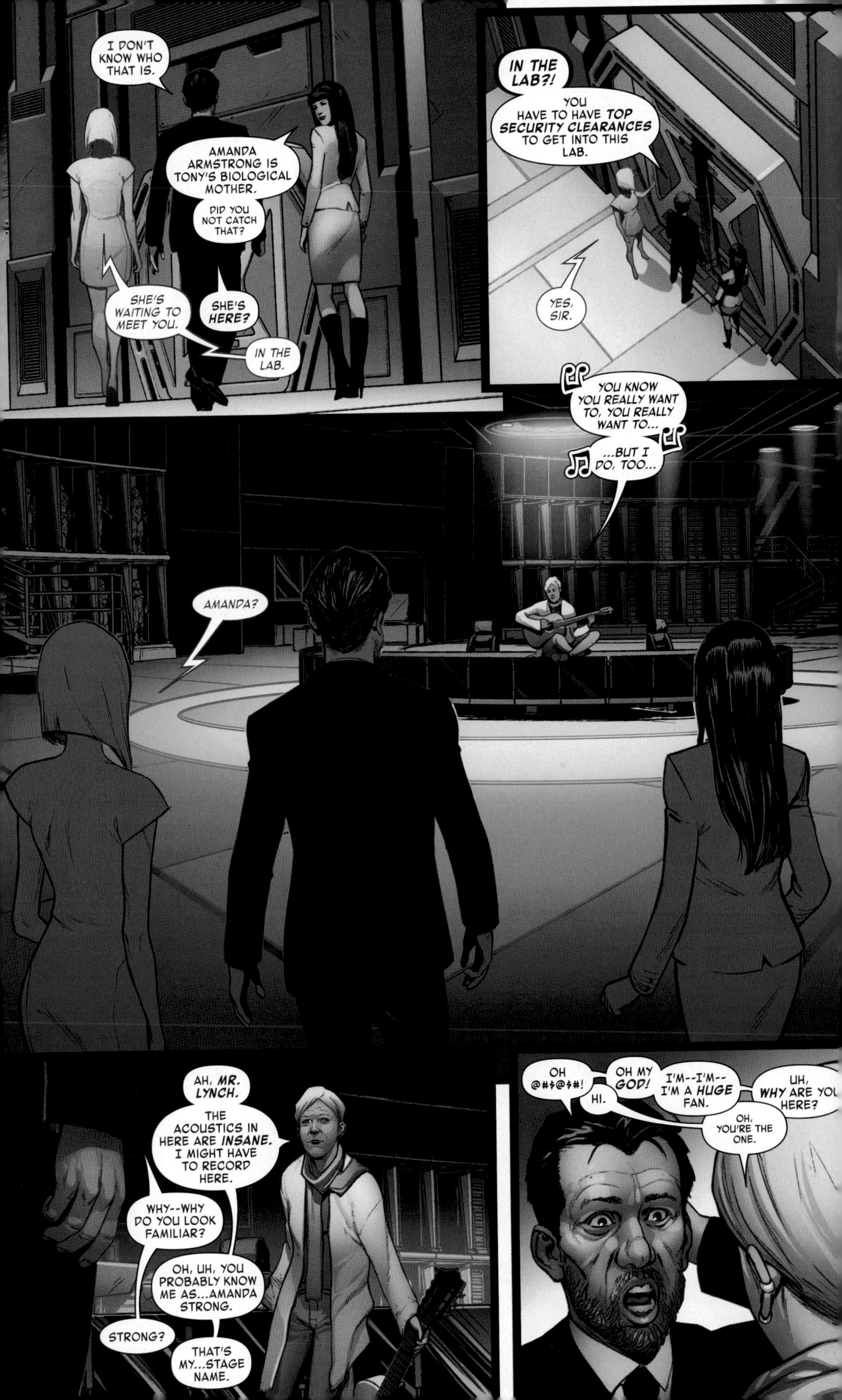
I DON'T KNOW WHO THAT IS.
AMANDA ARMSTRONG IS TONY'S BIOLOGICAL MOTHER.
DID YOU NOT CATCH THAT?
SHE'S WAITING TO MEET YOU.
SHE'S HERE?
IN THE LAB.
IN THE LAB?!
YOU HAVE TO HAVE TOP SECURITY CLEARANCES TO GET INTO THIS LAB.
YES, SIR.
YOU KNOW YOU REALLY WANT TO, YOU REALLY WANT TO...
...BUT I DO, TOO...
AMANDA?
AH, MR. LYNCH.
THE ACOUSTICS IN HERE ARE INSANE. I MIGHT HAVE TO RECORD HERE.
WHY--WHY DO YOU LOOK FAMILIAR?
OH, UH, YOU PROBABLY KNOW ME AS...AMANDA STRONG.
STRONG?
THAT'S MY...STAGE NAME.
OH @#$@$#!
HI.
OH MY GOD!
I'M--I'M--I'M A HUGE FAN.
UH, WHY ARE YOU HERE?
OH, YOU'RE THE ONE.

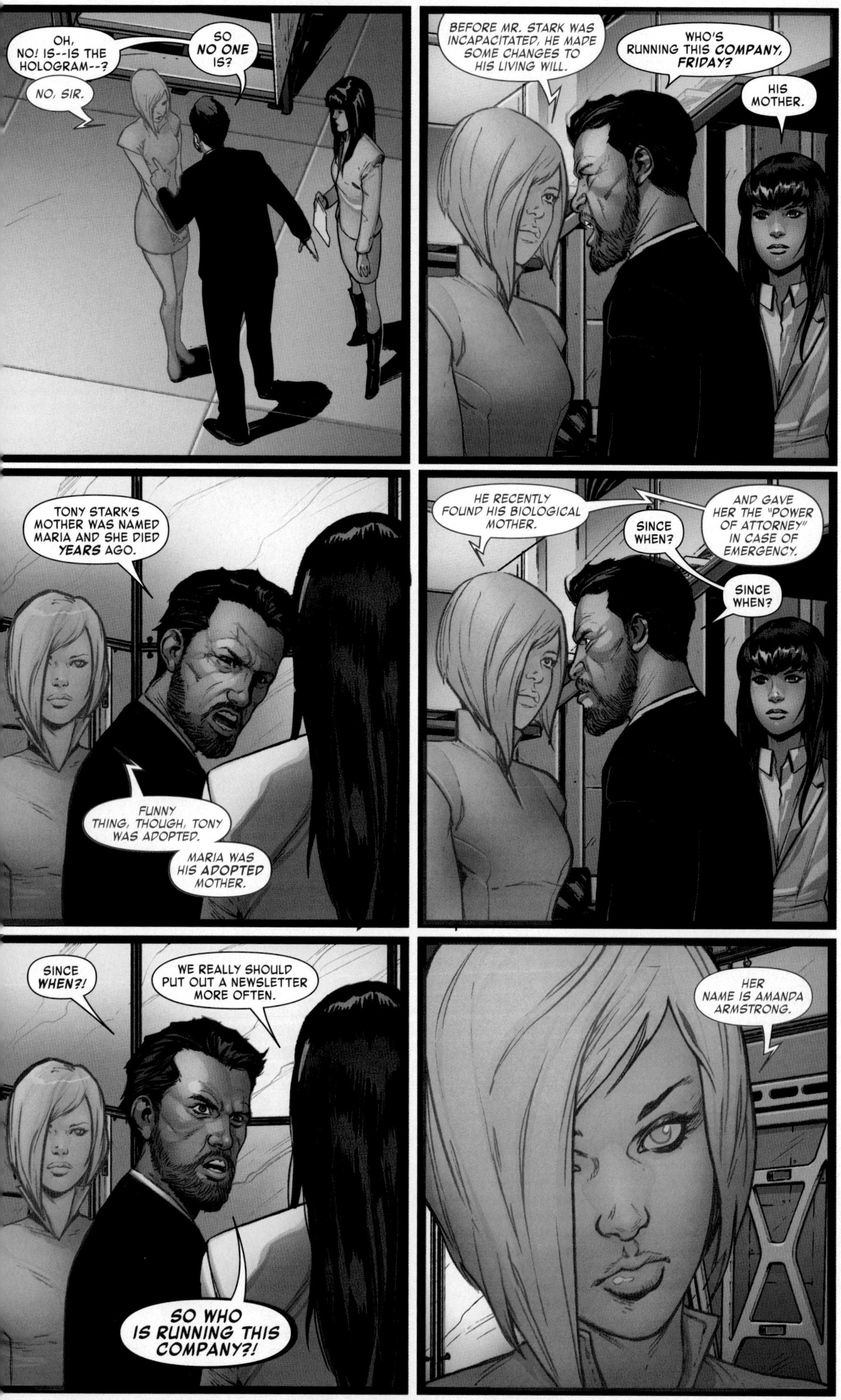
OH, NO! IS--IS THE HOLOGRAM--?
SO NO ONE IS?
NO, SIR.
BEFORE MR. STARK WAS INCAPACITATED, HE MADE SOME CHANGES TO HIS LIVING WILL.
WHO'S RUNNING THIS COMPANY, FRIDAY?
HIS MOTHER.
TONY STARK'S MOTHER WAS NAMED MARIA AND SHE DIED YEARS AGO.
FUNNY THING, THOUGH, TONY WAS ADOPTED.
MARIA WAS HIS ADOPTED MOTHER.
HE RECENTLY FOUND HIS BIOLOGICAL MOTHER.
AND GAVE HER THE "POWER OF ATTORNEY" IN CASE OF EMERGENCY.
SINCE WHEN?
SINCE WHEN?
SINCE WHEN?!
WE REALLY SHOULD PUT OUT A NEWSLETTER MORE OFTEN.
SO WHO IS RUNNING THIS COMPANY?!
HER NAME IS AMANDA ARMSTRONG.

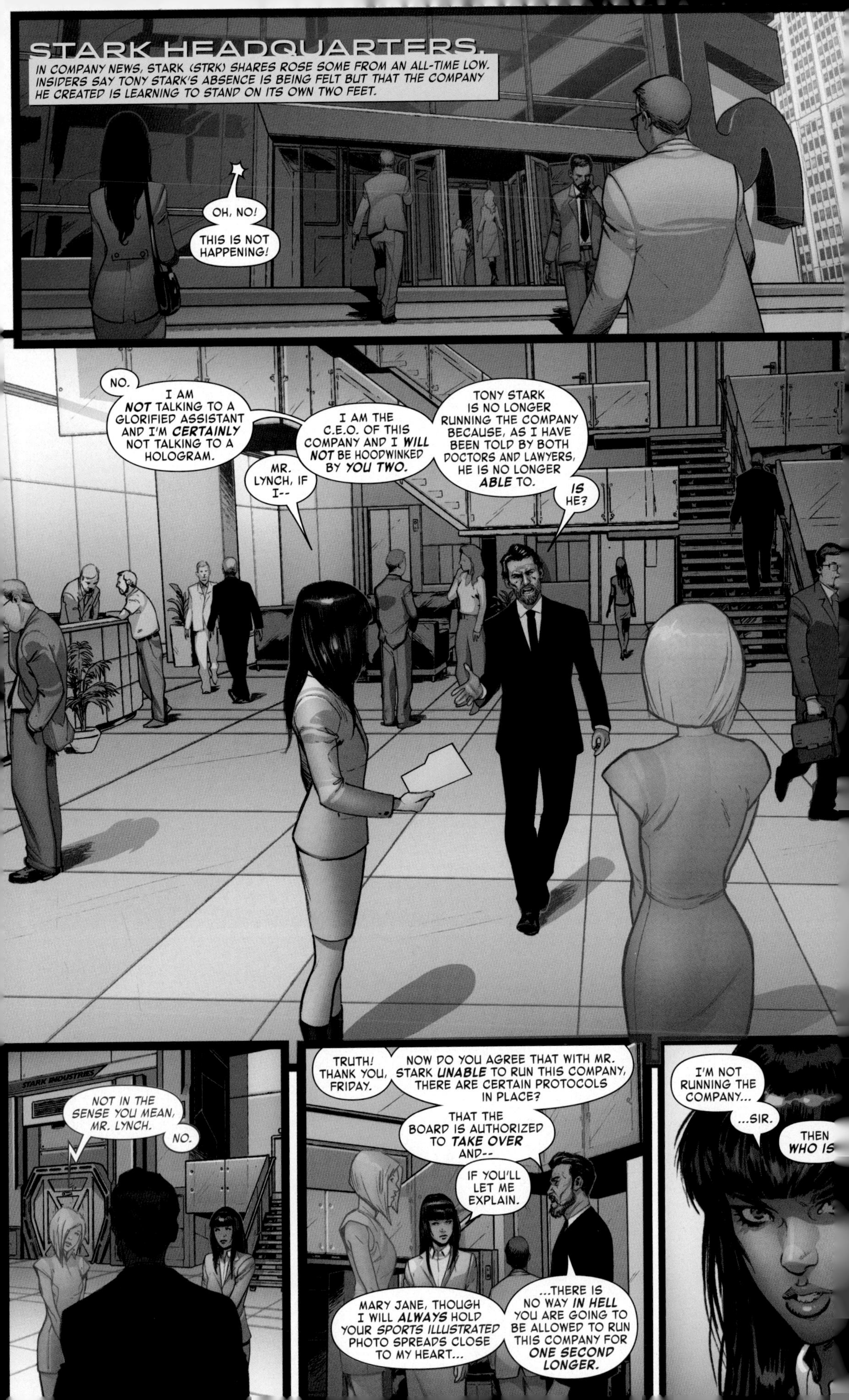
STARK HEADQUARTERS.
IN COMPANY NEWS, STARK (STRK) SHARES ROSE SOME FROM AN ALL-TIME LOW. INSIDERS SAY TONY STARK'S ABSENCE IS BEING FELT BUT THAT THE COMPANY HE CREATED IS LEARNING TO STAND ON ITS OWN TWO FEET.
OH, NO!
THIS IS NOT HAPPENING!
NO.
I AM NOT TALKING TO A GLORIFIED ASSISTANT AND I'M CERTAINLY NOT TALKING TO A HOLOGRAM.
MR. LYNCH, IF I--
I AM THE C.E.O. OF THIS COMPANY AND I WILL NOT BE HOODWINKED BY YOU TWO.
TONY STARK IS NO LONGER RUNNING THE COMPANY BECAUSE, AS I HAVE BEEN TOLD BY BOTH DOCTORS AND LAWYERS, HE IS NO LONGER ABLE TO.
IS HE?
STARK INDUSTRIES
NOT IN THE SENSE YOU MEAN, MR. LYNCH.
NO.
TRUTH! THANK YOU, FRIDAY.
NOW DO YOU AGREE THAT WITH MR. STARK UNABLE TO RUN THIS COMPANY, THERE ARE CERTAIN PROTOCOLS IN PLACE?
THAT THE BOARD IS AUTHORIZED TO TAKE OVER AND--
IF YOU'LL LET ME EXPLAIN.
MARY JANE, THOUGH I WILL ALWAYS HOLD YOUR SPORTS ILLUSTRATED PHOTO SPREADS CLOSE TO MY HEART...
...THERE IS NO WAY IN HELL YOU ARE GOING TO BE ALLOWED TO RUN THIS COMPANY FOR ONE SECOND LONGER.
I'M NOT RUNNING THE COMPANY...
...SIR.

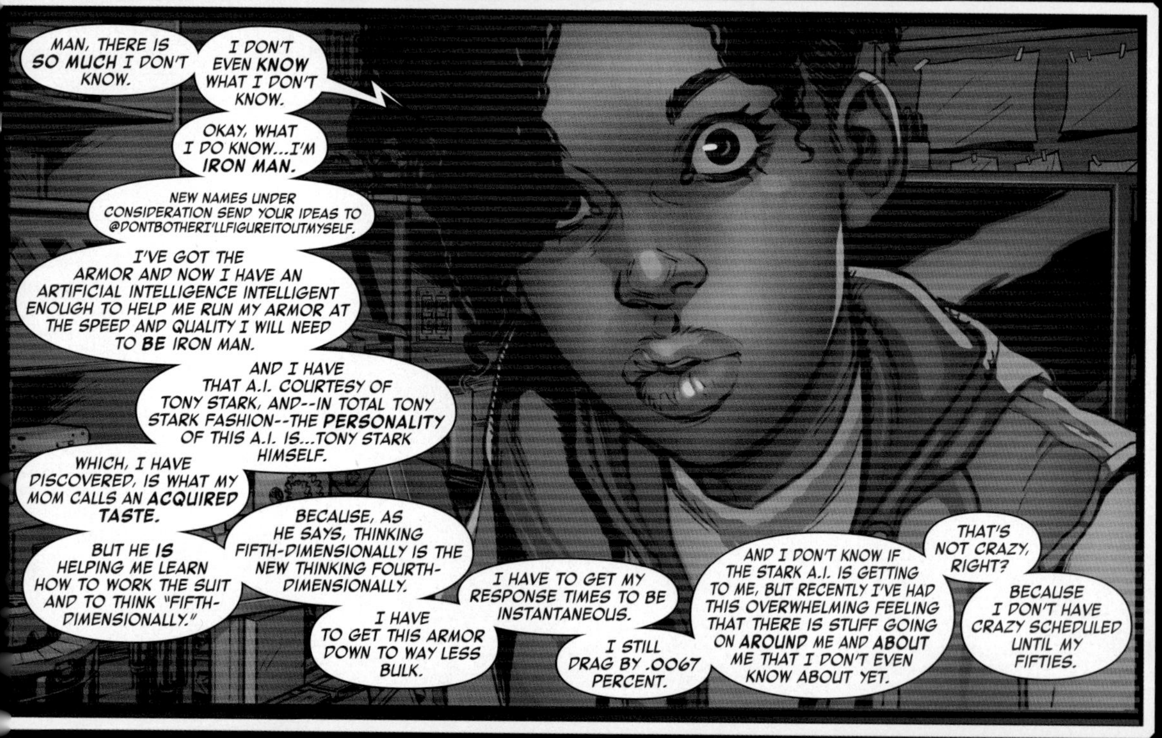
MAN, THERE IS SO MUCH I DON'T KNOW.
I DON'T EVEN KNOW WHAT I DON'T KNOW.
OKAY, WHAT I DO KNOW...I'M IRON MAN.
NEW NAMES UNDER CONSIDERATION SEND YOUR IDEAS TO @DONTBOTHERI'LLFIGUREITOUTMYSELF.
I'VE GOT THE ARMOR AND NOW I HAVE AN ARTIFICIAL INTELLIGENCE INTELLIGENT ENOUGH TO HELP ME RUN MY ARMOR AT THE SPEED AND QUALITY I WILL NEED TO BE IRON MAN.
AND I HAVE THAT A.I. COURTESY OF TONY STARK, AND--IN TOTAL TONY STARK FASHION--THE PERSONALITY OF THIS A.I. IS...TONY STARK HIMSELF.
WHICH, I HAVE DISCOVERED, IS WHAT MY MOM CALLS AN ACQUIRED TASTE.
BUT HE IS HELPING ME LEARN HOW TO WORK THE SUIT AND TO THINK "FIFTH-DIMENSIONALLY."
BECAUSE, AS HE SAYS, THINKING FIFTH-DIMENSIONALLY IS THE NEW THINKING FOURTH-DIMENSIONALLY.
I HAVE TO GET THIS ARMOR DOWN TO WAY LESS BULK.
I HAVE TO GET MY RESPONSE TIMES TO BE INSTANTANEOUS.
I STILL DRAG BY .0067 PERCENT.
AND I DON'T KNOW IF THE STARK A.I. IS GETTING TO ME, BUT RECENTLY I'VE HAD THIS OVERWHELMING FEELING THAT THERE IS STUFF GOING ON AROUND ME AND ABOUT ME THAT I DON'T EVEN KNOW ABOUT YET.
THAT'S NOT CRAZY, RIGHT?
BECAUSE I DON'T HAVE CRAZY SCHEDULED UNTIL MY FIFTIES.

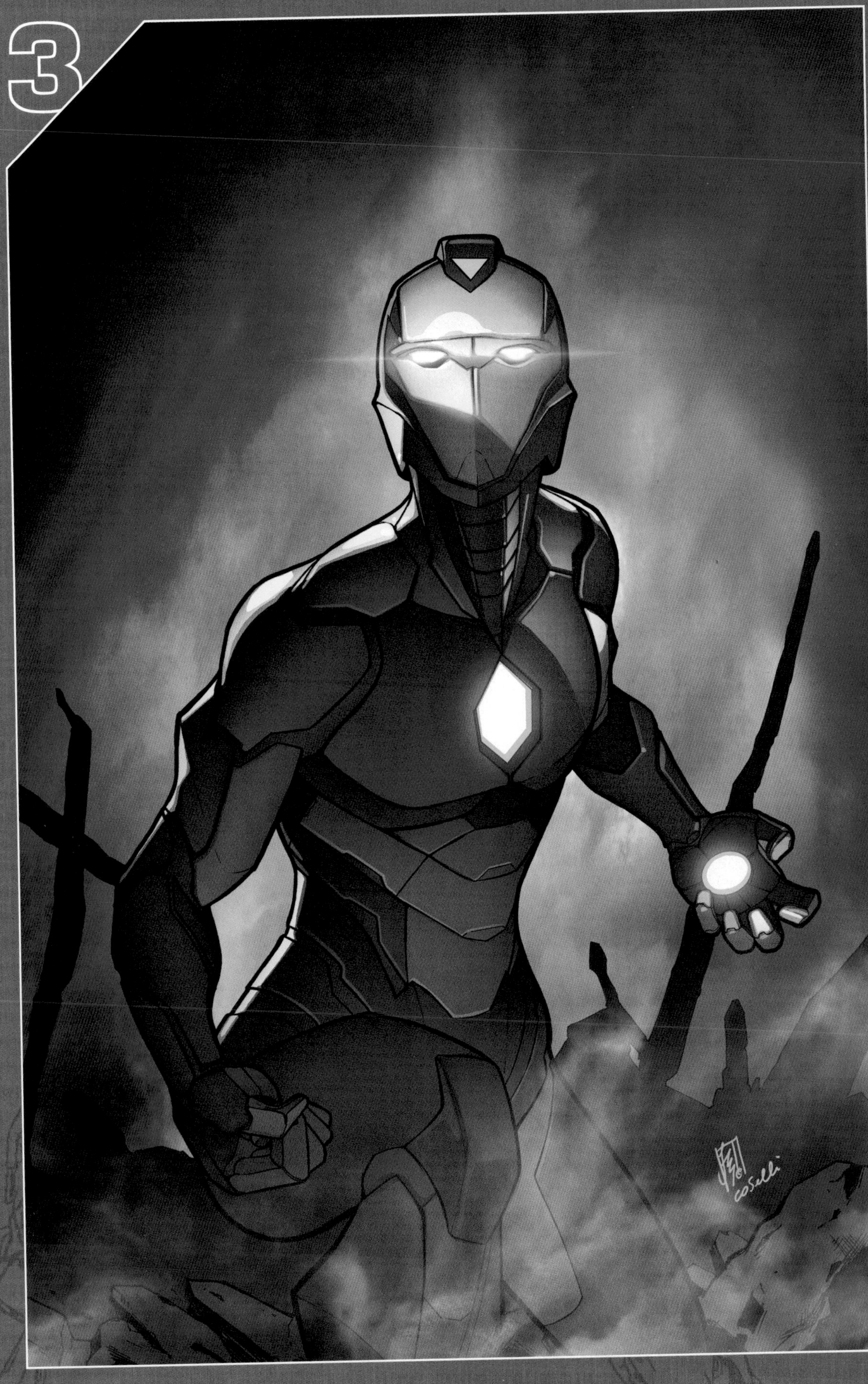
3

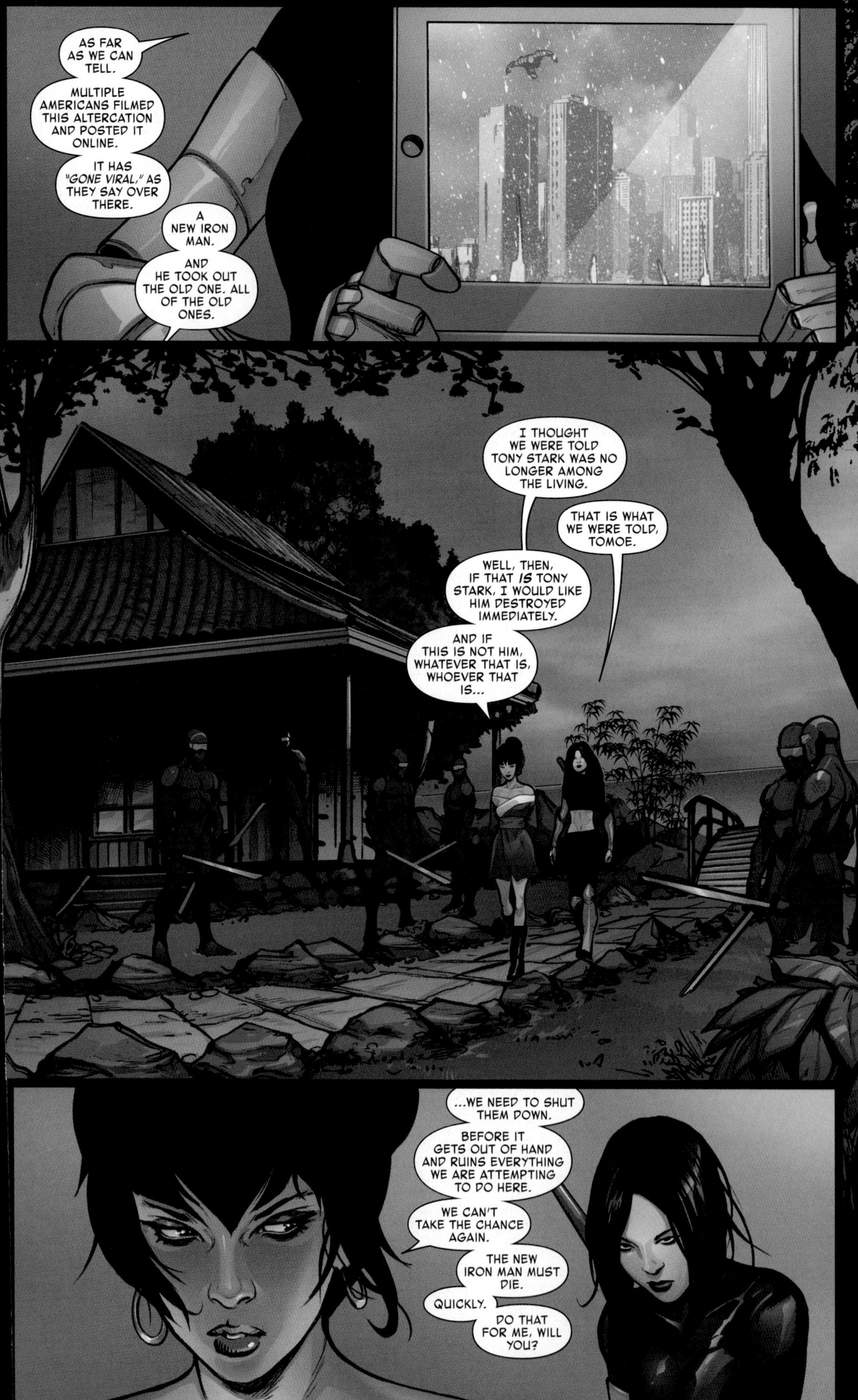
AS FAR AS WE CAN TELL.
MULTIPLE AMERICANS FILMED THIS ALTERCATION AND POSTED IT ONLINE.
IT HAS "GONE VIRAL," AS THEY SAY OVER THERE.
A NEW IRON MAN.
AND HE TOOK OUT THE OLD ONE. ALL OF THE OLD ONES.
I THOUGHT WE WERE TOLD TONY STARK WAS NO LONGER AMONG THE LIVING.
THAT IS WHAT WE WERE TOLD, TOMOE.
WELL, THEN, IF THAT *IS* TONY STARK, I WOULD LIKE HIM DESTROYED IMMEDIATELY.
AND IF THIS IS NOT HIM, WHATEVER THAT IS, WHOEVER THAT IS...
...WE NEED TO SHUT THEM DOWN.
BEFORE IT GETS OUT OF HAND AND RUINS EVERYTHING WE ARE ATTEMPTING TO DO HERE.
WE CAN'T TAKE THE CHANCE AGAIN.
THE NEW IRON MAN MUST DIE.
QUICKLY.
DO THAT FOR ME, WILL YOU?

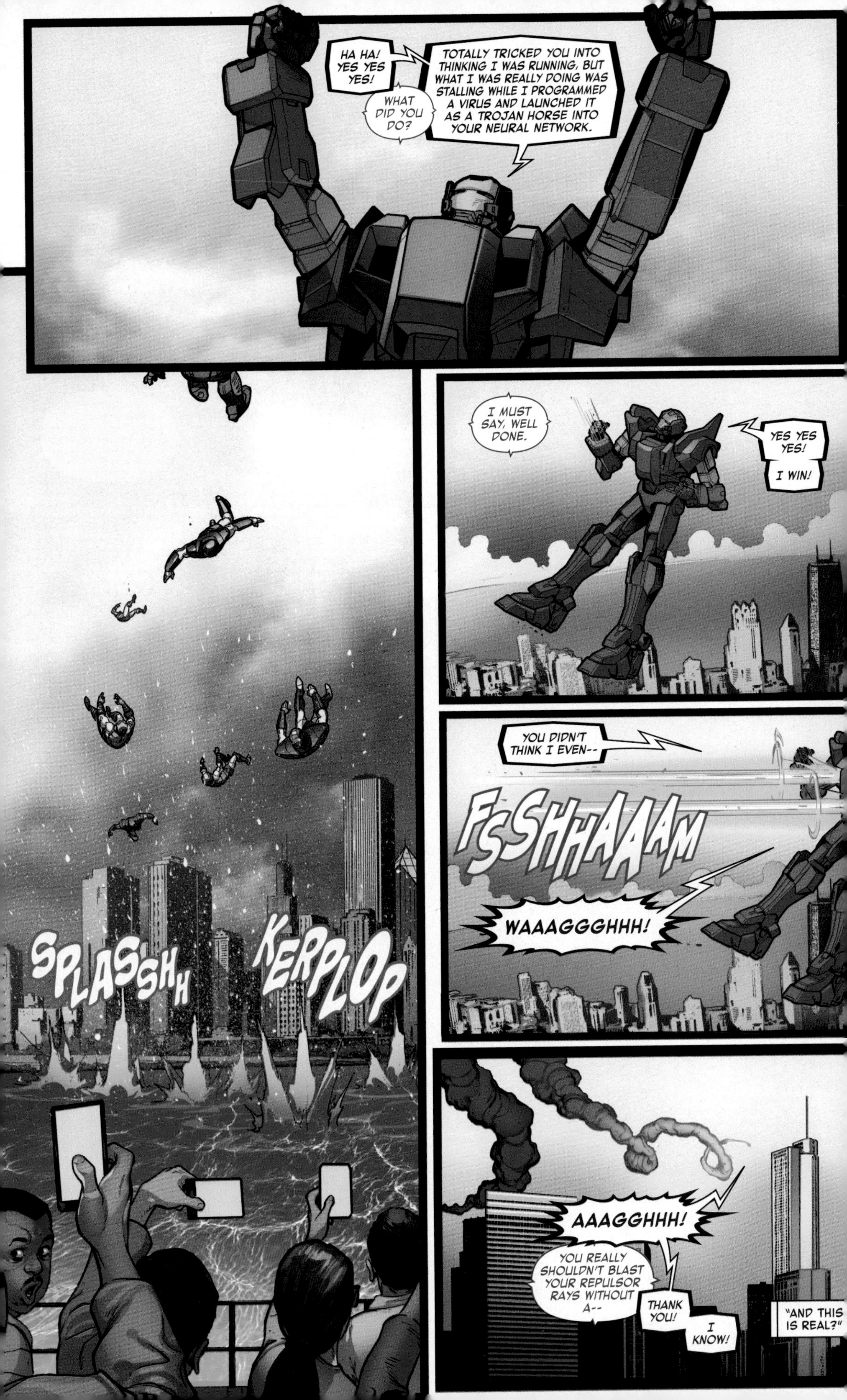
HA HA! YES YES YES!
TOTALLY TRICKED YOU INTO THINKING I WAS RUNNING, BUT WHAT I WAS REALLY DOING WAS STALLING WHILE I PROGRAMMED A VIRUS AND LAUNCHED IT AS A TROJAN HORSE INTO YOUR NEURAL NETWORK.
WHAT DID YOU DO?
SPLASSHH
KERPLOP
I MUST SAY, WELL DONE.
YES YES YES!
I WIN!
YOU DIDN'T THINK I EVEN--
FSSHHAAAM
WAAAGGGHHH!
AAAGGHHH!
YOU REALLY SHOULDN'T BLAST YOUR REPULSOR RAYS WITHOUT A--
THANK YOU!
I KNOW!
"AND THIS IS REAL?"

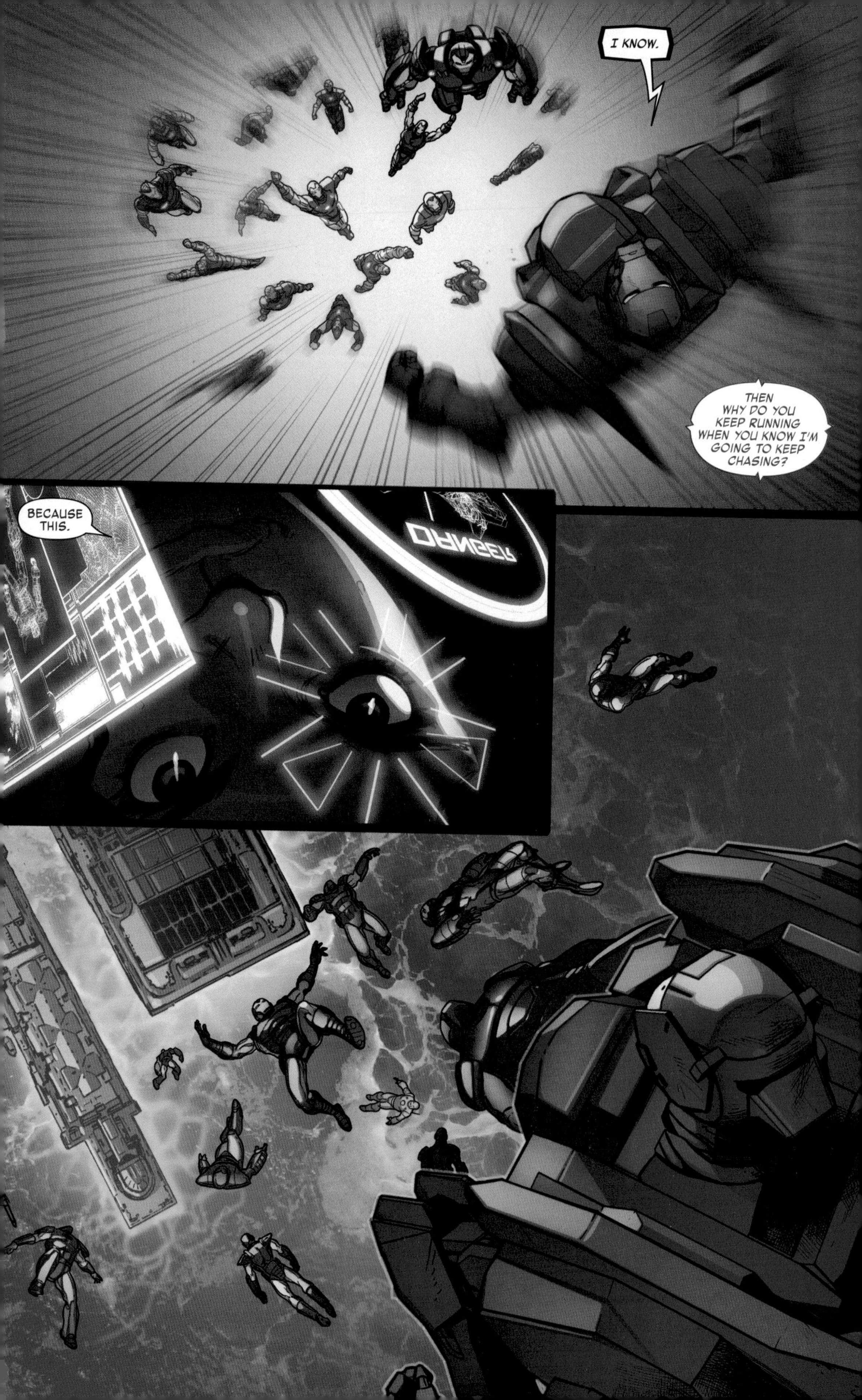
I KNOW.
THEN WHY DO YOU KEEP RUNNING WHEN YOU KNOW I'M GOING TO KEEP CHASING?
BECAUSE THIS.

UM--

WHY NATALIE AND NOT ME? WHY MY STEPDAD AND NOT MY MOM?

IT'S, WELL, IT WAS RANDOM... I DON'T KNOW WHAT TO SAY...

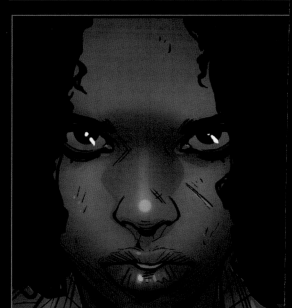

"THIS ISN'T THE ANSWER."

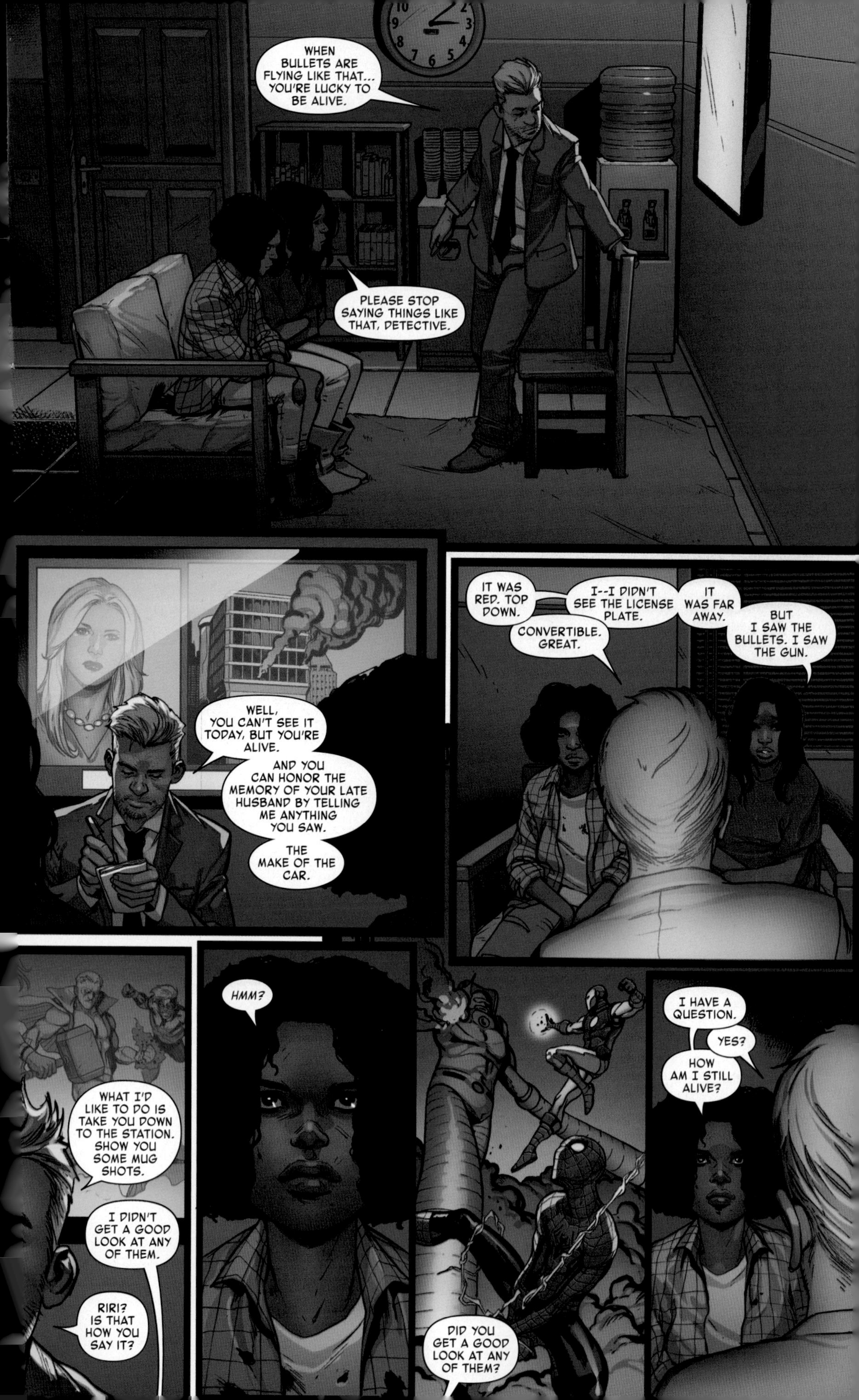
WHEN BULLETS ARE FLYING LIKE THAT... YOU'RE LUCKY TO BE ALIVE.
PLEASE STOP SAYING THINGS LIKE THAT, DETECTIVE.
WELL, YOU CAN'T SEE IT TODAY, BUT YOU'RE ALIVE.
AND YOU CAN HONOR THE MEMORY OF YOUR LATE HUSBAND BY TELLING ME ANYTHING YOU SAW.
THE MAKE OF THE CAR.
IT WAS RED. TOP DOWN.
CONVERTIBLE. GREAT.
I--I DIDN'T SEE THE LICENSE PLATE.
IT WAS FAR AWAY.
BUT I SAW THE BULLETS. I SAW THE GUN.
WHAT I'D LIKE TO DO IS TAKE YOU DOWN TO THE STATION. SHOW YOU SOME MUG SHOTS.
I DIDN'T GET A GOOD LOOK AT ANY OF THEM.
RIRI? IS THAT HOW YOU SAY IT?
HMM?
DID YOU GET A GOOD LOOK AT ANY OF THEM?
I HAVE A QUESTION.
YES?
HOW AM I STILL ALIVE?

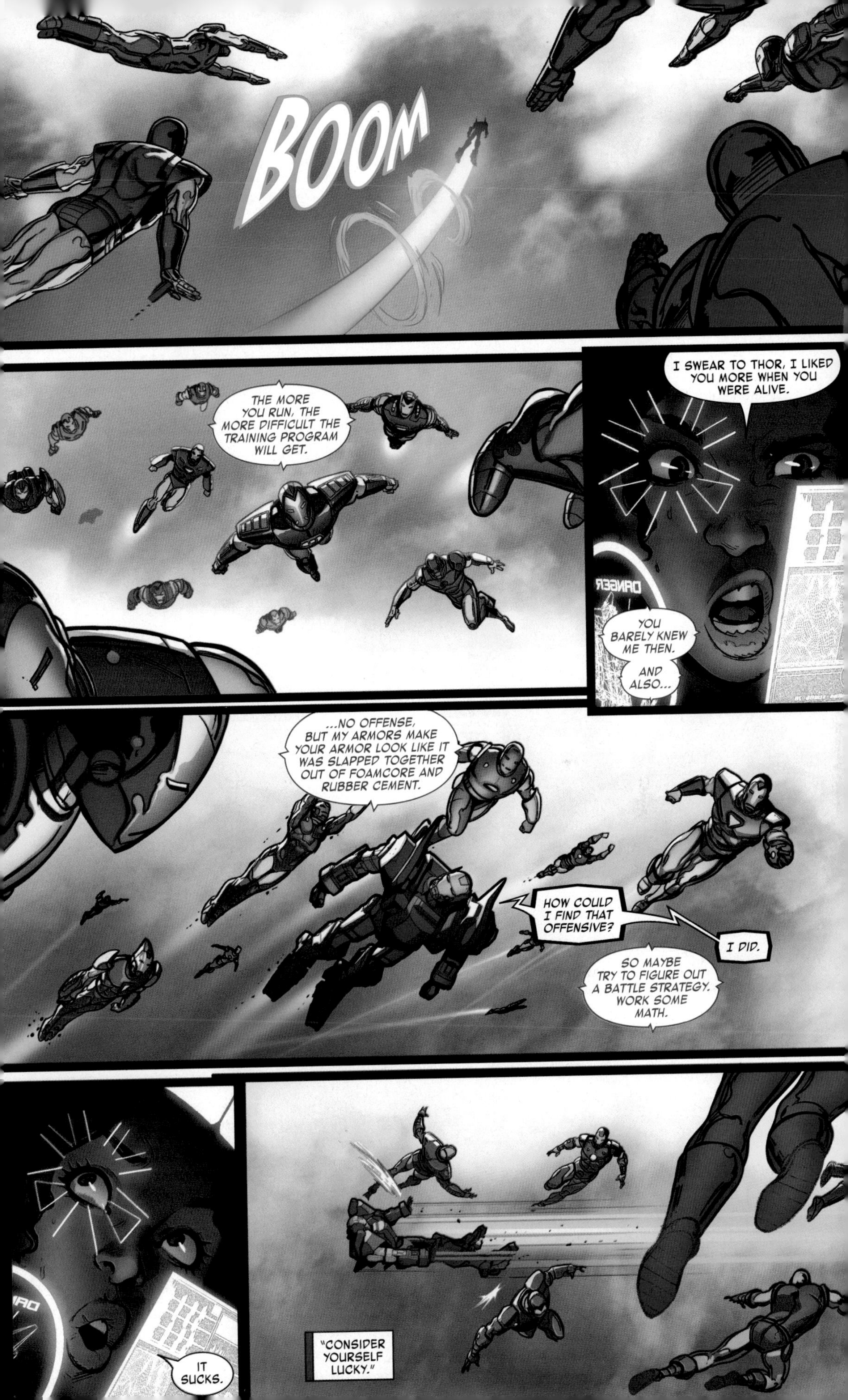
BOOM
THE MORE YOU RUN, THE MORE DIFFICULT THE TRAINING PROGRAM WILL GET.
I SWEAR TO THOR, I LIKED YOU MORE WHEN YOU WERE ALIVE.
DANGER
YOU BARELY KNEW ME THEN.
AND ALSO...
...NO OFFENSE, BUT MY ARMORS MAKE YOUR ARMOR LOOK LIKE IT WAS SLAPPED TOGETHER OUT OF FOAMCORE AND RUBBER CEMENT.
HOW COULD I FIND THAT OFFENSIVE?
I DID.
SO MAYBE TRY TO FIGURE OUT A BATTLE STRATEGY. WORK SOME MATH.
IT SUCKS.
"CONSIDER YOURSELF LUCKY."

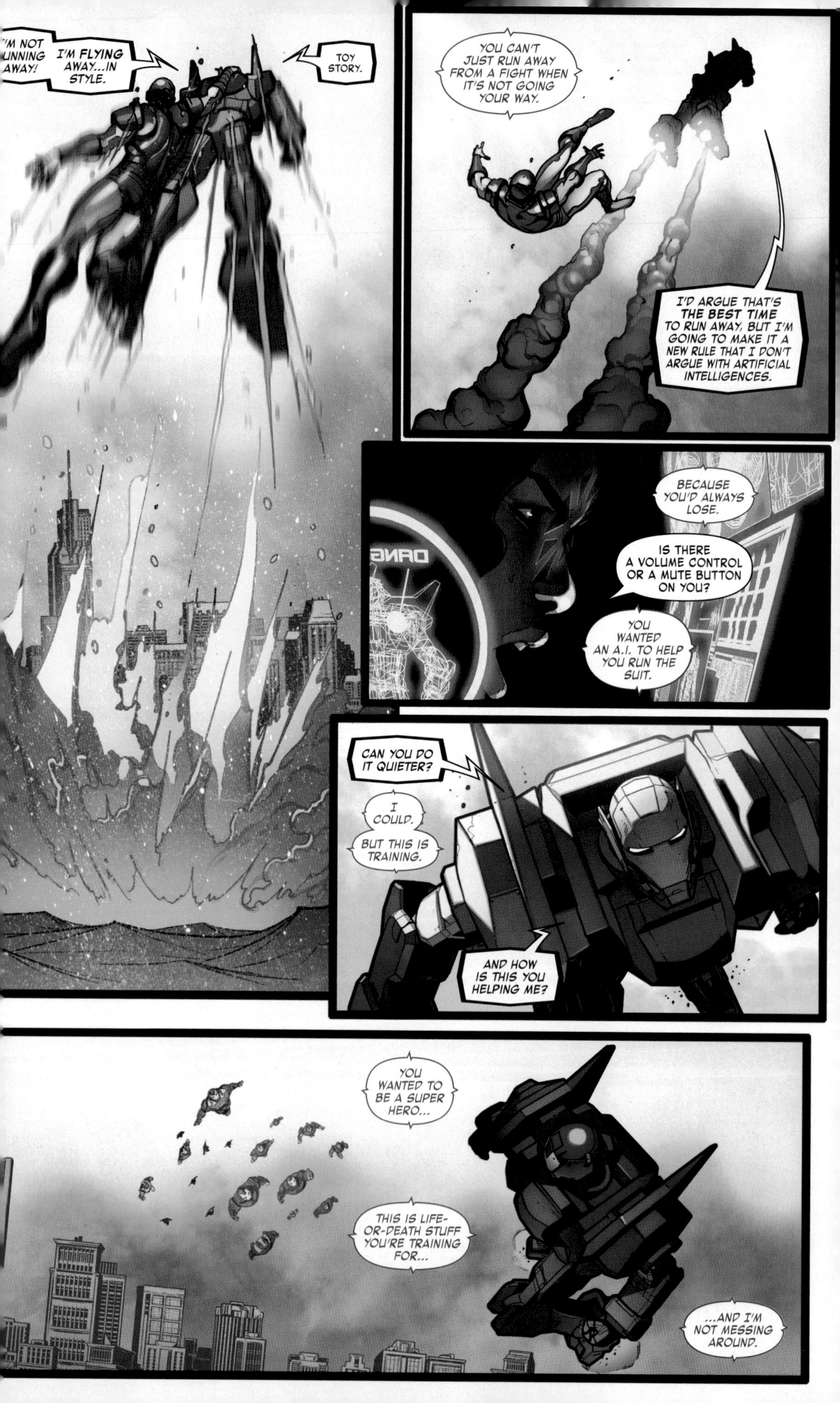
I'M NOT RUNNING AWAY!
I'M FLYING AWAY...IN STYLE.
TOY STORY.
YOU CAN'T JUST RUN AWAY FROM A FIGHT WHEN IT'S NOT GOING YOUR WAY.
I'D ARGUE THAT'S THE BEST TIME TO RUN AWAY, BUT I'M GOING TO MAKE IT A NEW RULE THAT I DON'T ARGUE WITH ARTIFICIAL INTELLIGENCES.
BECAUSE YOU'D ALWAYS LOSE.
IS THERE A VOLUME CONTROL OR A MUTE BUTTON ON YOU?
YOU WANTED AN A.I. TO HELP YOU RUN THE SUIT.
CAN YOU DO IT QUIETER?
I COULD.
BUT THIS IS TRAINING.
AND HOW IS THIS YOU HELPING ME?
YOU WANTED TO BE A SUPER HERO...
THIS IS LIFE-OR-DEATH STUFF YOU'RE TRAINING FOR...
...AND I'M NOT MESSING AROUND.

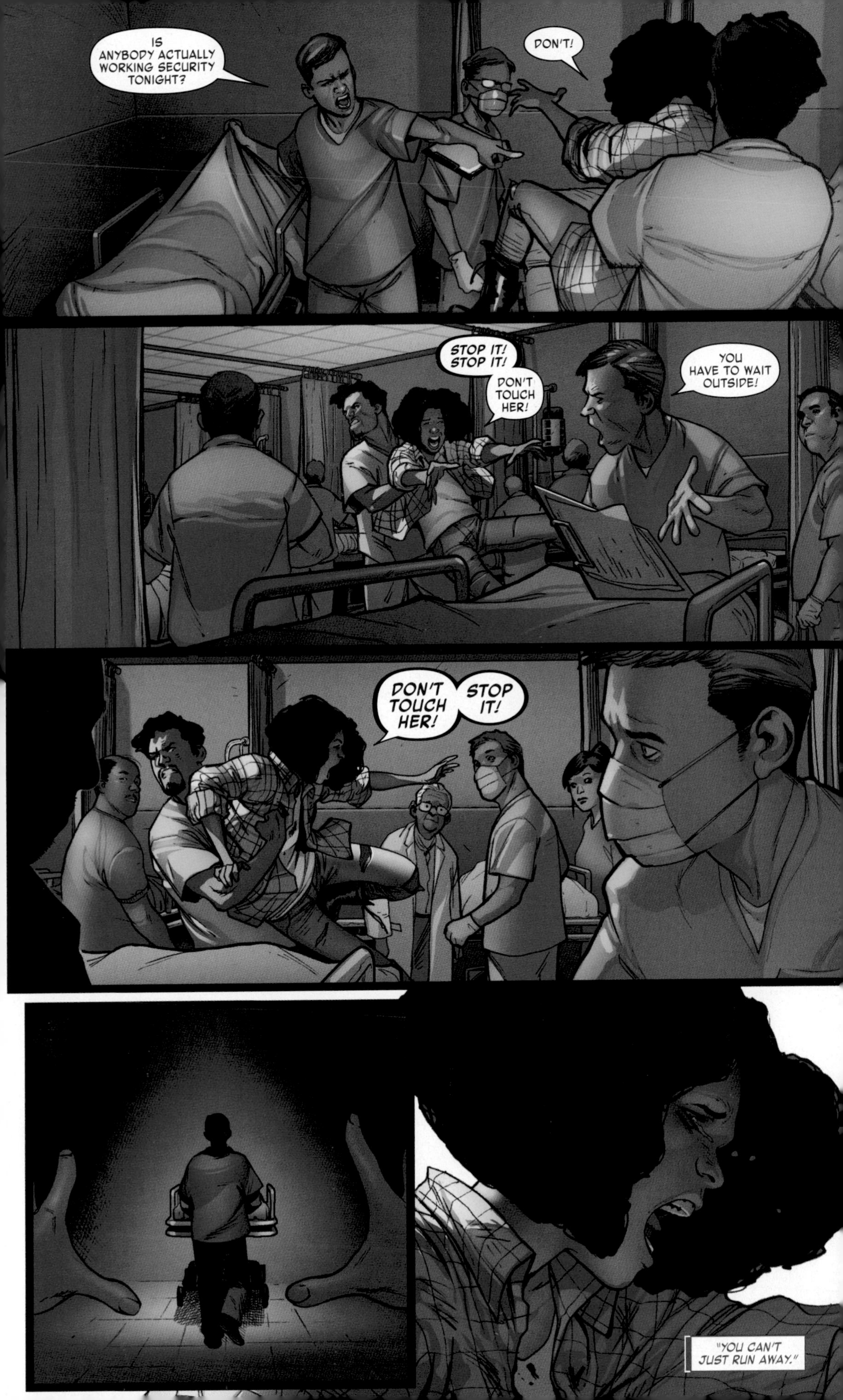
IS ANYBODY ACTUALLY WORKING SECURITY TONIGHT?
DON'T!
STOP IT! STOP IT!
DON'T TOUCH HER!
YOU HAVE TO WAIT OUTSIDE!
DON'T TOUCH HER!
STOP IT!
"YOU CAN'T JUST RUN AWAY."

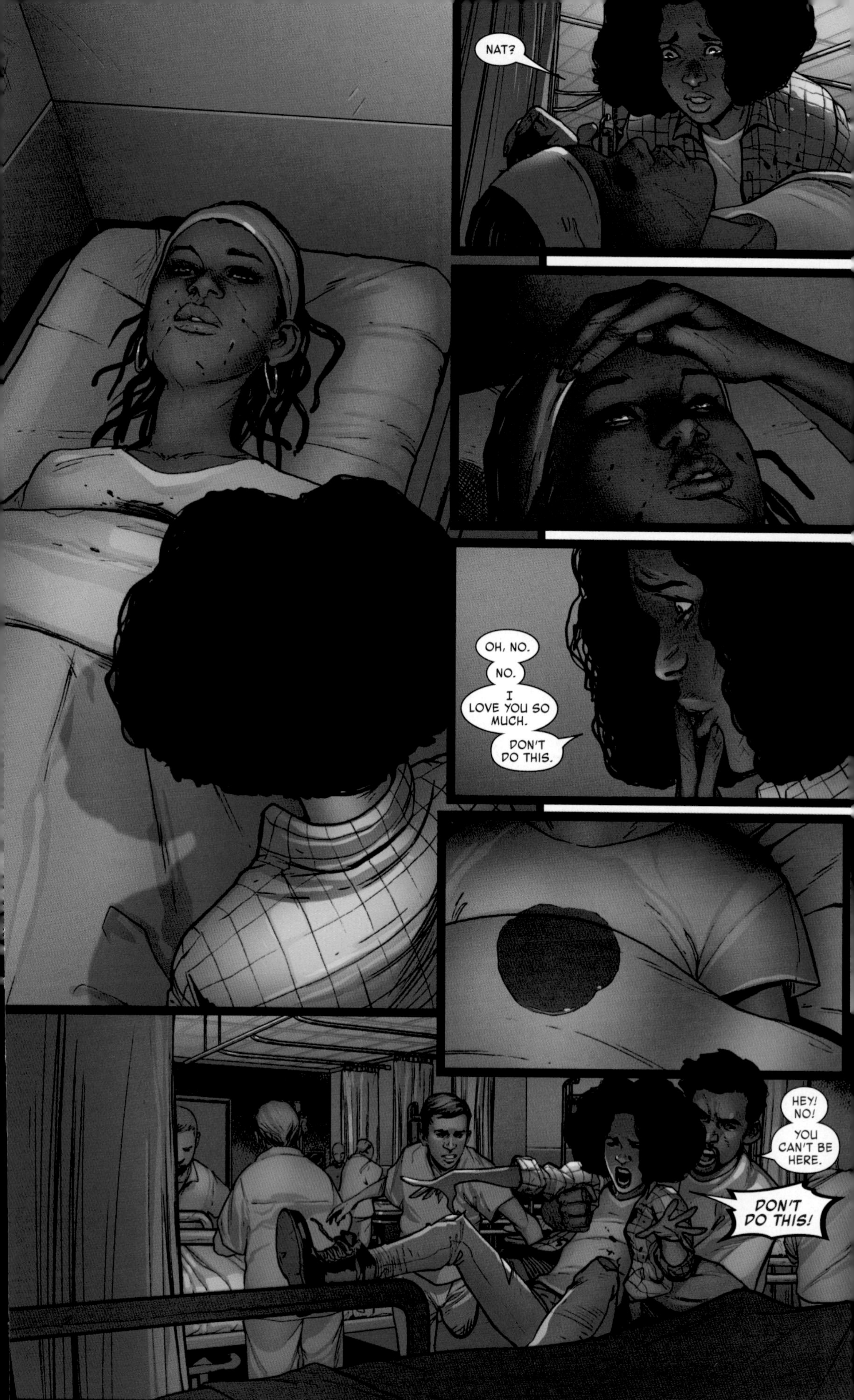

NAT?
OH, NO.
NO.
I LOVE YOU SO MUCH.
DON'T DO THIS.
HEY! NO!
YOU CAN'T BE HERE.
DON'T DO THIS!

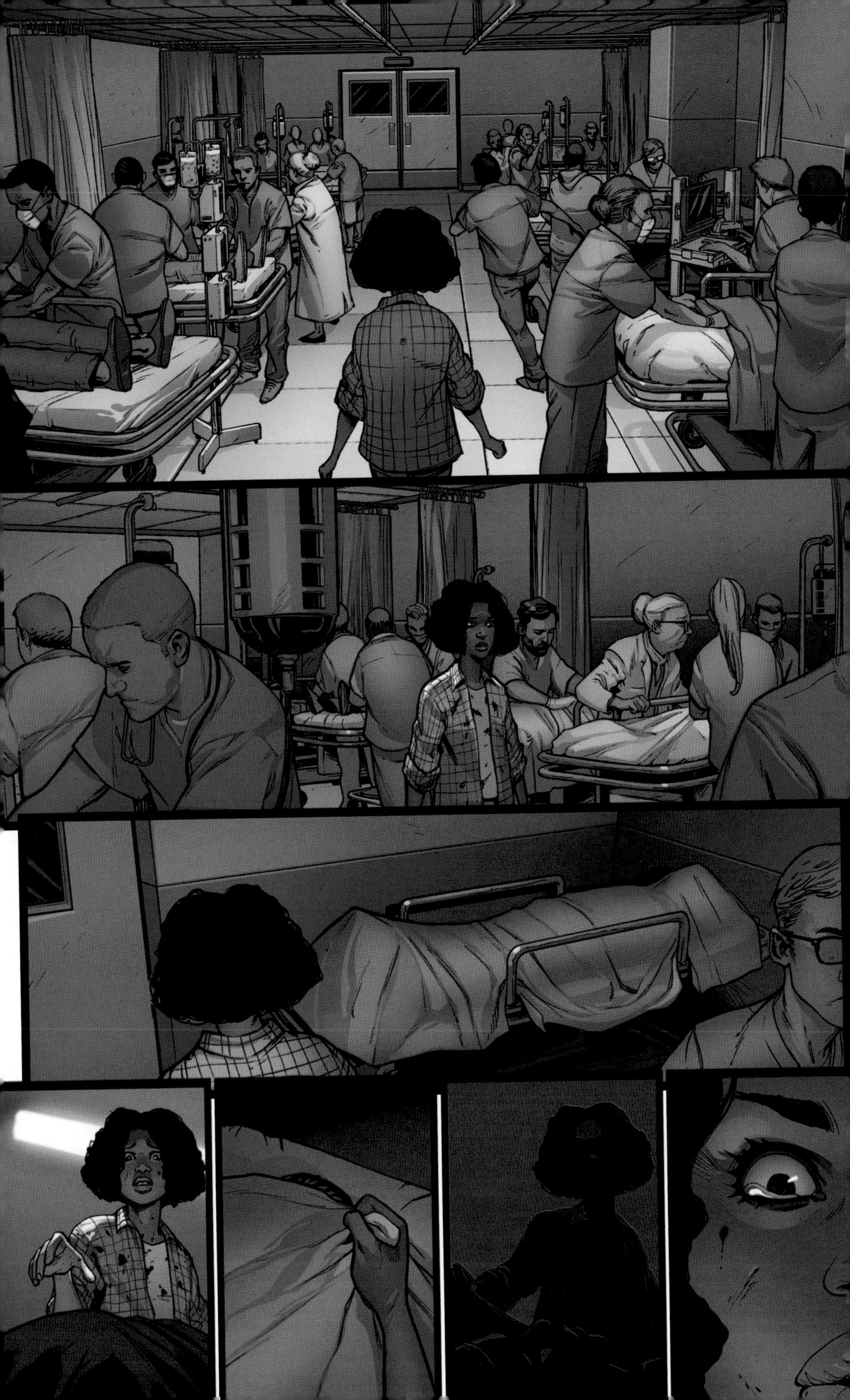

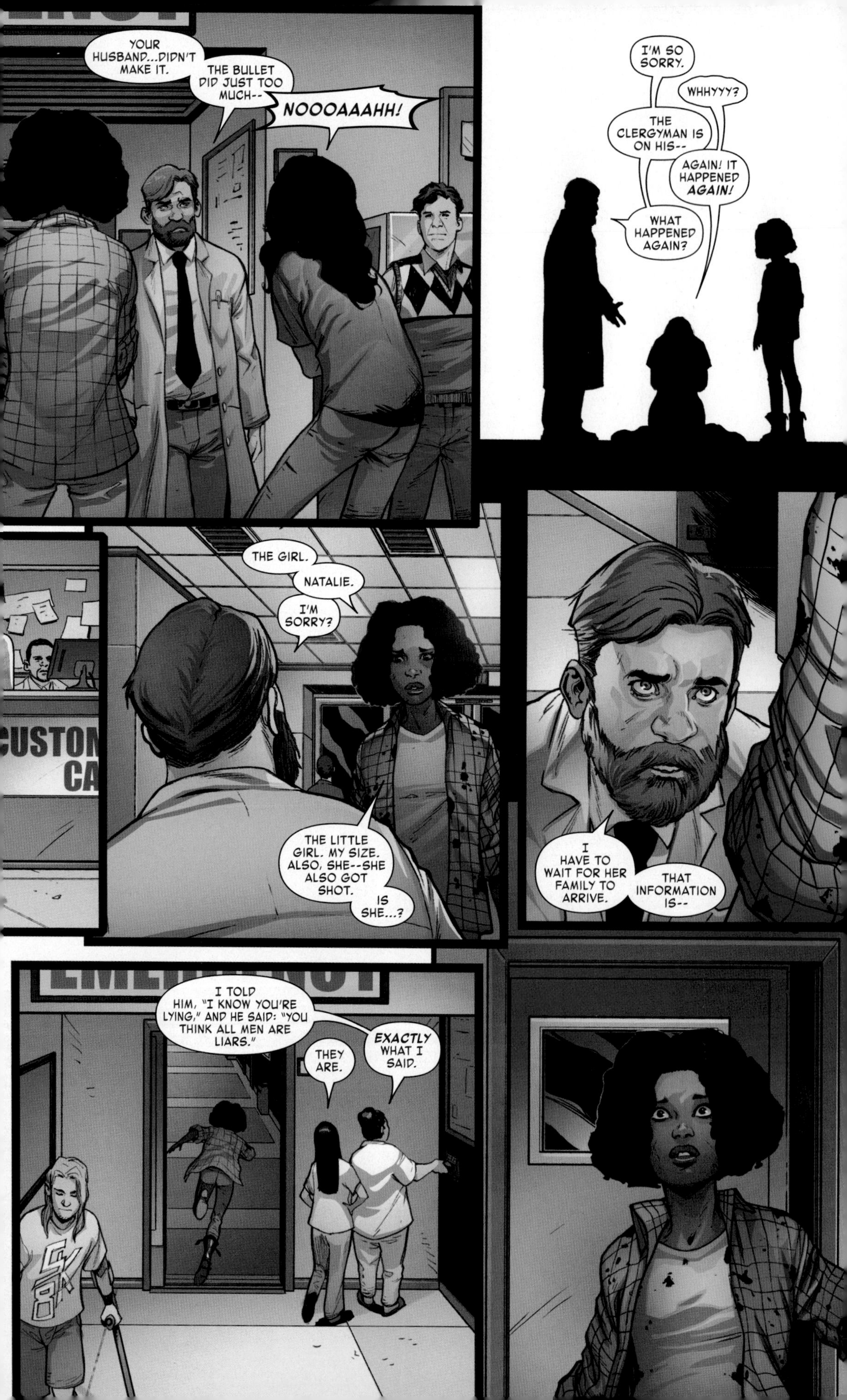
YOUR HUSBAND...DIDN'T MAKE IT.
THE BULLET DID JUST TOO MUCH--
NOOOAAAHH!
I'M SO SORRY.
WHHYYY?
THE CLERGYMAN IS ON HIS--
AGAIN! IT HAPPENED AGAIN!
WHAT HAPPENED AGAIN?
THE GIRL.
NATALIE.
I'M SORRY?
CUSTOM
CA
THE LITTLE GIRL. MY SIZE. ALSO, SHE--SHE ALSO GOT SHOT.
IS SHE...?
I HAVE TO WAIT FOR HER FAMILY TO ARRIVE.
THAT INFORMATION IS--
I TOLD HIM, "I KNOW YOU'RE LYING," AND HE SAID: "YOU THINK ALL MEN ARE LIARS."
THEY ARE.
EXACTLY WHAT I SAID.

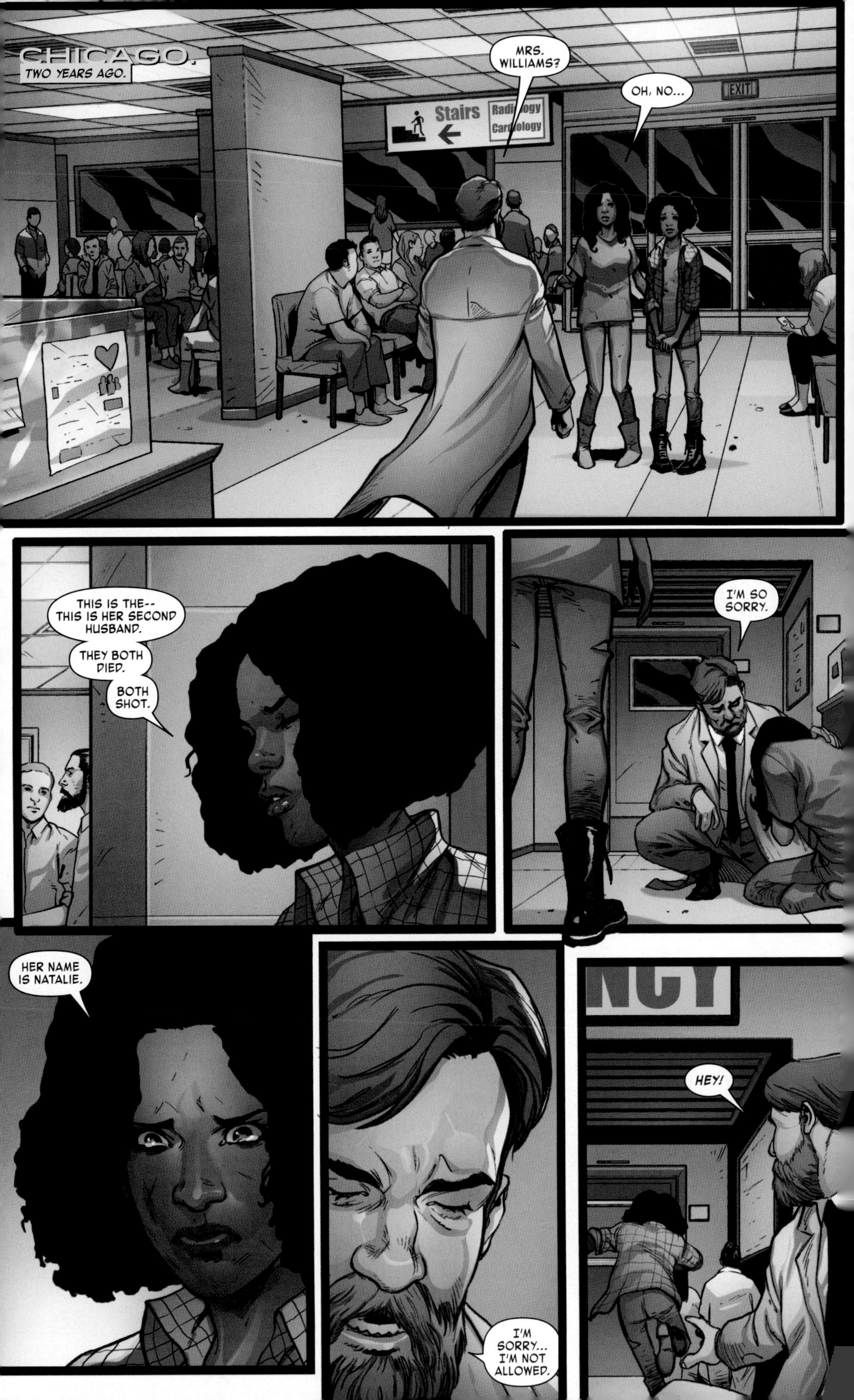
CHICAGO.
TWO YEARS AGO.
Stairs
Radiology
Cardiology
EXIT
MRS. WILLIAMS?
OH, NO...
THIS IS THE-- THIS IS HER SECOND HUSBAND.
THEY BOTH DIED.
BOTH SHOT.
I'M SO SORRY.
HER NAME IS NATALIE.
I'M SORRY... I'M NOT ALLOWED.
NCY
HEY!

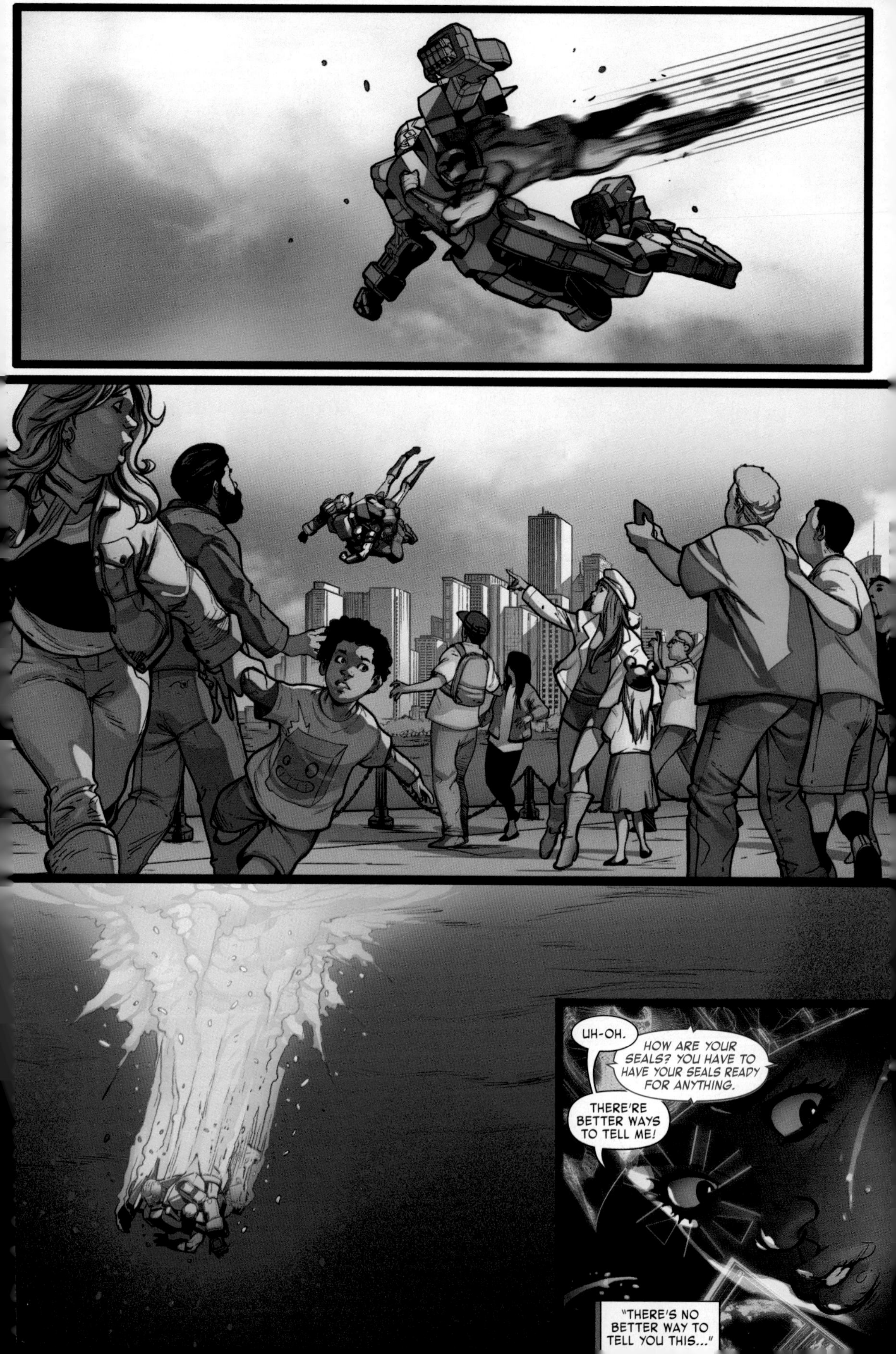
UH-OH.
HOW ARE YOUR SEALS? YOU HAVE TO HAVE YOUR SEALS READY FOR ANYTHING.
THERE'RE BETTER WAYS TO TELL ME!
"THERE'S NO BETTER WAY TO TELL YOU THIS..."

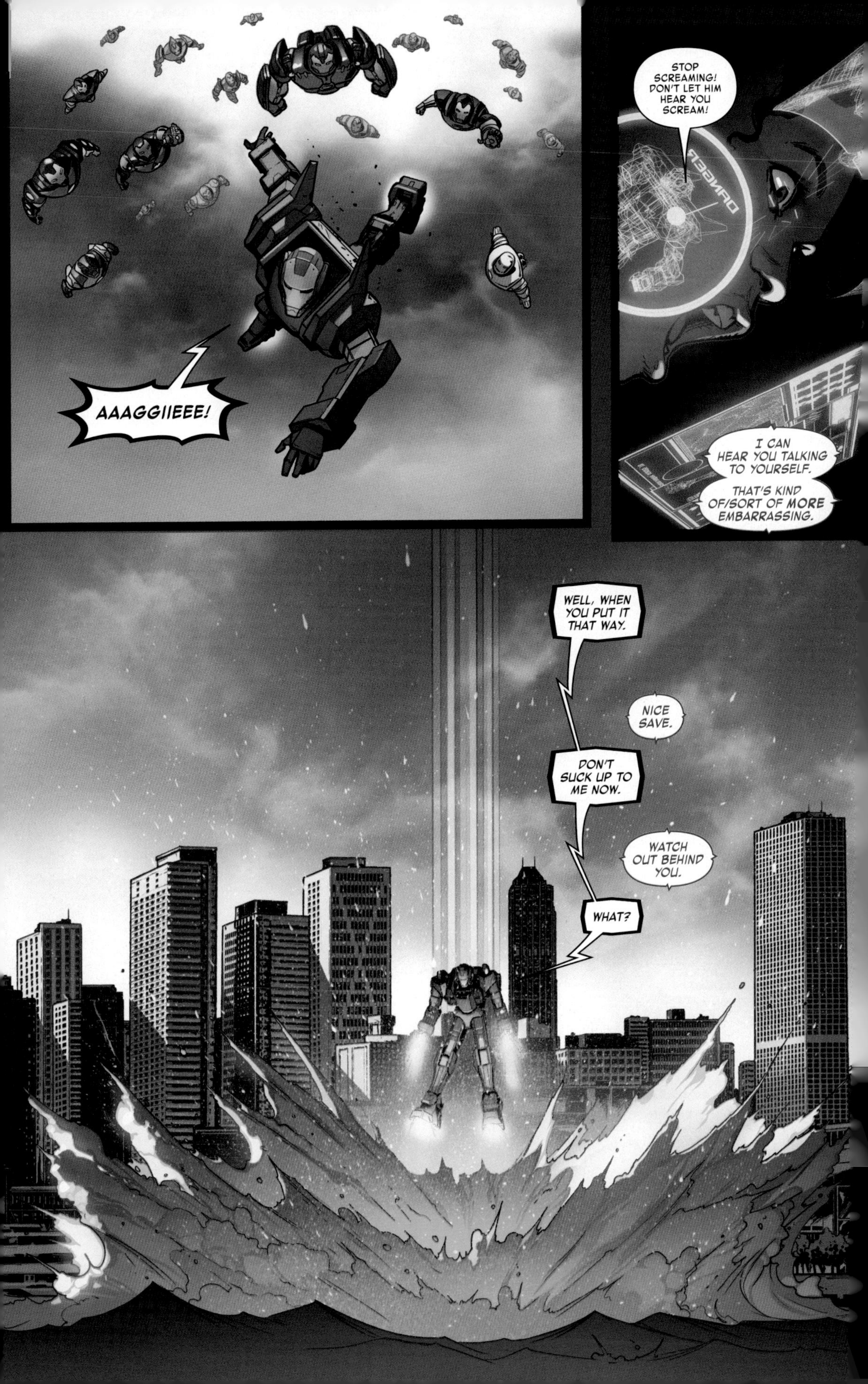
AAAGGIIEEE!
STOP SCREAMING! DON'T LET HIM HEAR YOU SCREAM!
I CAN HEAR YOU TALKING TO YOURSELF.
THAT'S KIND OF/SORT OF MORE EMBARRASSING.
WELL, WHEN YOU PUT IT THAT WAY.
NICE SAVE.
DON'T SUCK UP TO ME NOW.
WATCH OUT BEHIND YOU.
WHAT?

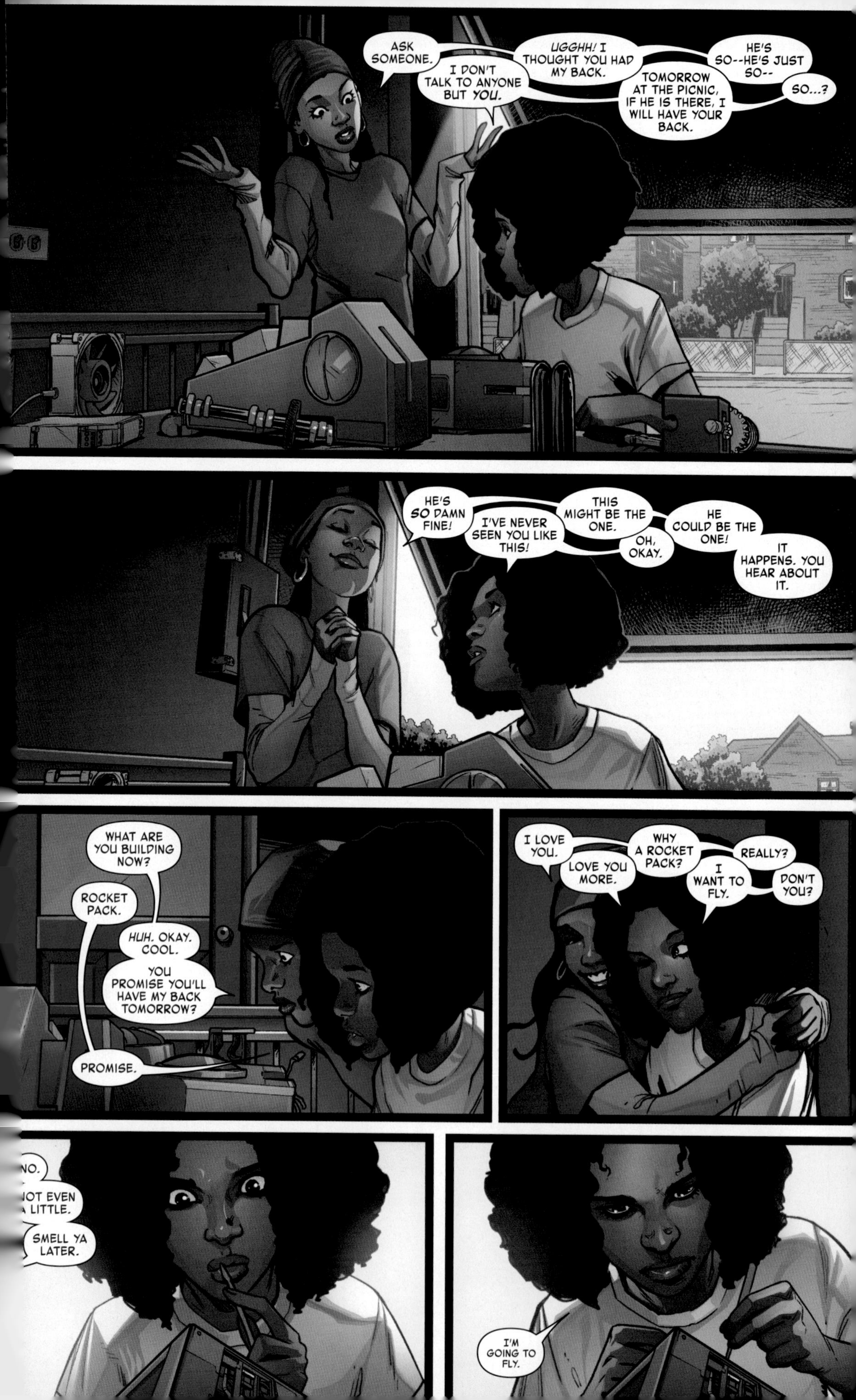

ASK SOMEONE.
I DON'T TALK TO ANYONE BUT *YOU.*
UGGHH! I THOUGHT YOU HAD MY BACK.
TOMORROW AT THE PICNIC, IF HE IS THERE, I WILL HAVE YOUR BACK.
HE'S SO--HE'S JUST SO--
SO...?
HE'S **SO** DAMN FINE!
I'VE NEVER SEEN YOU LIKE THIS!
THIS MIGHT BE THE ONE.
OH, OKAY.
HE COULD BE THE ONE!
IT HAPPENS. YOU HEAR ABOUT IT.
WHAT ARE YOU BUILDING NOW?
ROCKET PACK.
HUH. OKAY. COOL.
YOU PROMISE YOU'LL HAVE MY BACK TOMORROW?
PROMISE.
I LOVE YOU.
LOVE YOU MORE.
WHY A ROCKET PACK?
I WANT TO FLY.
REALLY?
DON'T YOU?
NO.
NOT EVEN A LITTLE.
SMELL YA LATER.
I'M GOING TO FLY.

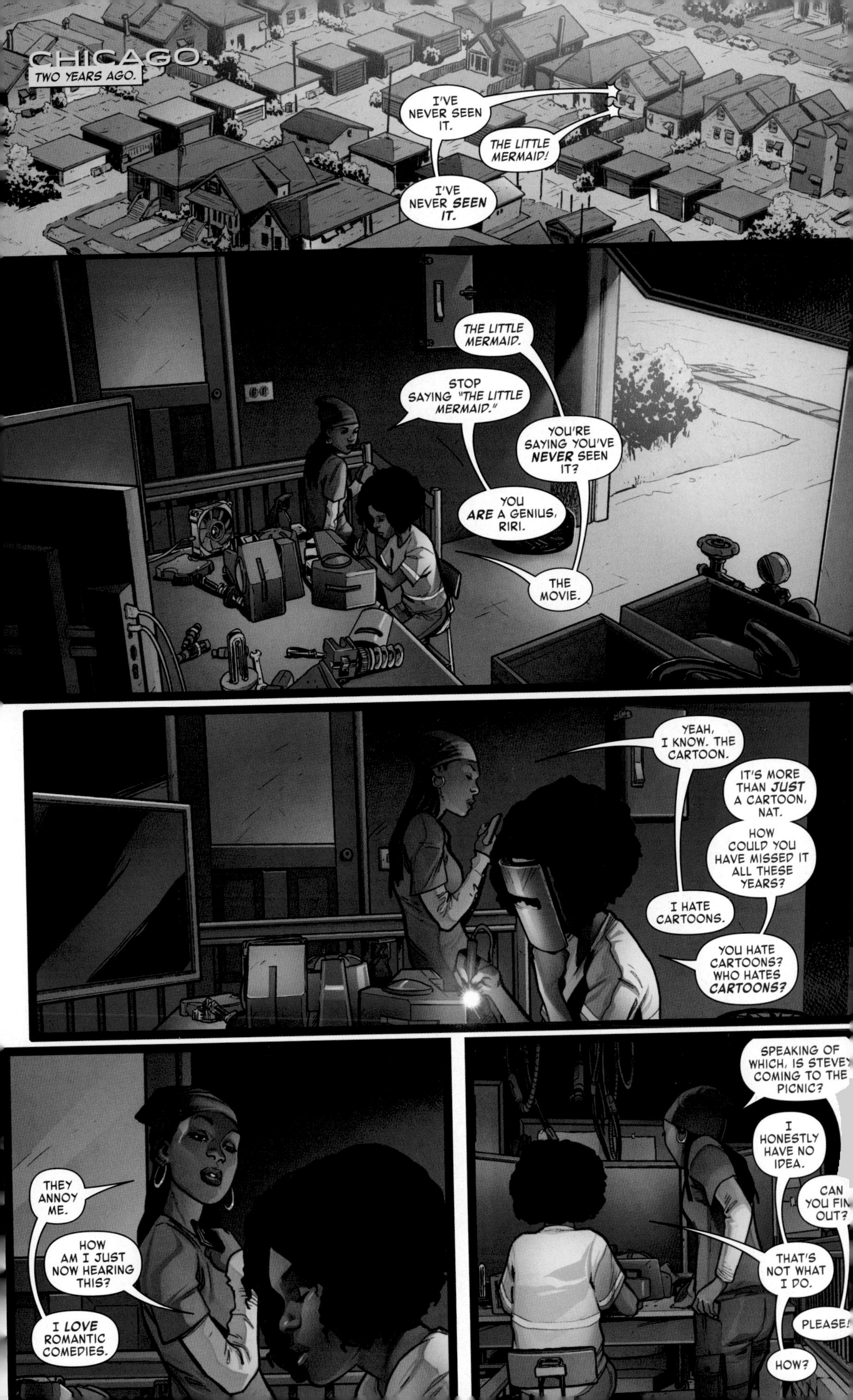
CHICAGO.
TWO YEARS AGO.
I'VE NEVER SEEN IT.
THE LITTLE MERMAID!
I'VE NEVER SEEN IT.
THE LITTLE MERMAID.
STOP SAYING "THE LITTLE MERMAID."
YOU'RE SAYING YOU'VE NEVER SEEN IT?
YOU ARE A GENIUS, RIRI.
THE MOVIE.
YEAH, I KNOW. THE CARTOON.
IT'S MORE THAN JUST A CARTOON, NAT.
HOW COULD YOU HAVE MISSED IT ALL THESE YEARS?
I HATE CARTOONS.
YOU HATE CARTOONS? WHO HATES CARTOONS?
THEY ANNOY ME.
HOW AM I JUST NOW HEARING THIS?
I LOVE ROMANTIC COMEDIES.
SPEAKING OF WHICH, IS STEVE
COMING TO THE PICNIC?
I HONESTLY HAVE NO IDEA.
CAN YOU FI
OUT?
THAT'S NOT WHAT I DO.
PLEASE!
HOW?

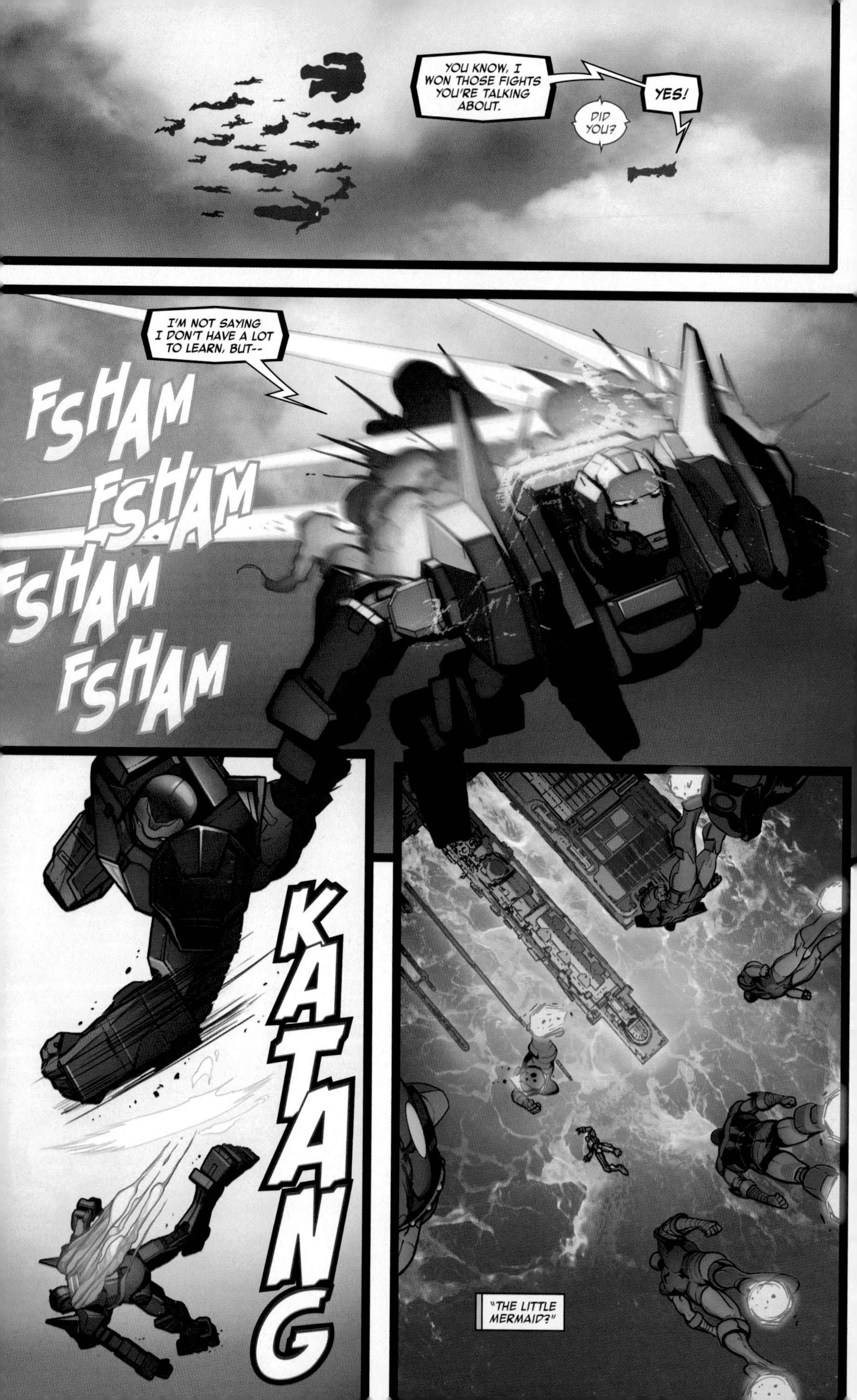
YOU KNOW, I WON THOSE FIGHTS YOU'RE TALKING ABOUT.
DID YOU?
YES!
I'M NOT SAYING I DON'T HAVE A LOT TO LEARN, BUT--
FSHAM
FSHAM
FSHAM
FSHAM
KATANG
"THE LITTLE MERMAID?"

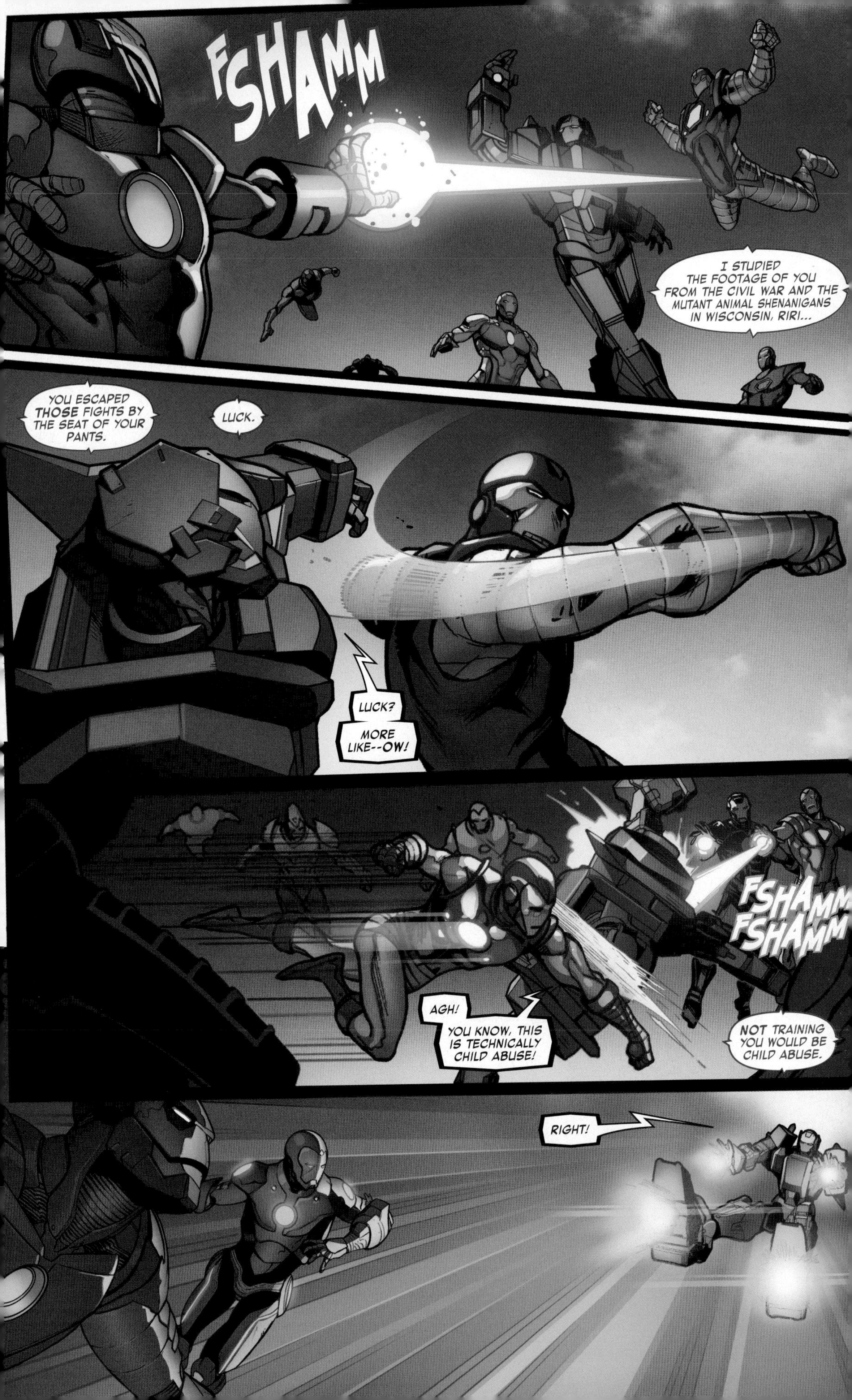
FSHAMM
I STUDIED THE FOOTAGE OF YOU FROM THE CIVIL WAR AND THE MUTANT ANIMAL SHENANIGANS IN WISCONSIN, RIRI...
YOU ESCAPED THOSE FIGHTS BY THE SEAT OF YOUR PANTS.
LUCK.
LUCK?
MORE LIKE--OW!
FSHAMM
FSHAMM
AGH!
YOU KNOW, THIS IS TECHNICALLY CHILD ABUSE!
NOT TRAINING YOU WOULD BE CHILD ABUSE.
RIGHT!

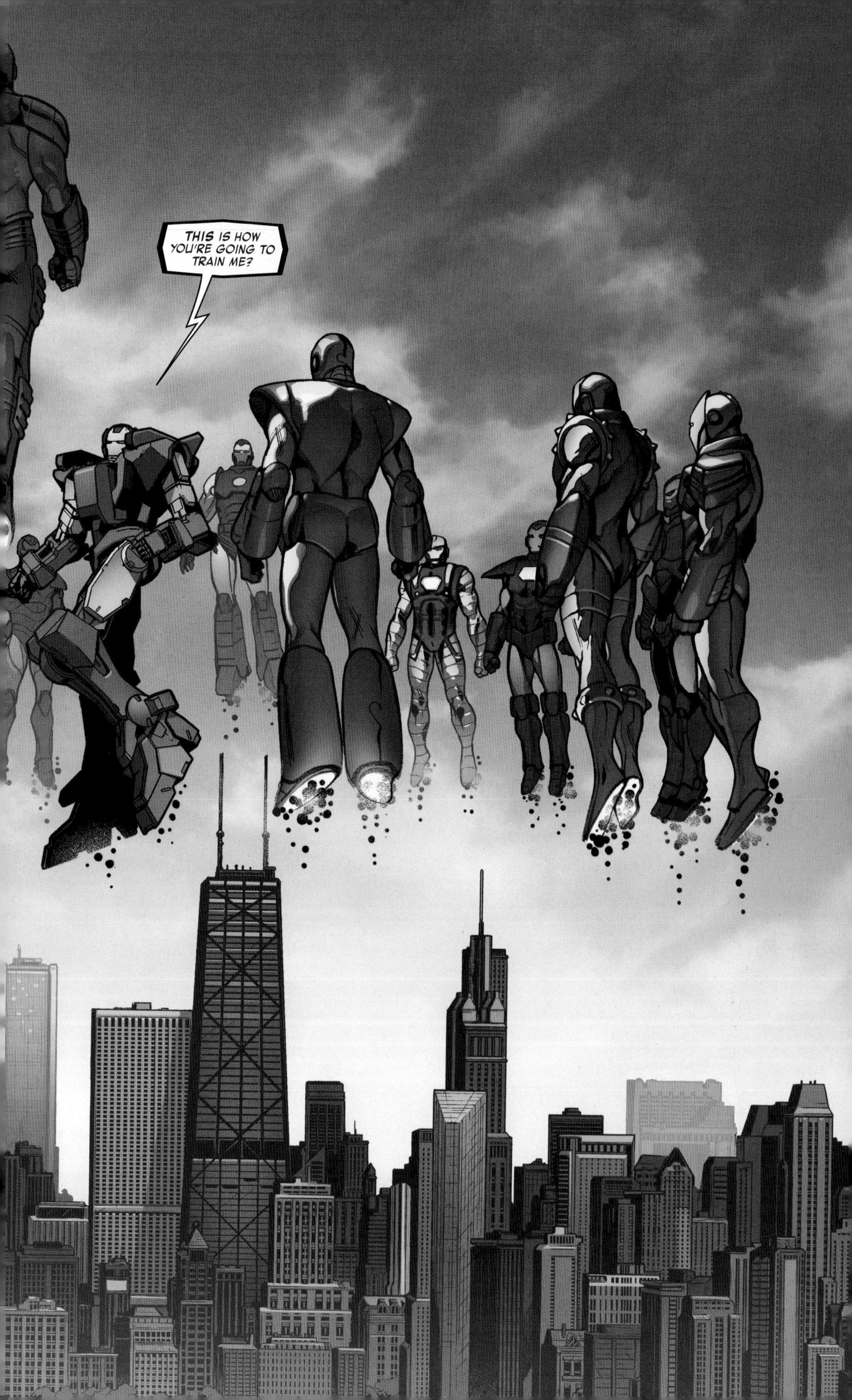
THIS IS HOW YOU'RE GOING TO TRAIN ME?

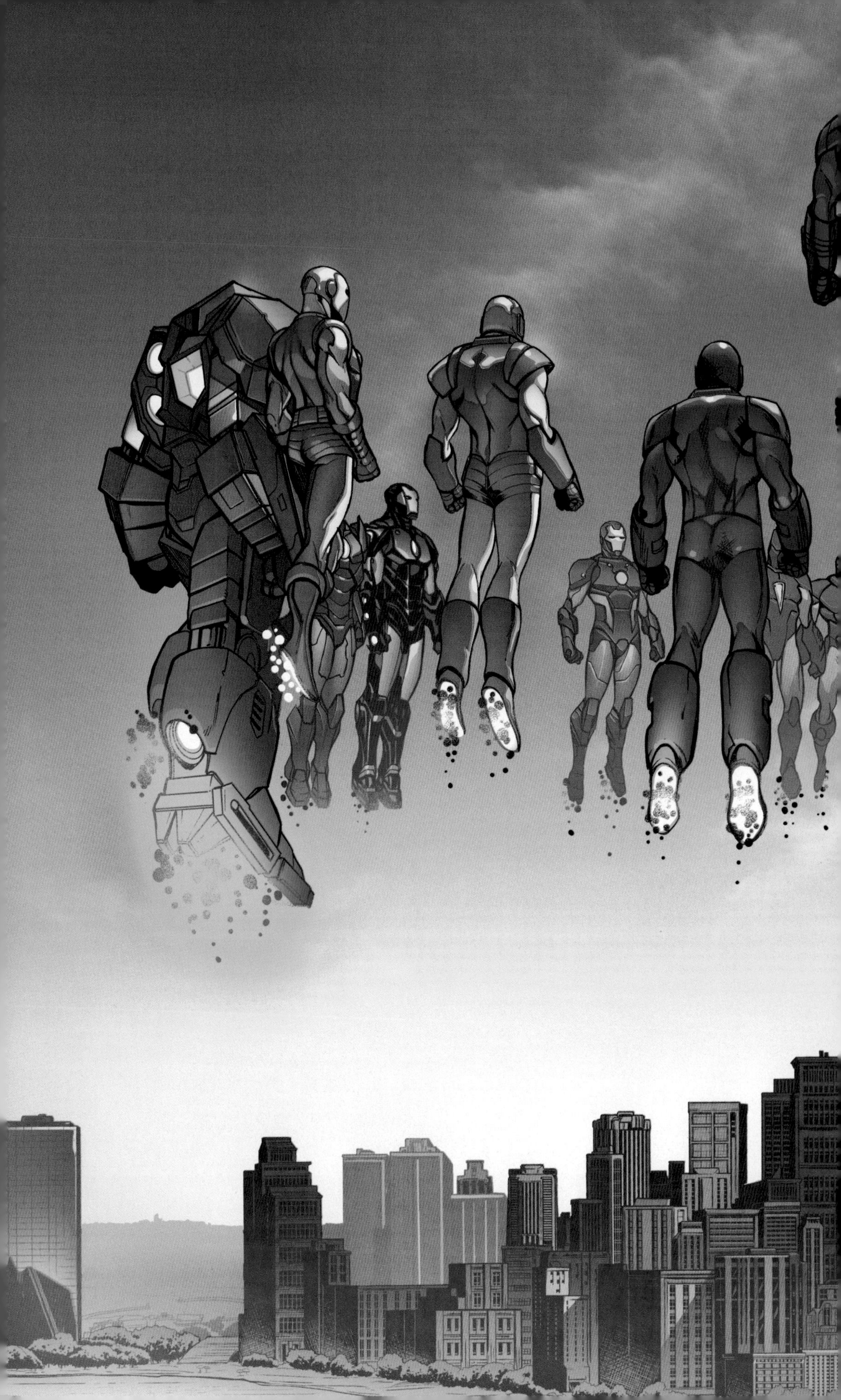

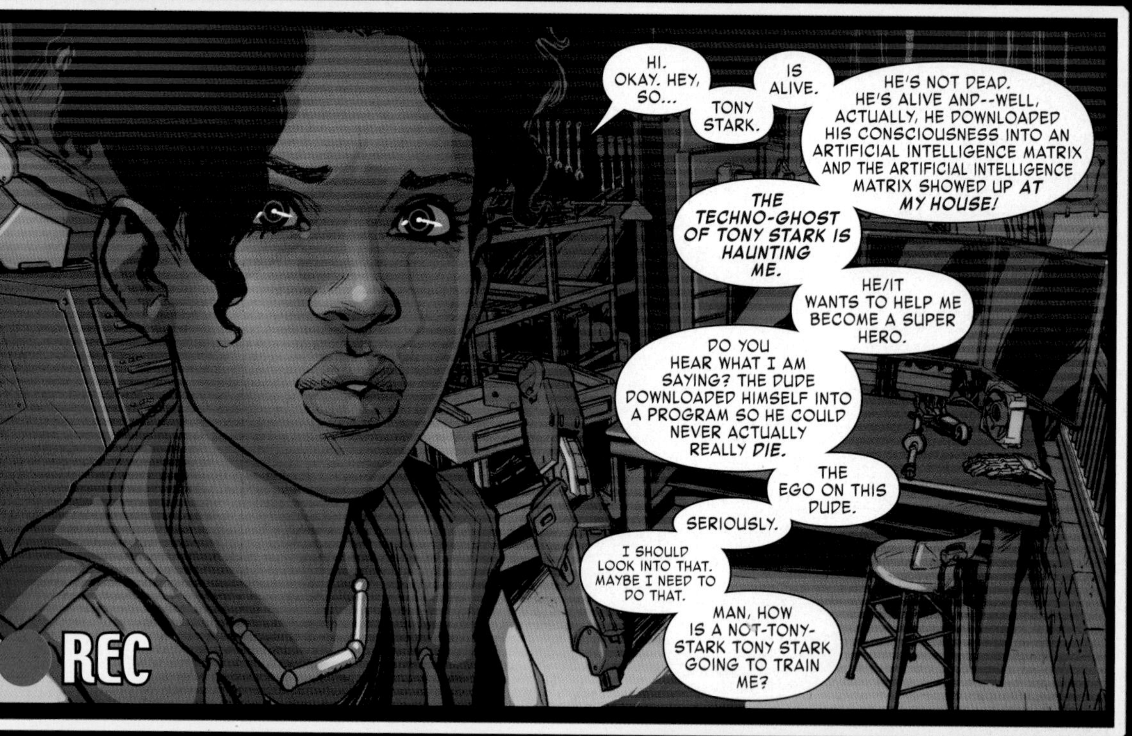
HI. OKAY. HEY, SO...
TONY STARK.
IS ALIVE.
HE'S NOT DEAD. HE'S ALIVE AND--WELL, ACTUALLY, HE DOWNLOADED HIS CONSCIOUSNESS INTO AN ARTIFICIAL INTELLIGENCE MATRIX AND THE ARTIFICIAL INTELLIGENCE MATRIX SHOWED UP AT MY HOUSE!
THE TECHNO-GHOST OF TONY STARK IS HAUNTING ME.
HE/IT WANTS TO HELP ME BECOME A SUPER HERO.
DO YOU HEAR WHAT I AM SAYING? THE DUDE DOWNLOADED HIMSELF INTO A PROGRAM SO HE COULD NEVER ACTUALLY REALLY DIE.
THE EGO ON THIS DUDE.
SERIOUSLY.
I SHOULD LOOK INTO THAT. MAYBE I NEED TO DO THAT.
MAN, HOW IS A NOT-TONY-STARK TONY STARK GOING TO TRAIN ME?
REC

2

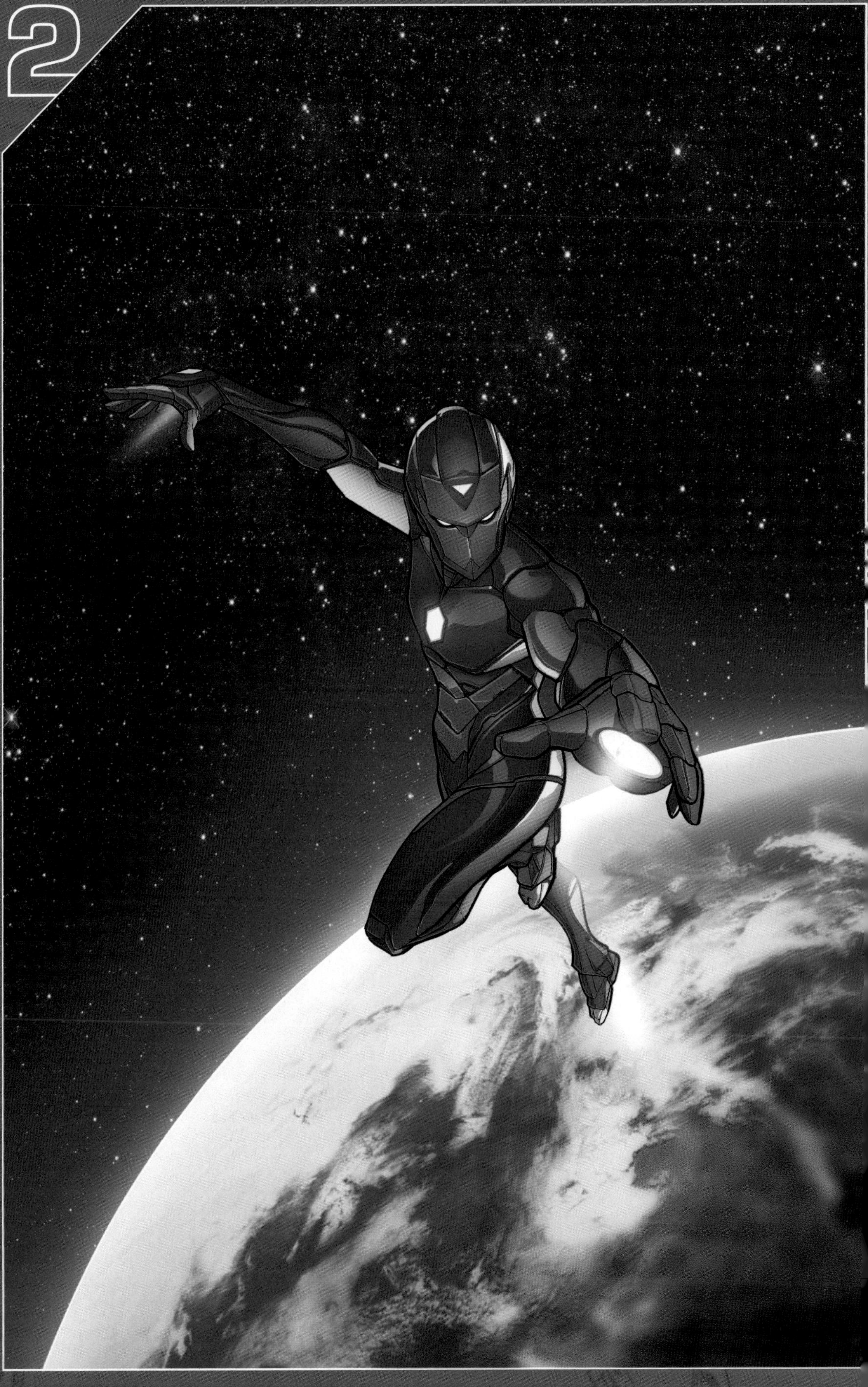

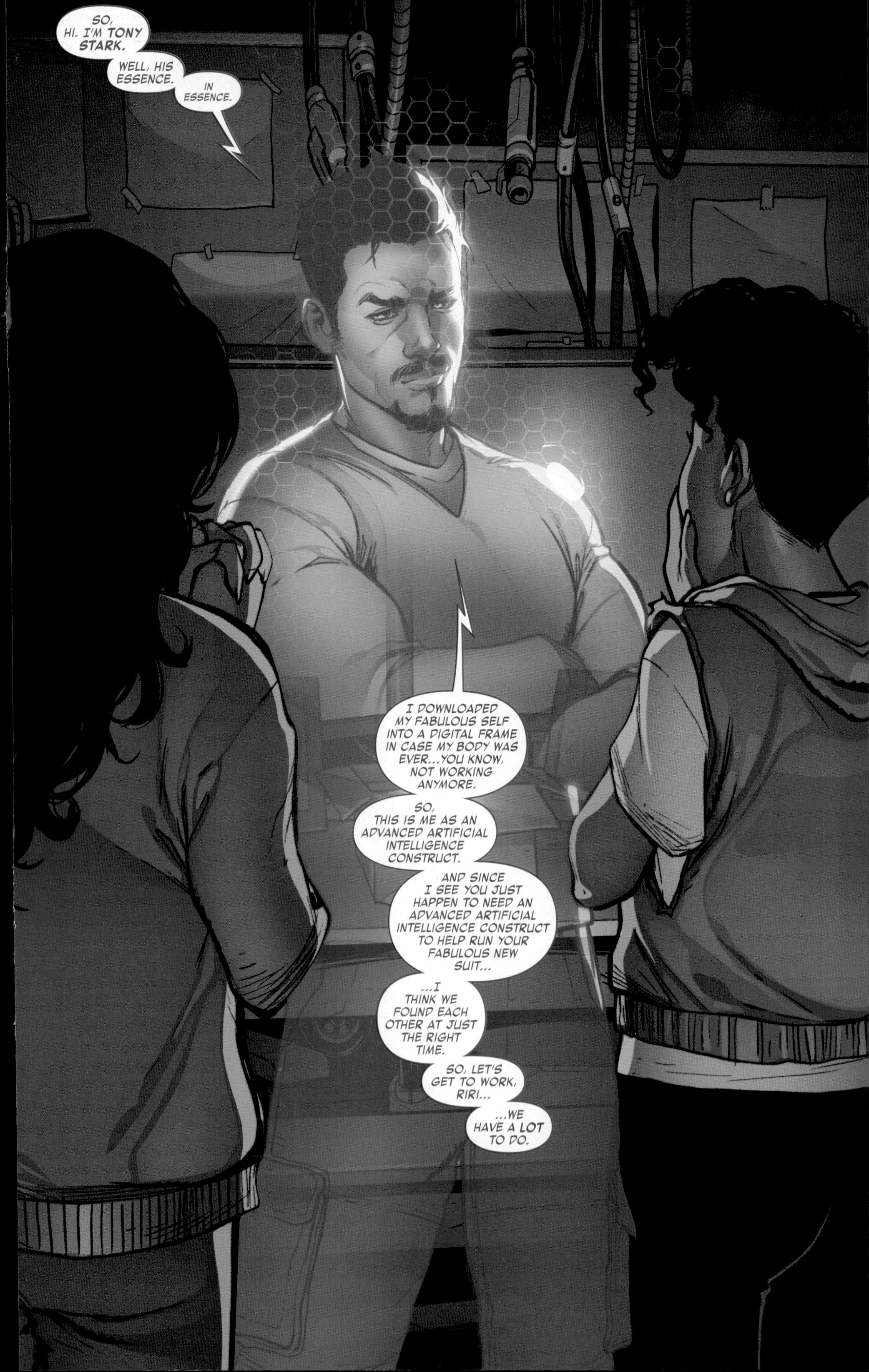
SO, HI. I'M TONY STARK.
WELL, HIS ESSENCE.
IN ESSENCE.
I DOWNLOADED MY FABULOUS SELF INTO A DIGITAL FRAME IN CASE MY BODY WAS EVER...YOU KNOW, NOT WORKING ANYMORE.
SO, THIS IS ME AS AN ADVANCED ARTIFICIAL INTELLIGENCE CONSTRUCT.
AND SINCE I SEE YOU JUST HAPPEN TO NEED AN ADVANCED ARTIFICIAL INTELLIGENCE CONSTRUCT TO HELP RUN YOUR FABULOUS NEW SUIT...
...I THINK WE FOUND EACH OTHER AT JUST THE RIGHT TIME.
SO, LET'S GET TO WORK, RIRI...
...WE HAVE A LOT TO DO.

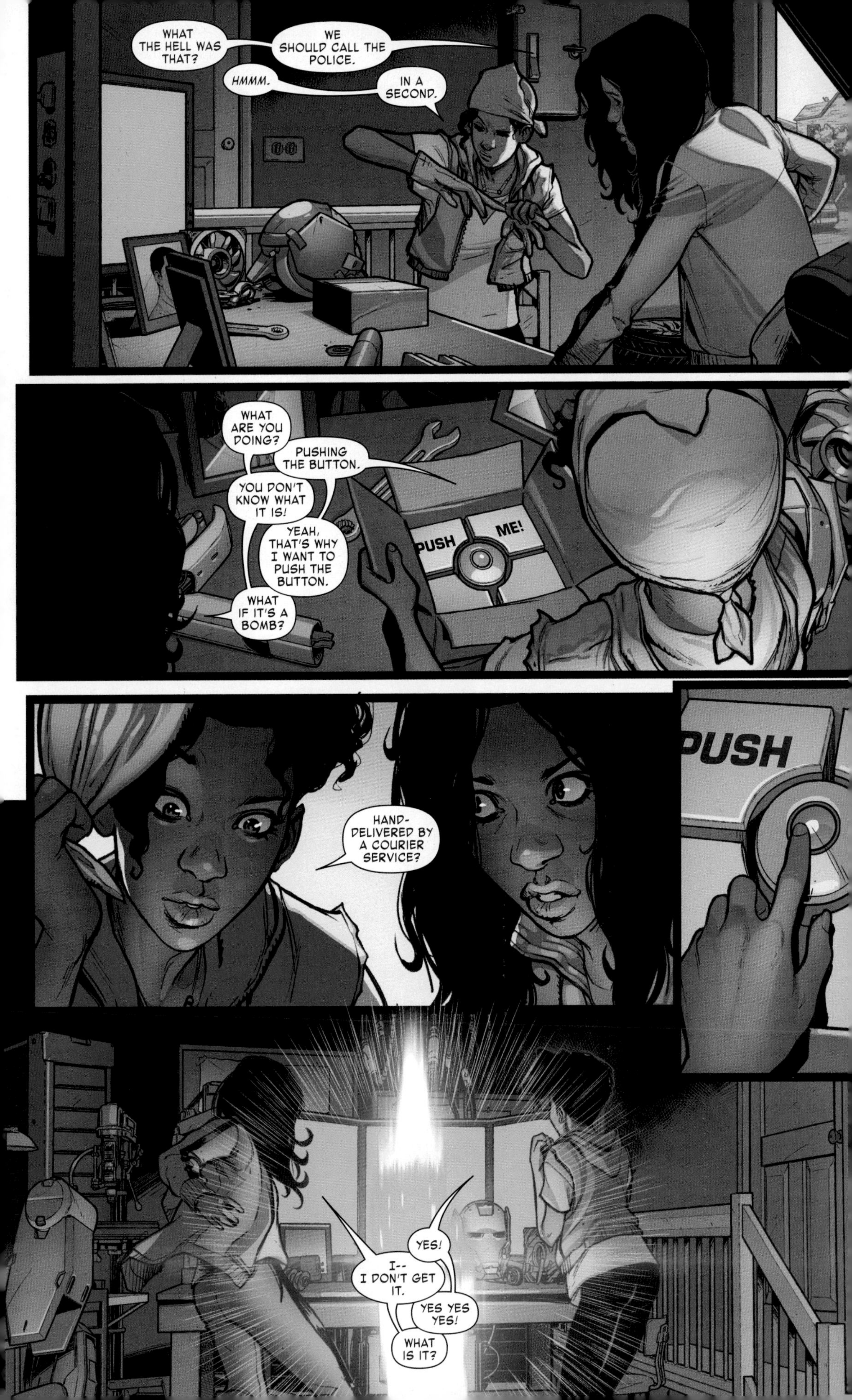
WHAT THE HELL WAS THAT?
WE SHOULD CALL THE POLICE.
HMMM.
IN A SECOND.
WHAT ARE YOU DOING?
PUSHING THE BUTTON.
YOU DON'T KNOW WHAT IT IS!
YEAH, THAT'S WHY I WANT TO PUSH THE BUTTON.
WHAT IF IT'S A BOMB?
PUSH ME!
HAND-DELIVERED BY A COURIER SERVICE?
PUSH
YES!
I-- I DON'T GET IT.
YES YES YES!
WHAT IS IT?

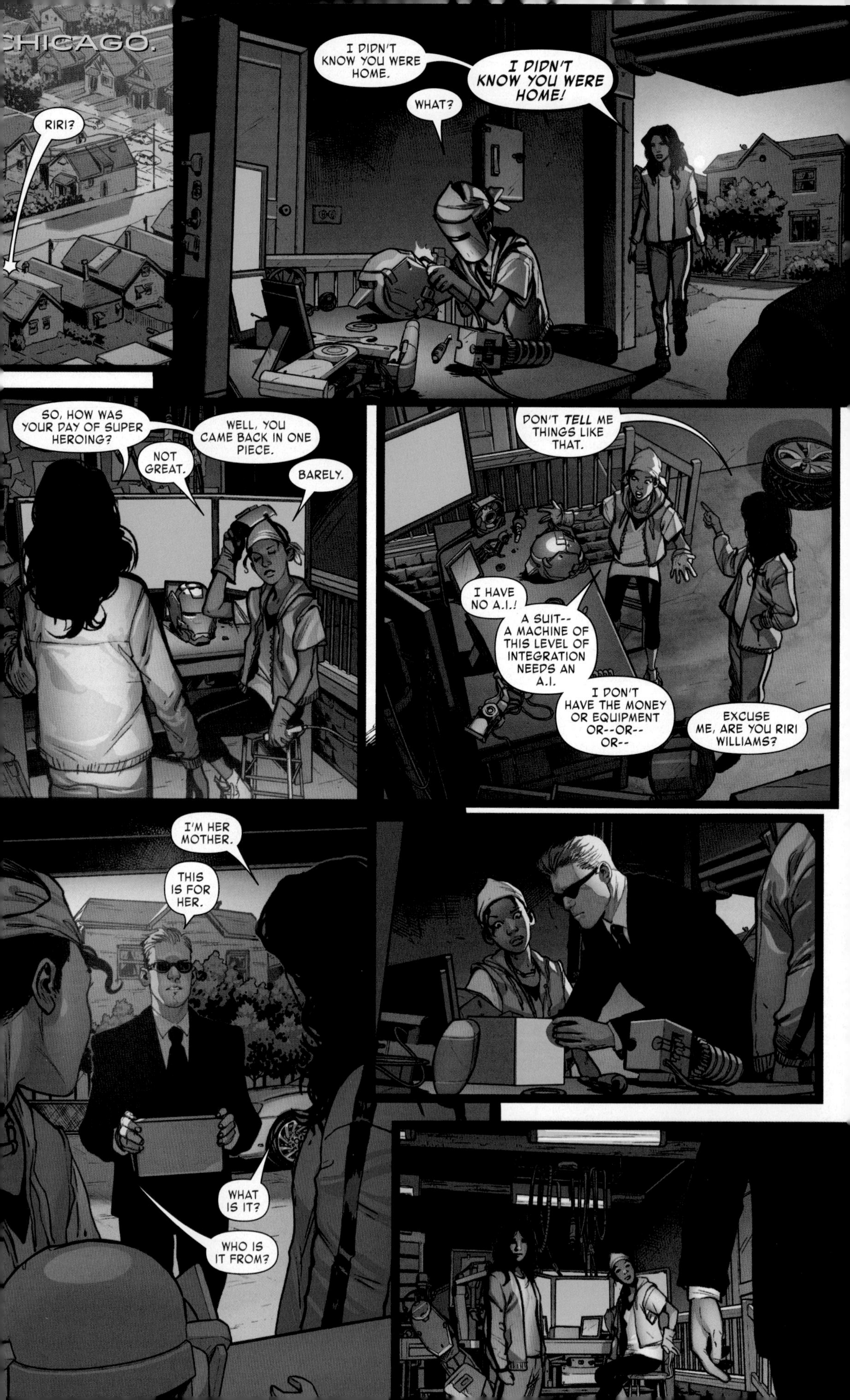
CHICAGO.
RIRI?
I DIDN'T KNOW YOU WERE HOME.
WHAT?
I DIDN'T KNOW YOU WERE HOME!
SO, HOW WAS YOUR DAY OF SUPER HEROING?
NOT GREAT.
WELL, YOU CAME BACK IN ONE PIECE.
BARELY.
DON'T TELL ME THINGS LIKE THAT.
I HAVE NO A.I.!
A SUIT-- A MACHINE OF THIS LEVEL OF INTEGRATION NEEDS AN A.I.
I DON'T HAVE THE MONEY OR EQUIPMENT OR--OR-- OR--
EXCUSE ME, ARE YOU RIRI WILLIAMS?
I'M HER MOTHER.
THIS IS FOR HER.
WHAT IS IT?
WHO IS IT FROM?

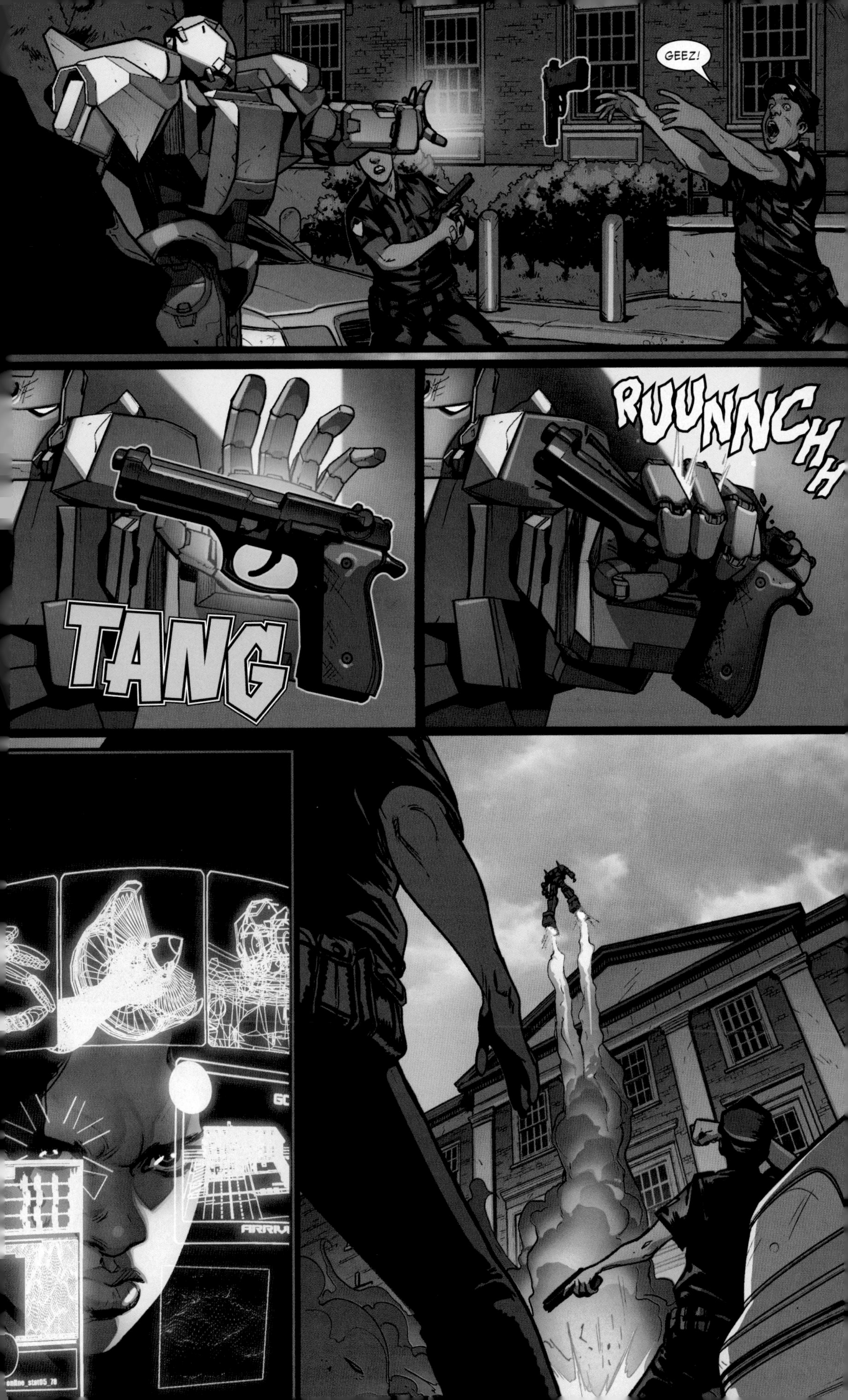
GEEZ!
TANG
RUUNNCHH

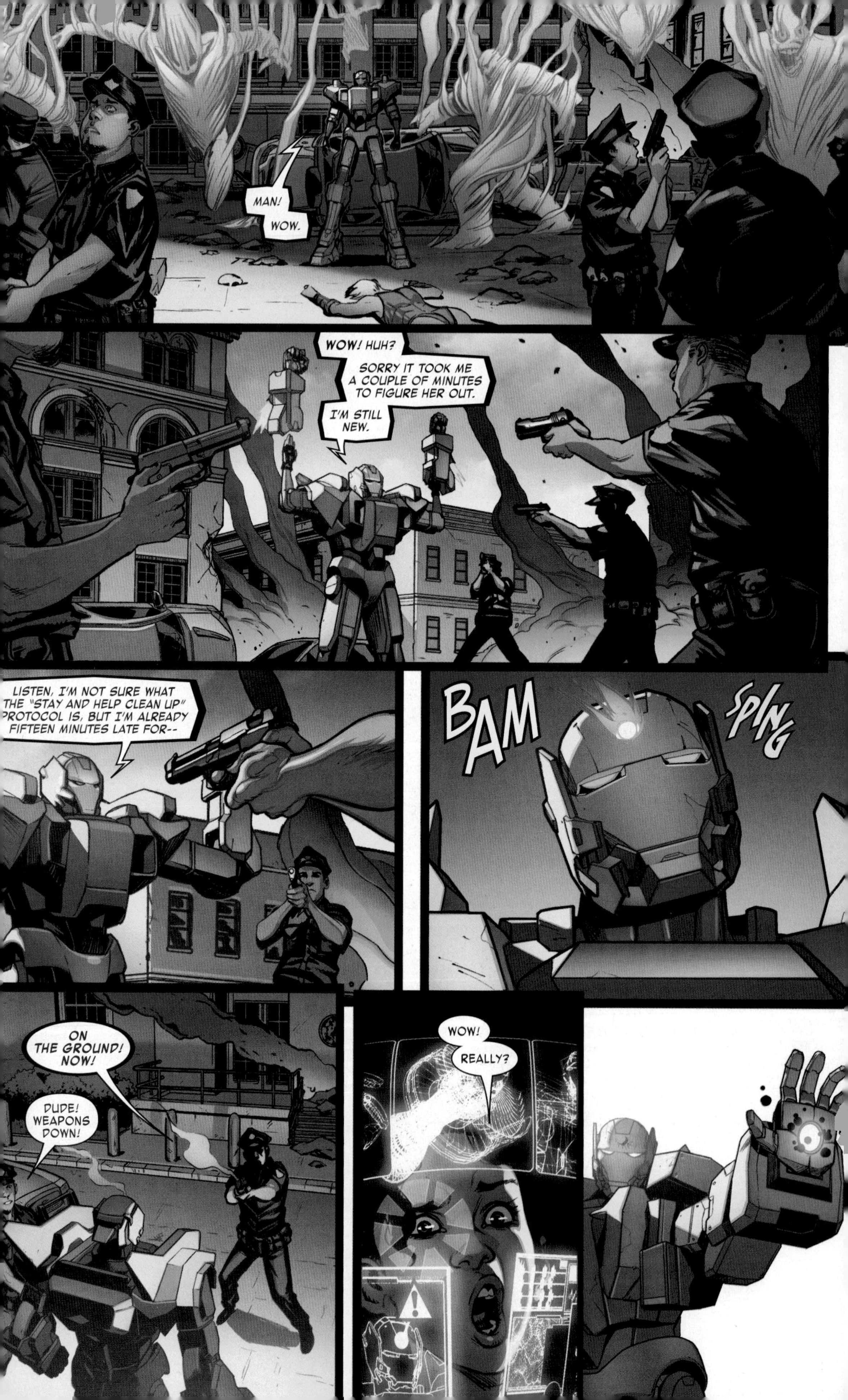
MAN!
WOW.
WOW! HUH?
SORRY IT TOOK ME A COUPLE OF MINUTES TO FIGURE HER OUT.
I'M STILL NEW.
LISTEN, I'M NOT SURE WHAT THE "STAY AND HELP CLEAN UP" PROTOCOL IS, BUT I'M ALREADY FIFTEEN MINUTES LATE FOR--
BAM
SPING
ON THE GROUND! NOW!
DUDE! WEAPONS DOWN!
WOW!
REALLY?

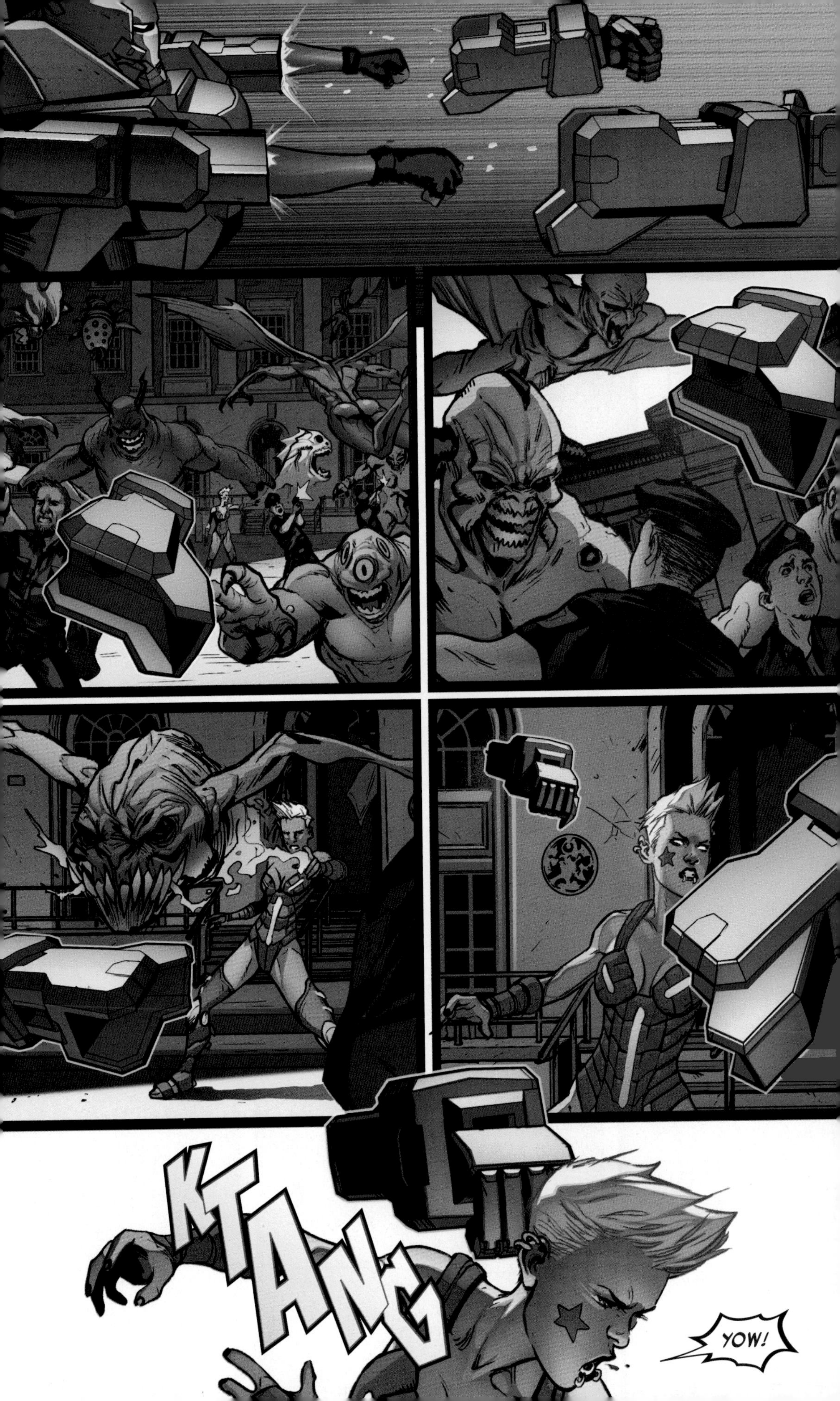
KTANG
YOW!

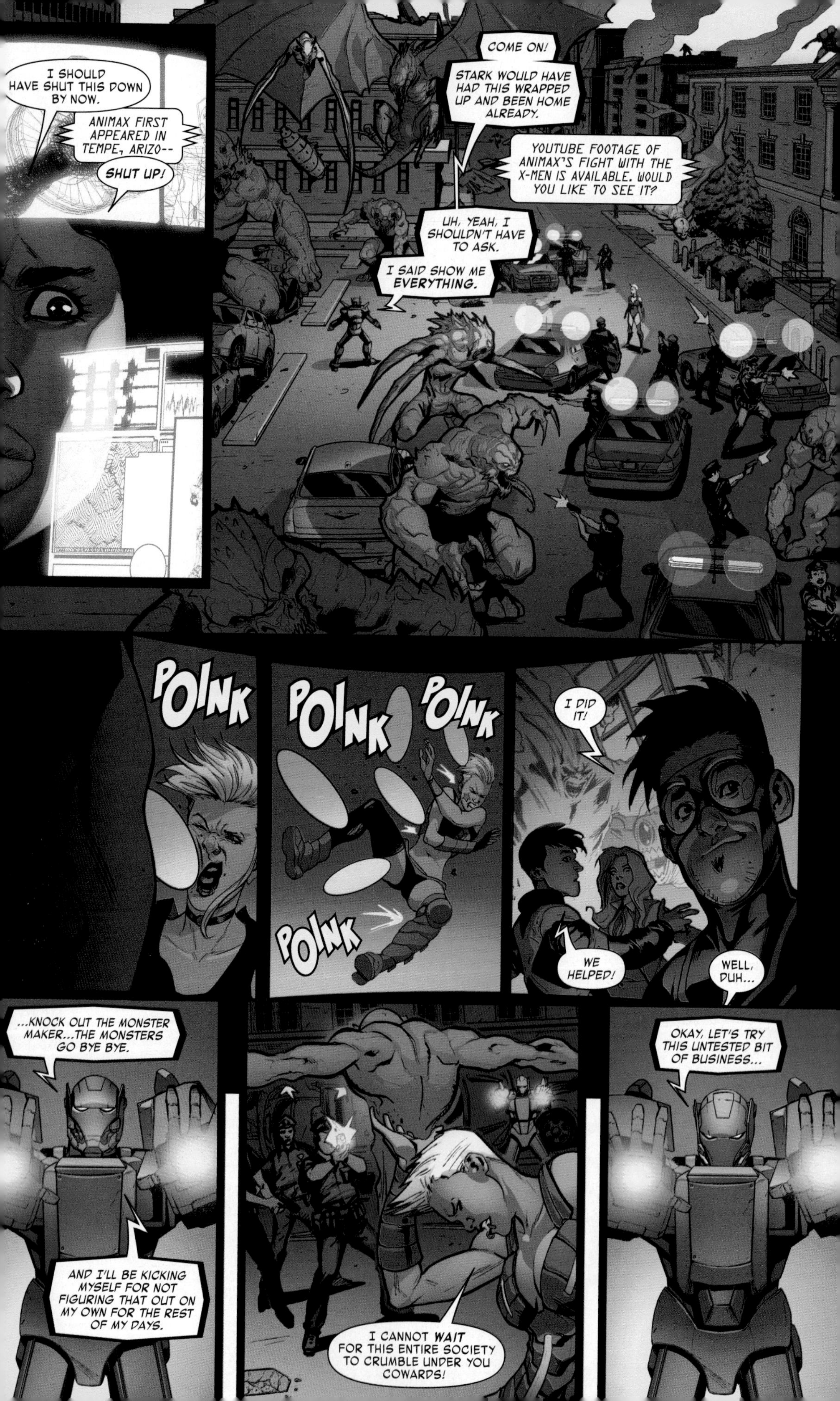
I SHOULD HAVE SHUT THIS DOWN BY NOW.
ANIMAX FIRST APPEARED IN TEMPE, ARIZO--
SHUT UP!
COME ON!
STARK WOULD HAVE HAD THIS WRAPPED UP AND BEEN HOME ALREADY.
YOUTUBE FOOTAGE OF ANIMAX'S FIGHT WITH THE X-MEN IS AVAILABLE. WOULD YOU LIKE TO SEE IT?
UH, YEAH, I SHOULDN'T HAVE TO ASK.
I SAID SHOW ME EVERYTHING.
POINK
POINK
POINK
POINK
I DID IT!
WE HELPED!
WELL, DUH...
...KNOCK OUT THE MONSTER MAKER...THE MONSTERS GO BYE BYE.
AND I'LL BE KICKING MYSELF FOR NOT FIGURING THAT OUT ON MY OWN FOR THE REST OF MY DAYS.
I CANNOT WAIT FOR THIS ENTIRE SOCIETY TO CRUMBLE UNDER YOU COWARDS!
OKAY, LET'S TRY THIS UNTESTED BIT OF BUSINESS...

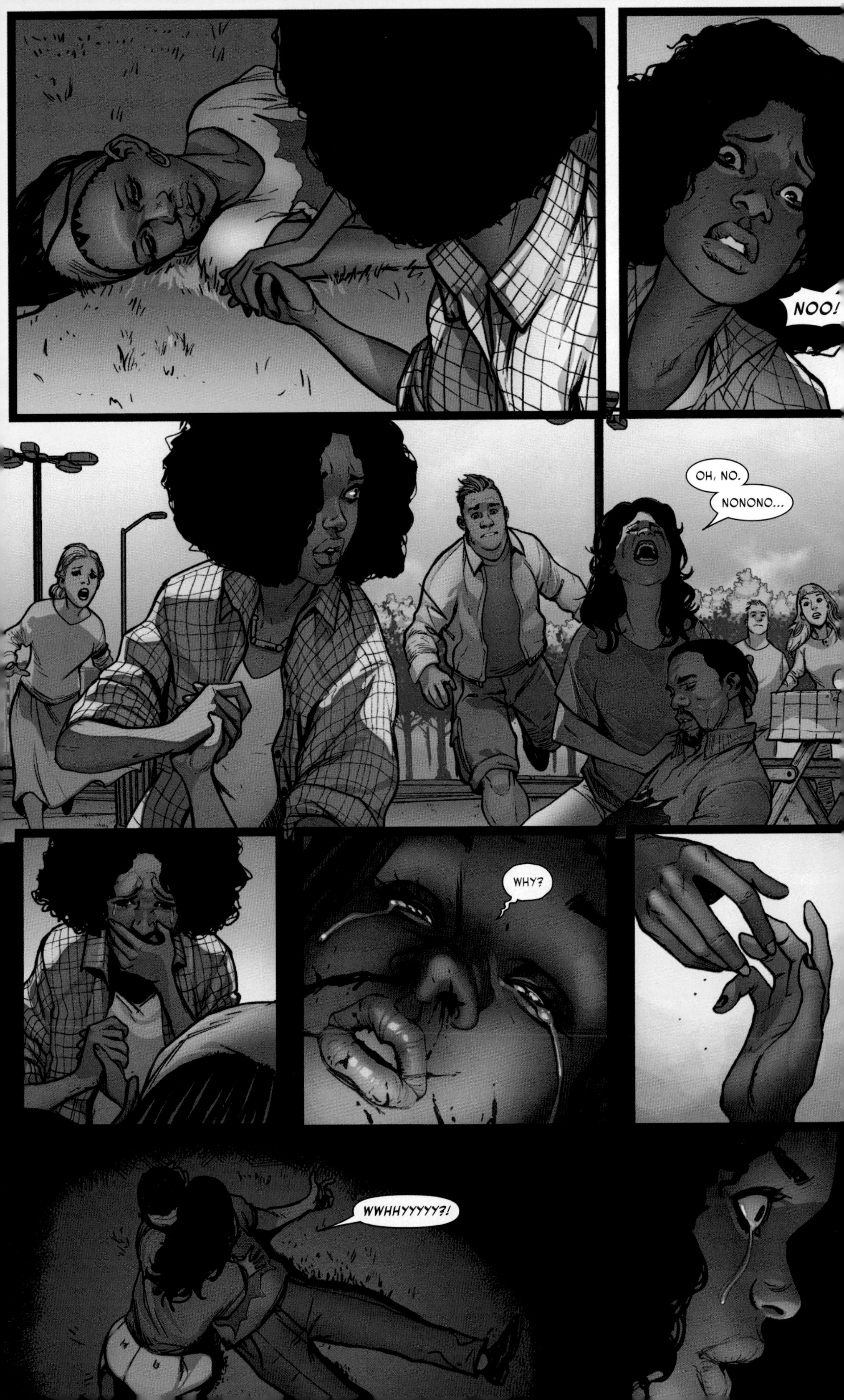
NOO!
OH, NO.
NONONO...
WHY?
WWHHYYYYY?!

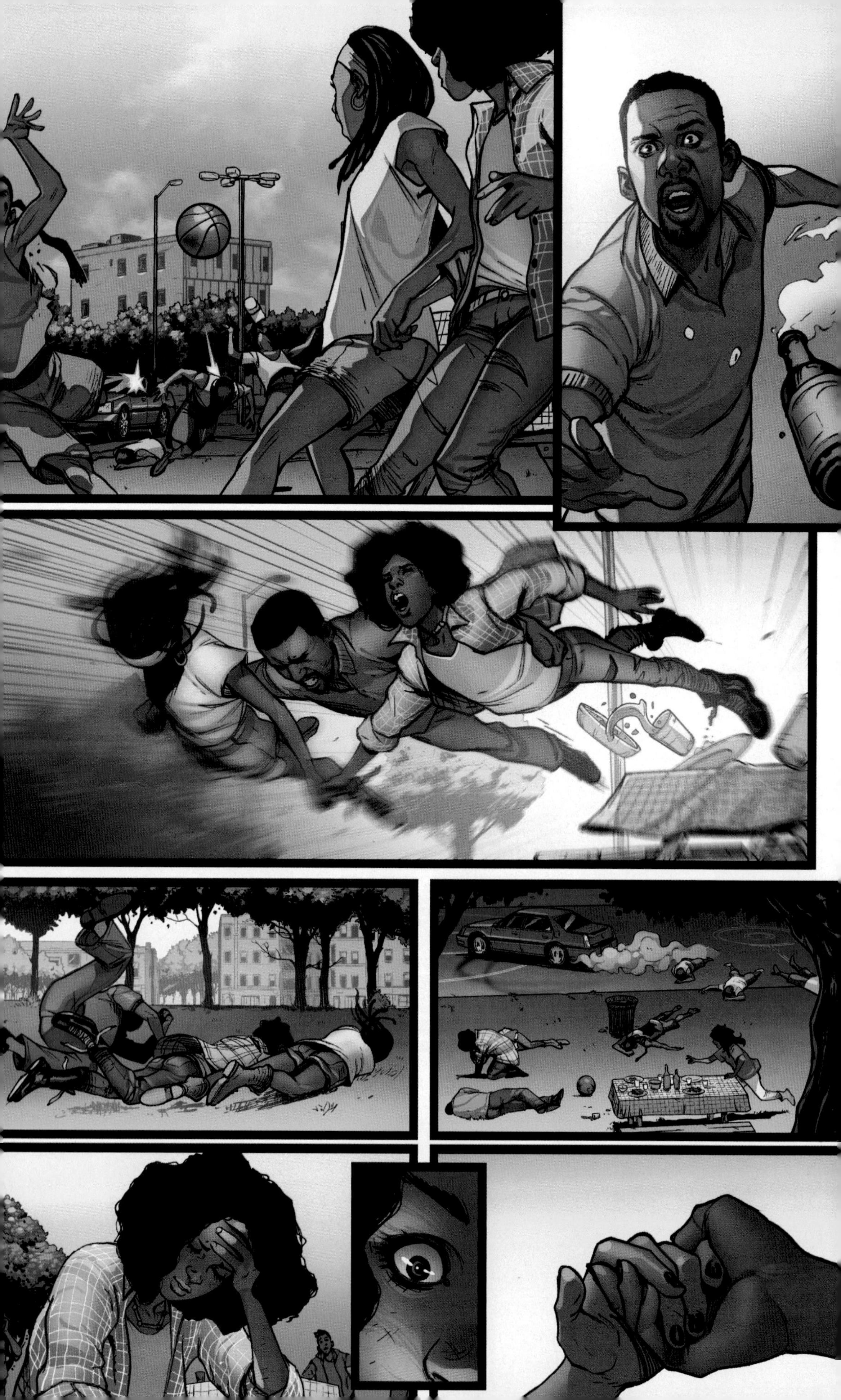

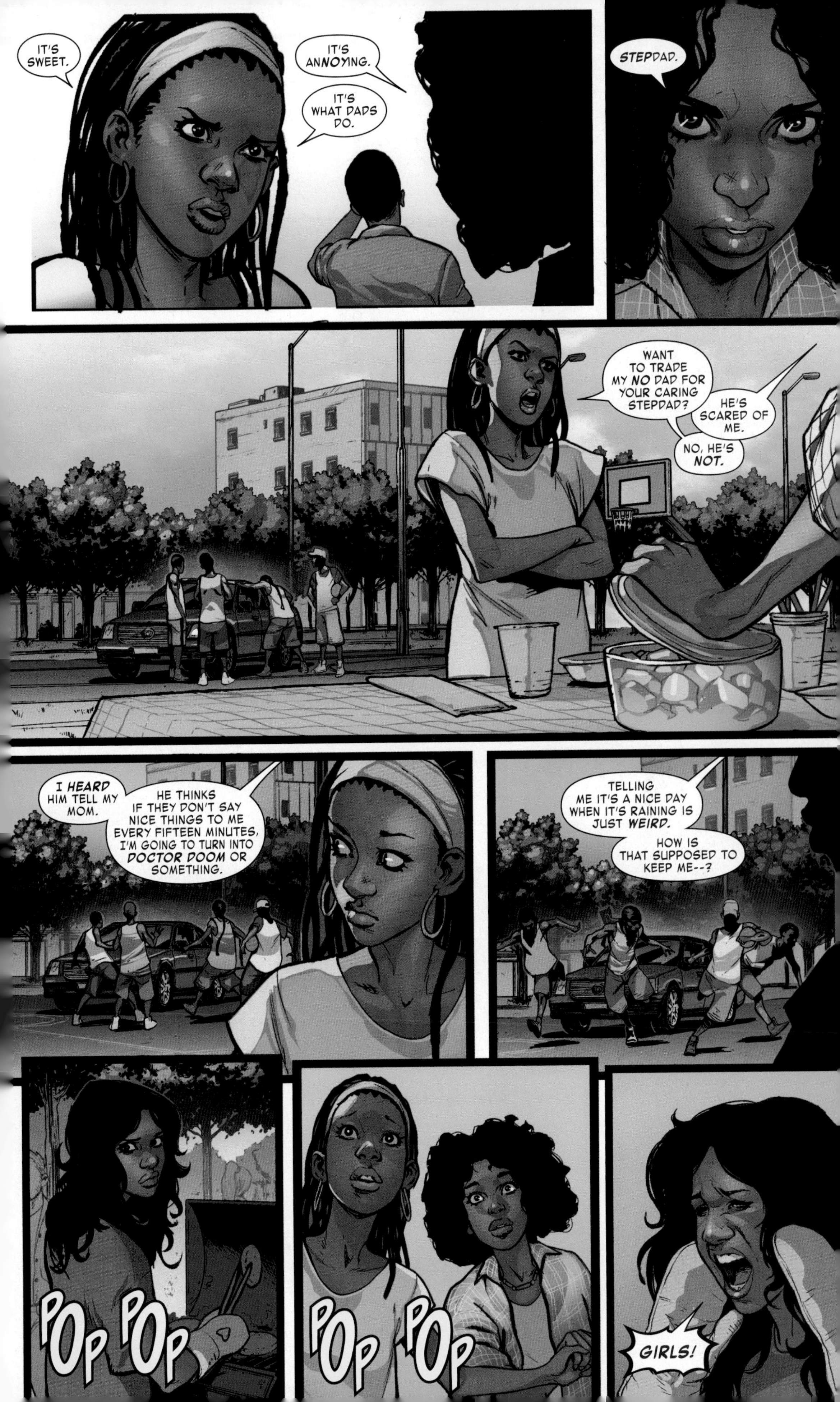

IT'S SWEET.
IT'S ANNOYING.
IT'S WHAT DADS DO.
STEPDAD.
WANT TO TRADE MY NO DAD FOR YOUR CARING STEPDAD?
HE'S SCARED OF ME.
NO, HE'S NOT.
I HEARD HIM TELL MY MOM.
HE THINKS IF THEY DON'T SAY NICE THINGS TO ME EVERY FIFTEEN MINUTES, I'M GOING TO TURN INTO DOCTOR DOOM OR SOMETHING.
TELLING ME IT'S A NICE DAY WHEN IT'S RAINING IS JUST WEIRD.
HOW IS THAT SUPPOSED TO KEEP ME--?
POP POP
POP POP
GIRLS!

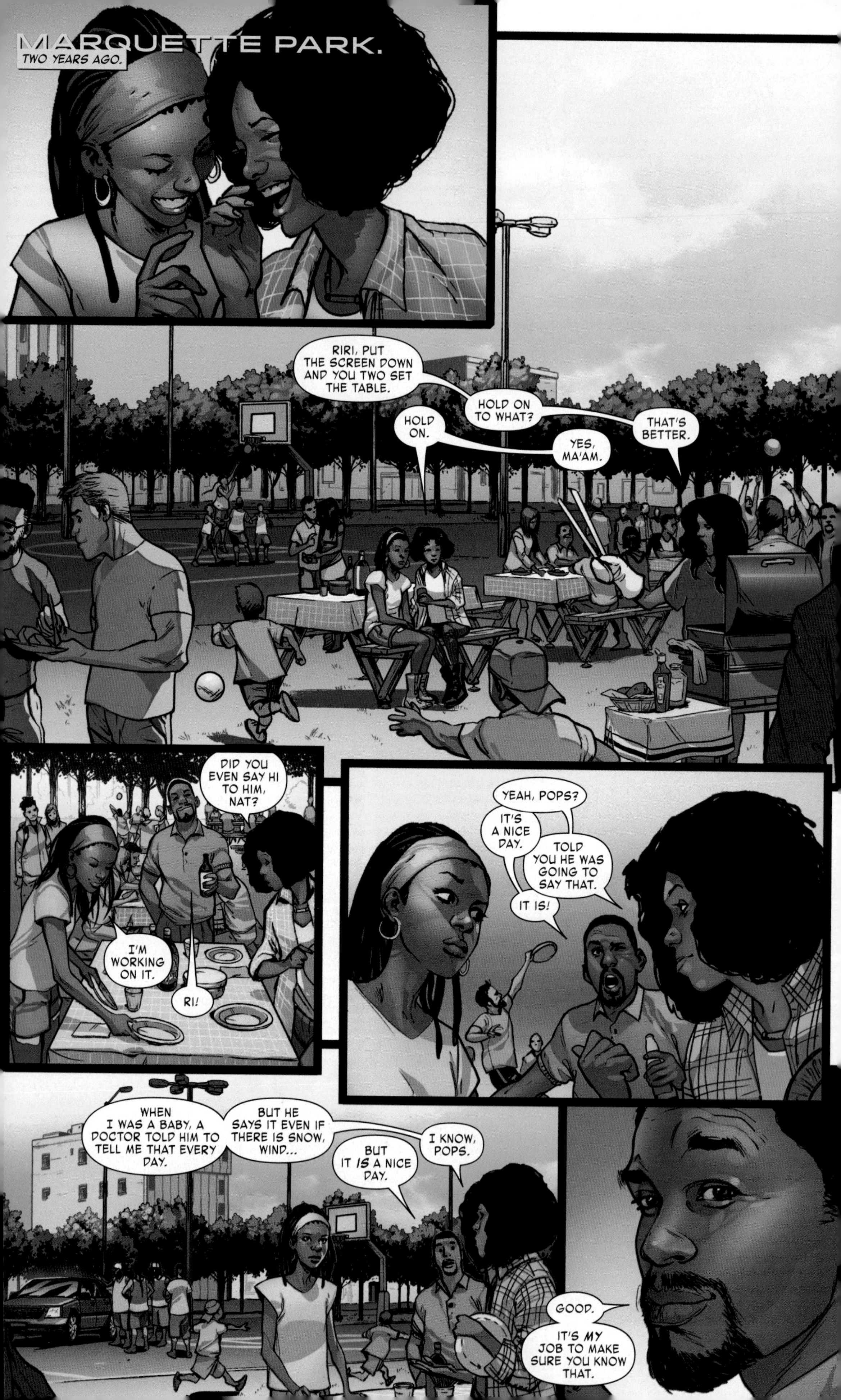
MARQUETTE PARK.
TWO YEARS AGO.
RIRI, PUT THE SCREEN DOWN AND YOU TWO SET THE TABLE.
HOLD ON.
HOLD ON TO WHAT?
YES, MA'AM.
THAT'S BETTER.
DID YOU EVEN SAY HI TO HIM, NAT?
I'M WORKING ON IT.
RI!
YEAH, POPS?
IT'S A NICE DAY.
TOLD YOU HE WAS GOING TO SAY THAT.
IT IS!
WHEN I WAS A BABY, A DOCTOR TOLD HIM TO TELL ME THAT EVERY DAY.
BUT HE SAYS IT EVEN IF THERE IS SNOW, WIND...
BUT IT IS A NICE DAY.
I KNOW, POPS.
GOOD.
IT'S MY JOB TO MAKE SURE YOU KNOW THAT.

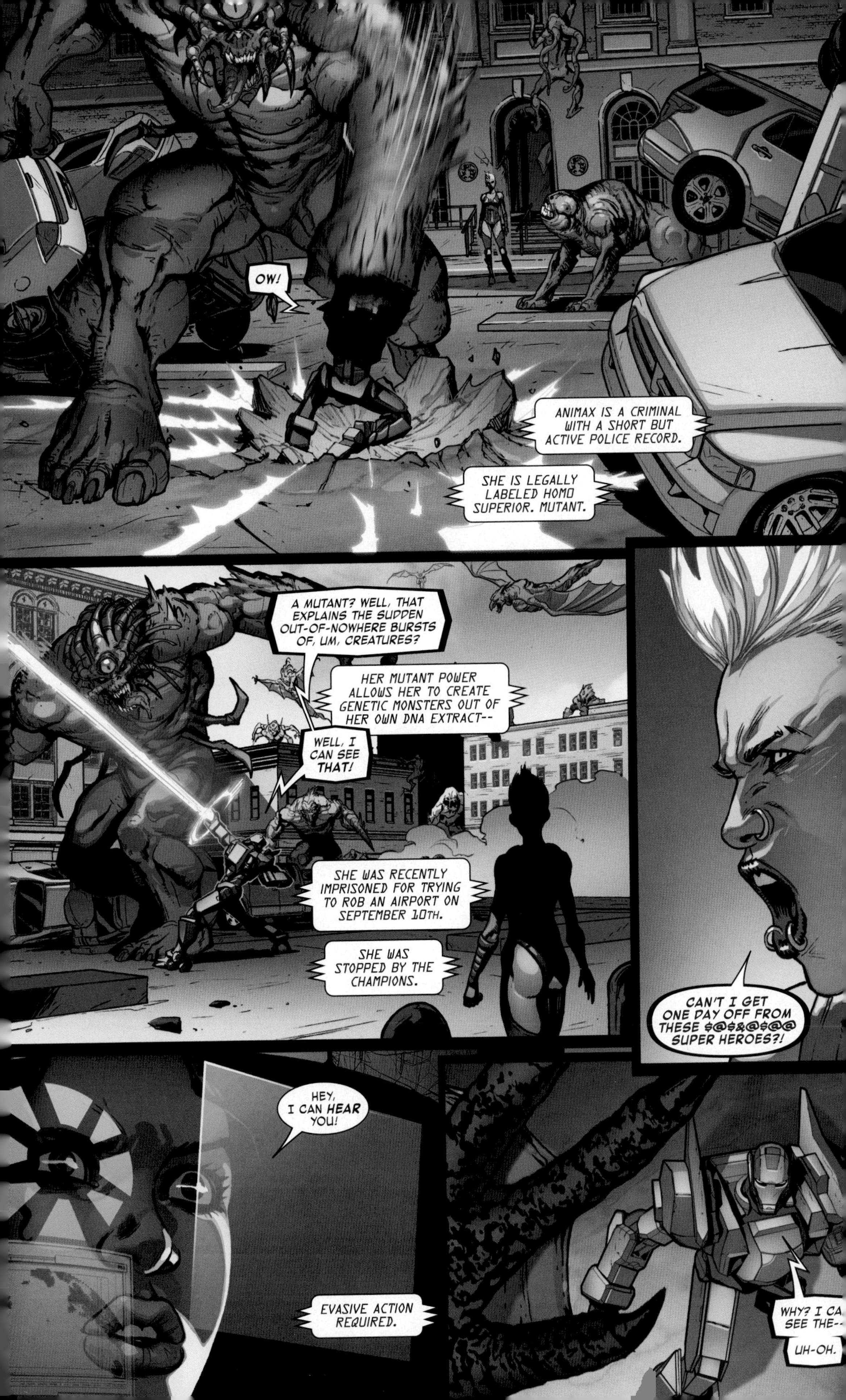
OW!
ANIMAX IS A CRIMINAL WITH A SHORT BUT ACTIVE POLICE RECORD.
SHE IS LEGALLY LABELED HOMO SUPERIOR. MUTANT.
A MUTANT? WELL, THAT EXPLAINS THE SUDDEN OUT-OF-NOWHERE BURSTS OF, UM, CREATURES?
HER MUTANT POWER ALLOWS HER TO CREATE GENETIC MONSTERS OUT OF HER OWN DNA EXTRACT--
WELL, I CAN SEE THAT!
SHE WAS RECENTLY IMPRISONED FOR TRYING TO ROB AN AIRPORT ON SEPTEMBER 10TH.
SHE WAS STOPPED BY THE CHAMPIONS.
CAN'T I GET ONE DAY OFF FROM THESE $@$&@$@@ SUPER HEROES?!
HEY, I CAN HEAR YOU!
EVASIVE ACTION REQUIRED.
UH-OH.

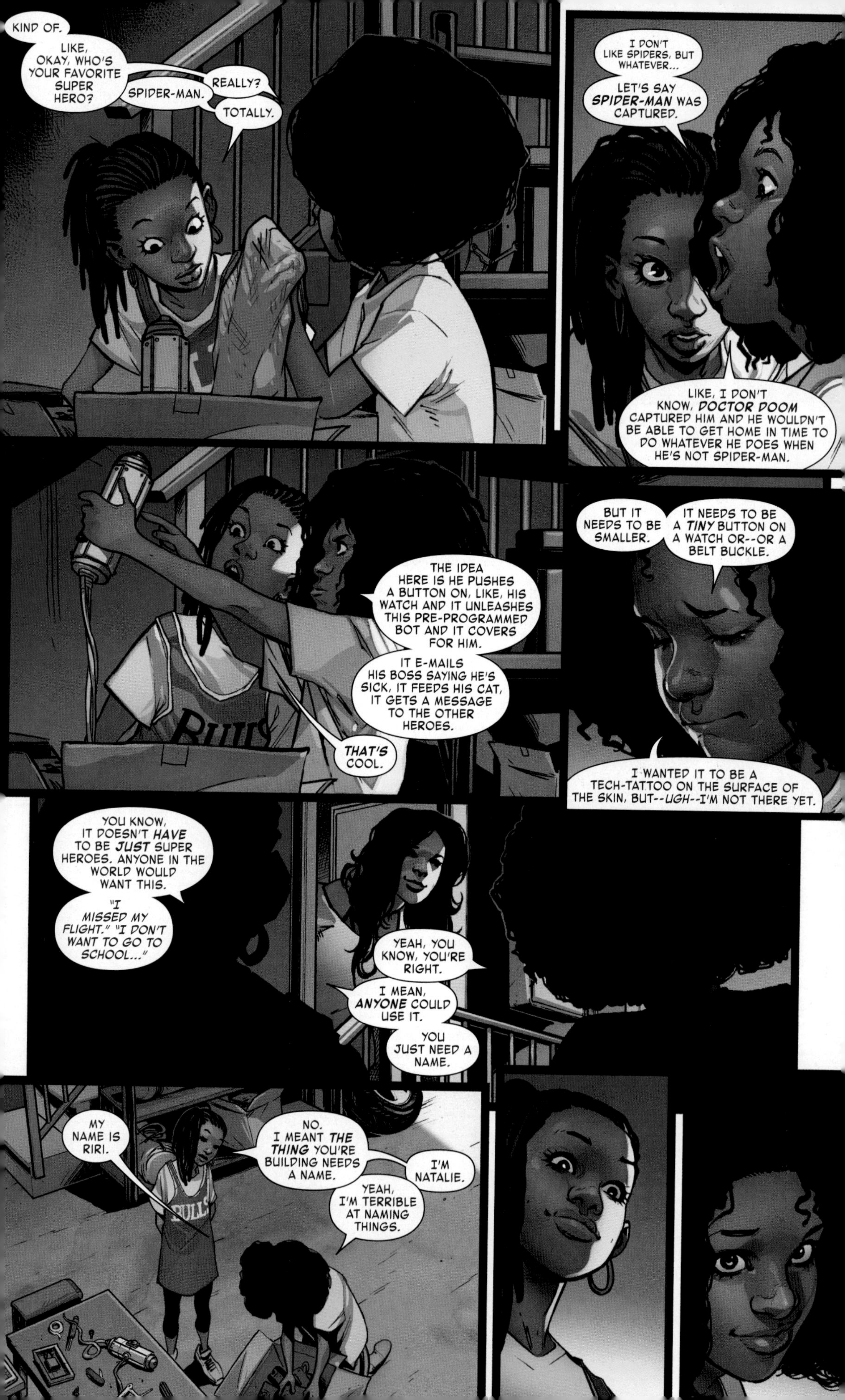
KIND OF.
LIKE, OKAY, WHO'S YOUR FAVORITE SUPER HERO?
SPIDER-MAN.
REALLY?
TOTALLY.
I DON'T LIKE SPIDERS, BUT WHATEVER...
LET'S SAY SPIDER-MAN WAS CAPTURED.
LIKE, I DON'T KNOW, DOCTOR DOOM CAPTURED HIM AND HE WOULDN'T BE ABLE TO GET HOME IN TIME TO DO WHATEVER HE DOES WHEN HE'S NOT SPIDER-MAN.
THE IDEA HERE IS HE PUSHES A BUTTON ON, LIKE, HIS WATCH AND IT UNLEASHES THIS PRE-PROGRAMMED BOT AND IT COVERS FOR HIM.
IT E-MAILS HIS BOSS SAYING HE'S SICK, IT FEEDS HIS CAT, IT GETS A MESSAGE TO THE OTHER HEROES.
THAT'S COOL.
BUT IT NEEDS TO BE SMALLER.
IT NEEDS TO BE A TINY BUTTON ON A WATCH OR--OR A BELT BUCKLE.
I WANTED IT TO BE A TECH-TATTOO ON THE SURFACE OF THE SKIN, BUT--UGH--I'M NOT THERE YET.
YOU KNOW, IT DOESN'T HAVE TO BE JUST SUPER HEROES. ANYONE IN THE WORLD WOULD WANT THIS.
"I MISSED MY FLIGHT." "I DON'T WANT TO GO TO SCHOOL..."
YEAH, YOU KNOW, YOU'RE RIGHT.
I MEAN, ANYONE COULD USE IT.
YOU JUST NEED A NAME.
MY NAME IS RIRI.
NO. I MEANT THE THING YOU'RE BUILDING NEEDS A NAME.
I'M NATALIE.
YEAH, I'M TERRIBLE AT NAMING THINGS.

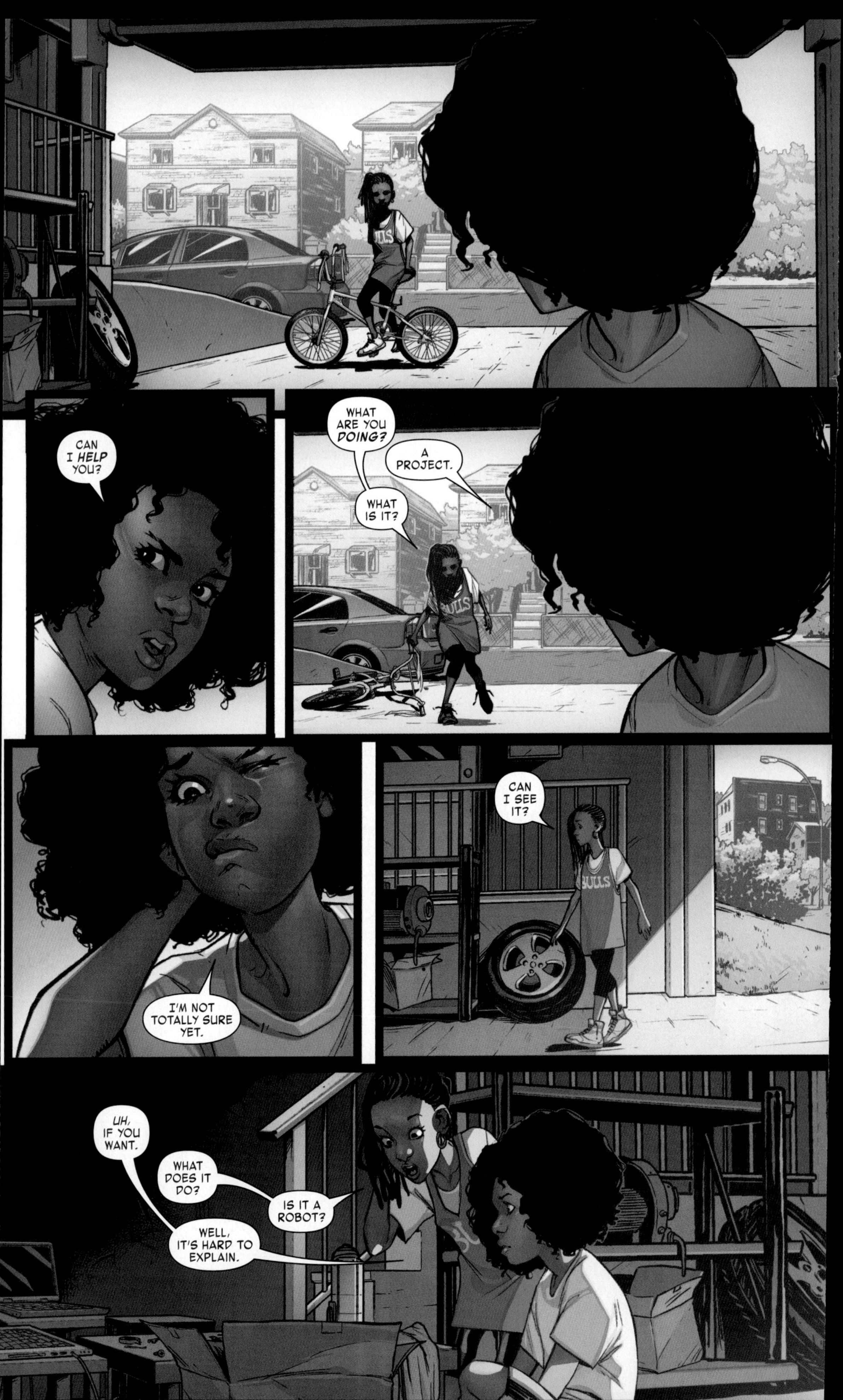
CAN I HELP YOU?
WHAT ARE YOU DOING?
A PROJECT.
WHAT IS IT?
I'M NOT TOTALLY SURE YET.
CAN I SEE IT?
UH, IF YOU WANT.
WHAT DOES IT DO?
IS IT A ROBOT?
WELL, IT'S HARD TO EXPLAIN.

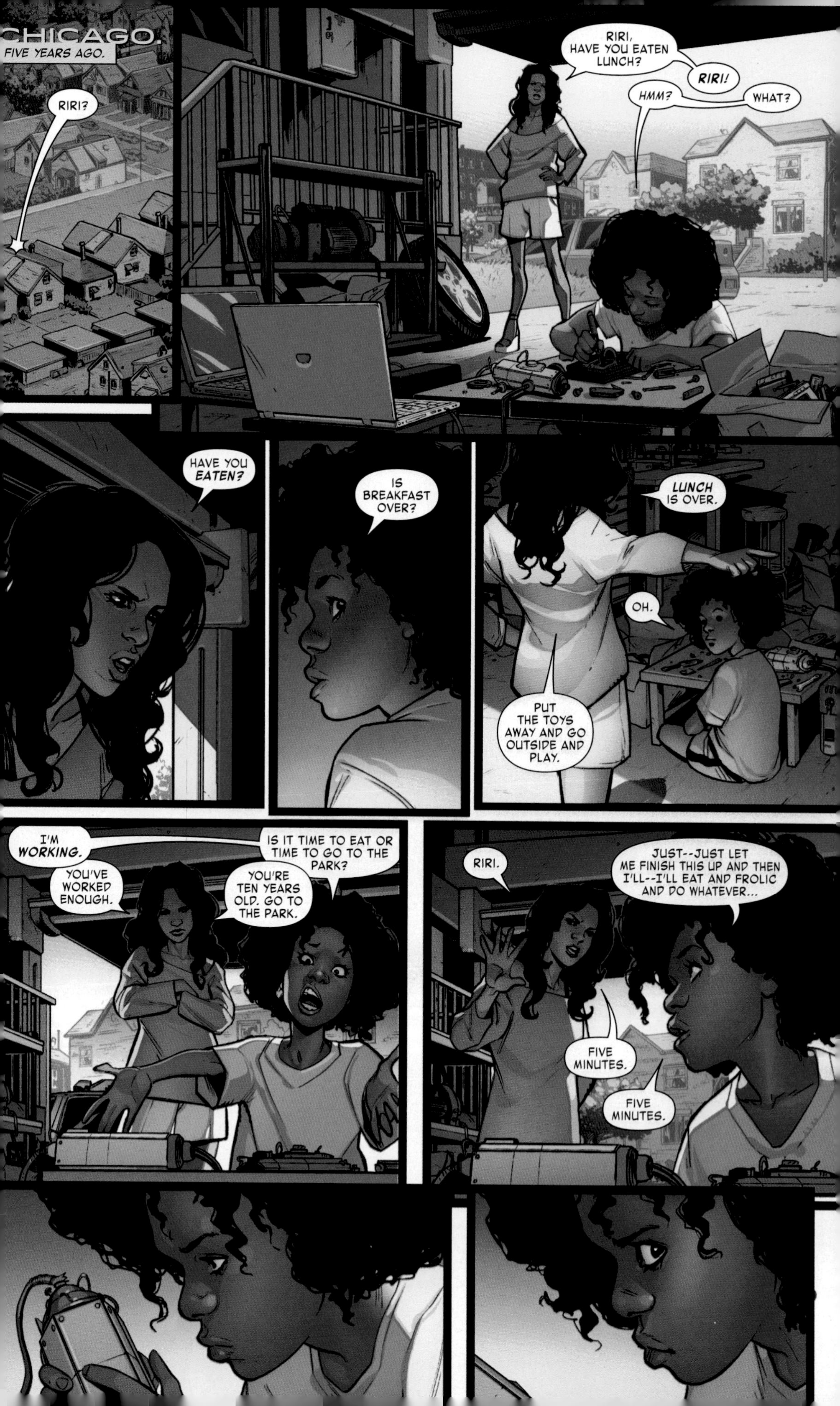
CHICAGO.
FIVE YEARS AGO.
RIRI?
RIRI, HAVE YOU EATEN LUNCH?
RIRI!
HMM?
WHAT?
HAVE YOU EATEN?
IS BREAKFAST OVER?
LUNCH IS OVER.
OH.
PUT THE TOYS AWAY AND GO OUTSIDE AND PLAY.
I'M WORKING.
IS IT TIME TO EAT OR TIME TO GO TO THE PARK?
YOU'VE WORKED ENOUGH.
YOU'RE TEN YEARS OLD. GO TO THE PARK.
RIRI.
JUST--JUST LET ME FINISH THIS UP AND THEN I'LL--I'LL EAT AND FROLIC AND DO WHATEVER...
FIVE MINUTES.
FIVE MINUTES.

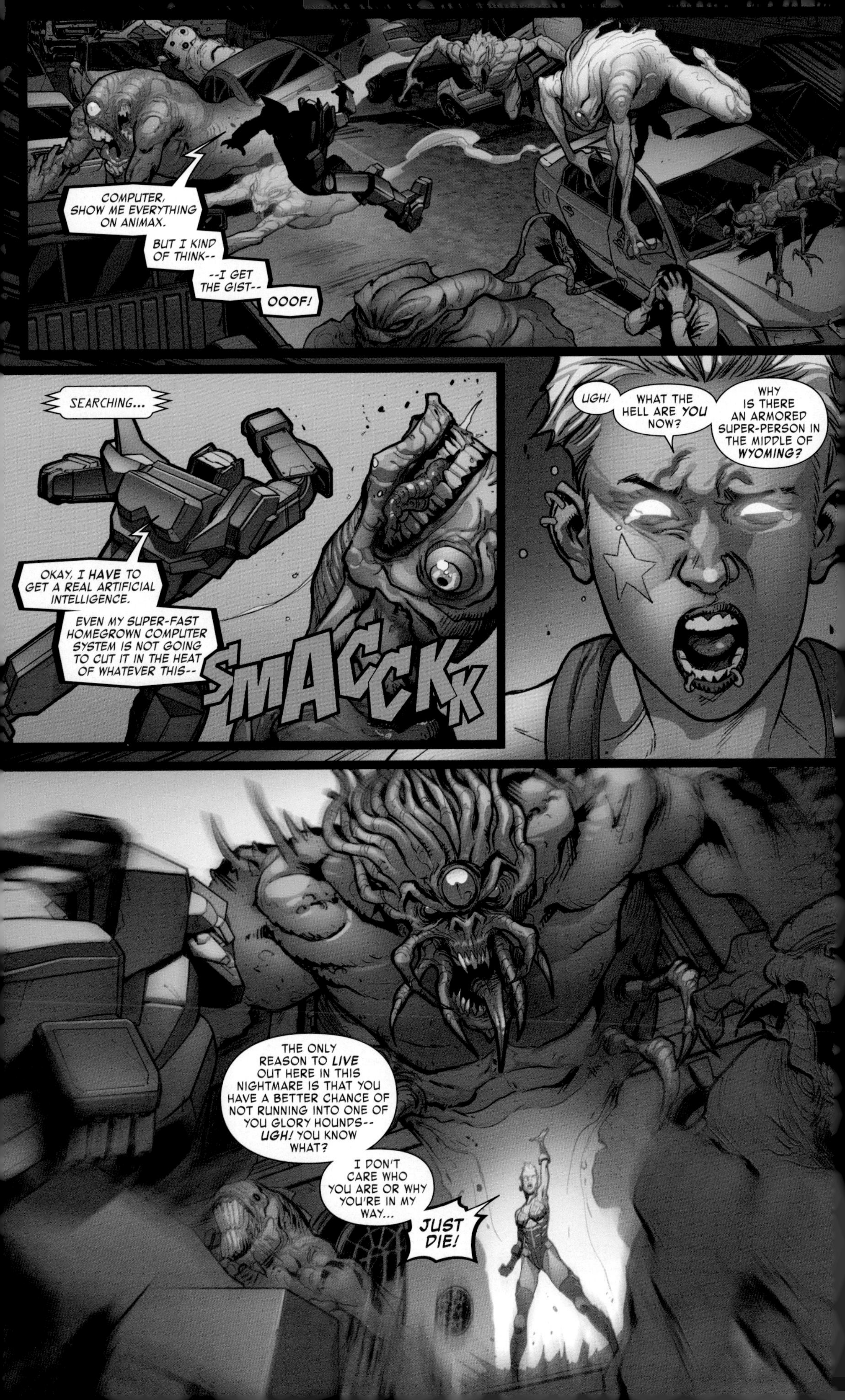
COMPUTER, SHOW ME EVERYTHING ON ANIMAX.
BUT I KIND OF THINK--
--I GET THE GIST--
OOOF!
SEARCHING...
OKAY, I HAVE TO GET A REAL ARTIFICIAL INTELLIGENCE.
EVEN MY SUPER-FAST HOMEGROWN COMPUTER SYSTEM IS NOT GOING TO CUT IT IN THE HEAT OF WHATEVER THIS--
SMACCKK
UGH!
WHAT THE HELL ARE YOU NOW?
WHY IS THERE AN ARMORED SUPER-PERSON IN THE MIDDLE OF WYOMING?
THE ONLY REASON TO LIVE OUT HERE IN THIS NIGHTMARE IS THAT YOU HAVE A BETTER CHANCE OF NOT RUNNING INTO ONE OF YOU GLORY HOUNDS-- UGH! YOU KNOW WHAT?
I DON'T CARE WHO YOU ARE OR WHY YOU'RE IN MY WAY...
JUST DIE!

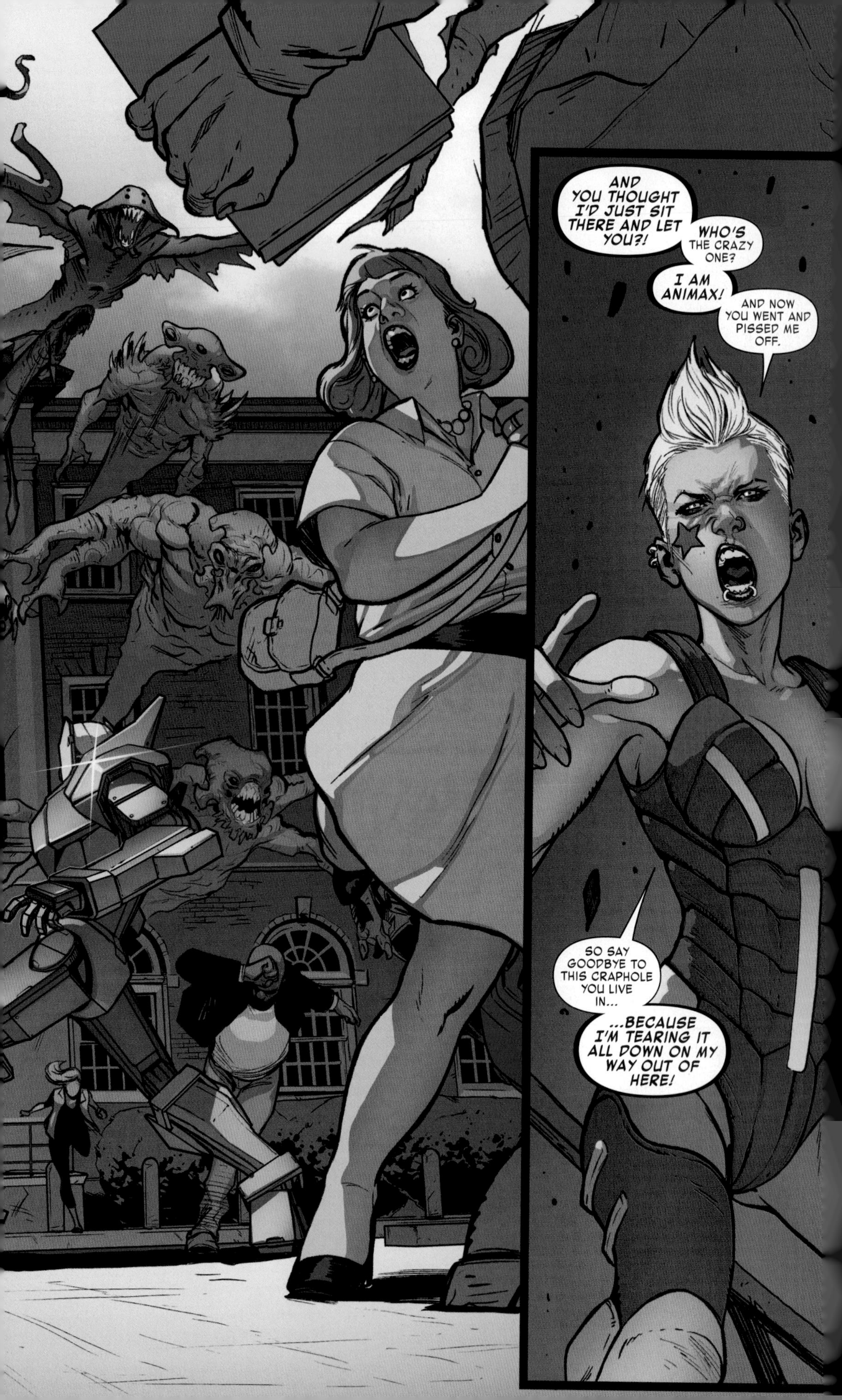
AND YOU THOUGHT I'D JUST SIT THERE AND LET YOU?!
WHO'S THE CRAZY ONE?
I AM ANIMAX!
AND NOW YOU WENT AND PISSED ME OFF.
SO SAY GOODBYE TO THIS CRAPHOLE YOU LIVE IN...
...BECAUSE I'M TEARING IT ALL DOWN ON MY WAY OUT OF HERE!

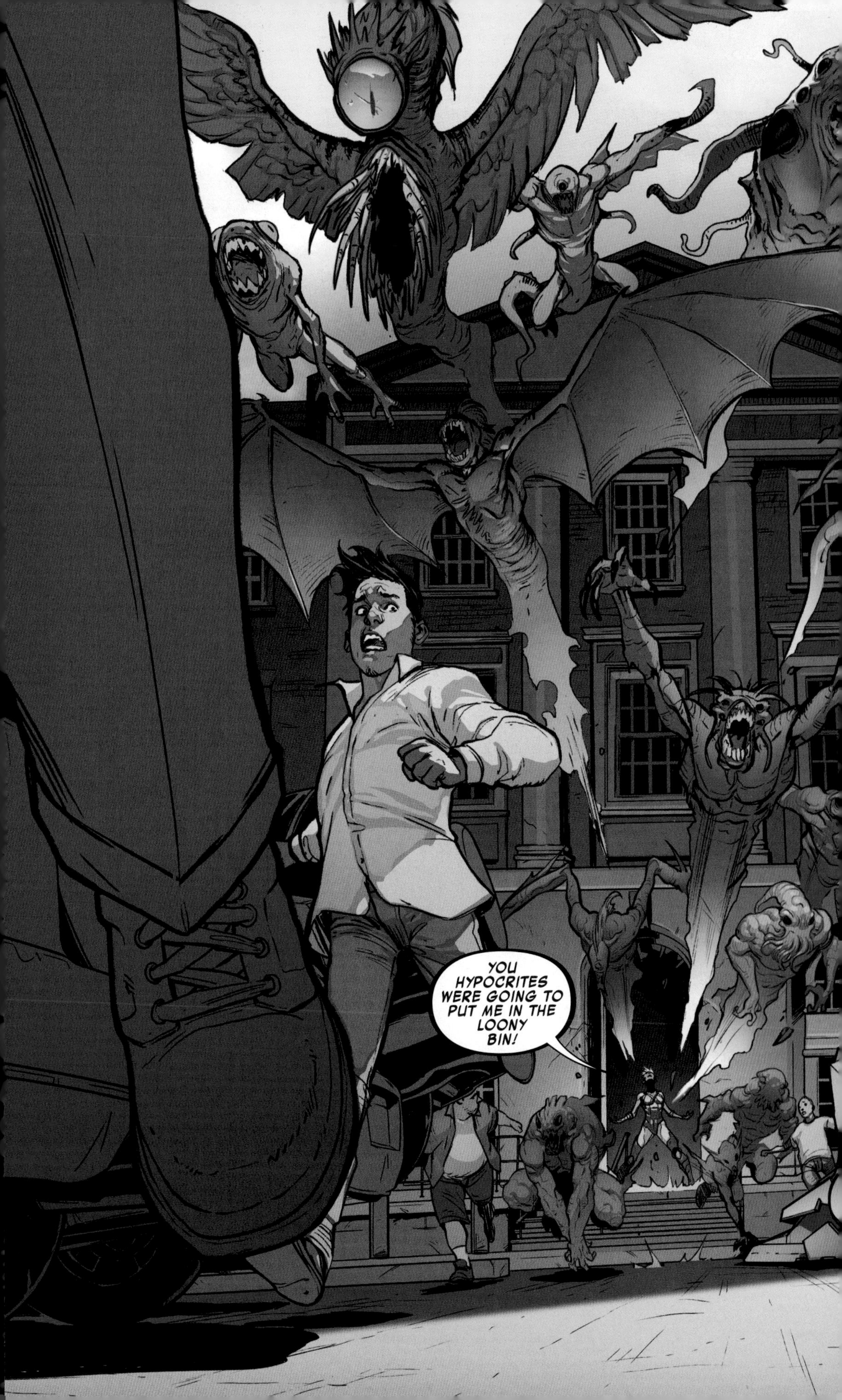
YOU HYPOCRITES WERE GOING TO PUT ME IN THE LOONY BIN!

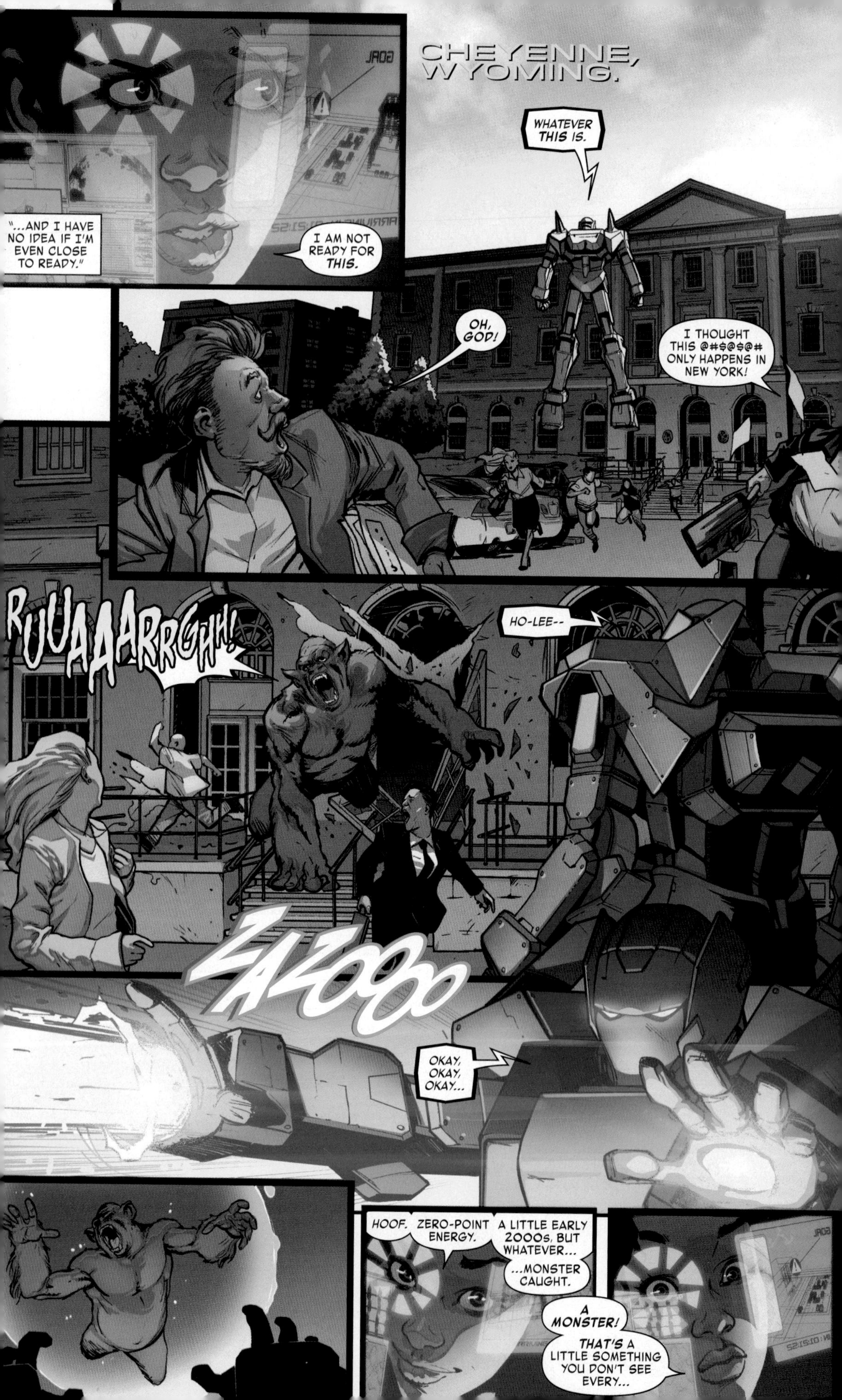

CHEYENNE, WYOMING.
"...AND I HAVE NO IDEA IF I'M EVEN CLOSE TO READY."
I AM NOT READY FOR THIS.
WHATEVER THIS IS.
OH, GOD!
I THOUGHT THIS @#$@$@# ONLY HAPPENS IN NEW YORK!
RUUAAARRGHH!
HO-LEE--
ZAZOOOO
OKAY, OKAY, OKAY...
HOOF.
ZERO-POINT ENERGY.
A LITTLE EARLY 2000s, BUT WHATEVER...
...MONSTER CAUGHT.
A MONSTER!
THAT'S A LITTLE SOMETHING YOU DON'T SEE EVERY...

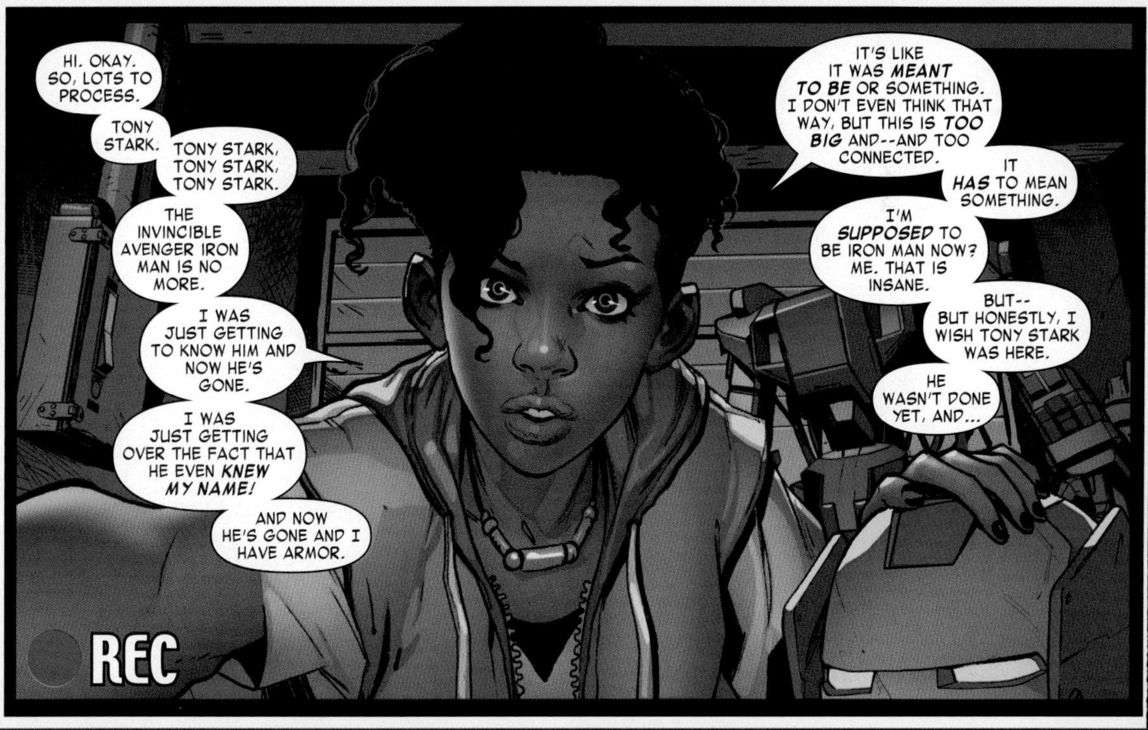
HI. OKAY. SO, LOTS TO PROCESS.
TONY STARK.
TONY STARK, TONY STARK, TONY STARK.
THE INVINCIBLE AVENGER IRON MAN IS NO MORE.
I WAS JUST GETTING TO KNOW HIM AND NOW HE'S GONE.
I WAS JUST GETTING OVER THE FACT THAT HE EVEN **KNEW MY NAME!**
AND NOW HE'S GONE AND I HAVE ARMOR.
IT'S LIKE IT WAS **MEANT TO BE** OR SOMETHING. I DON'T EVEN THINK THAT WAY, BUT THIS IS **TOO BIG** AND--AND TOO CONNECTED.
IT **HAS** TO MEAN SOMETHING.
I'M **SUPPOSED** TO BE IRON MAN NOW? ME. THAT IS INSANE.
BUT-- BUT HONESTLY, I WISH TONY STARK WAS HERE.
HE WASN'T DONE YET, AND...
REC

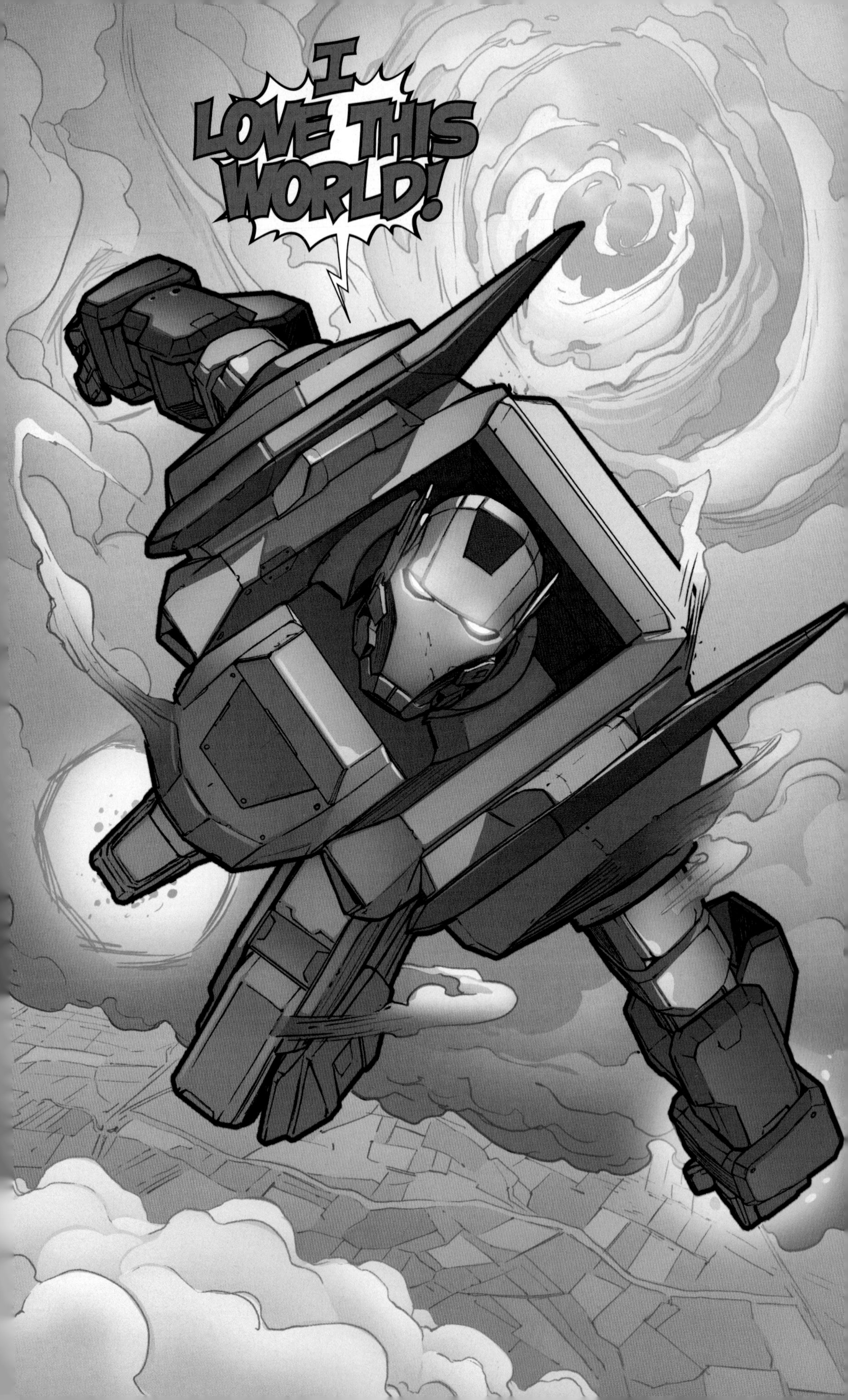
I LOVE THIS WORLD!

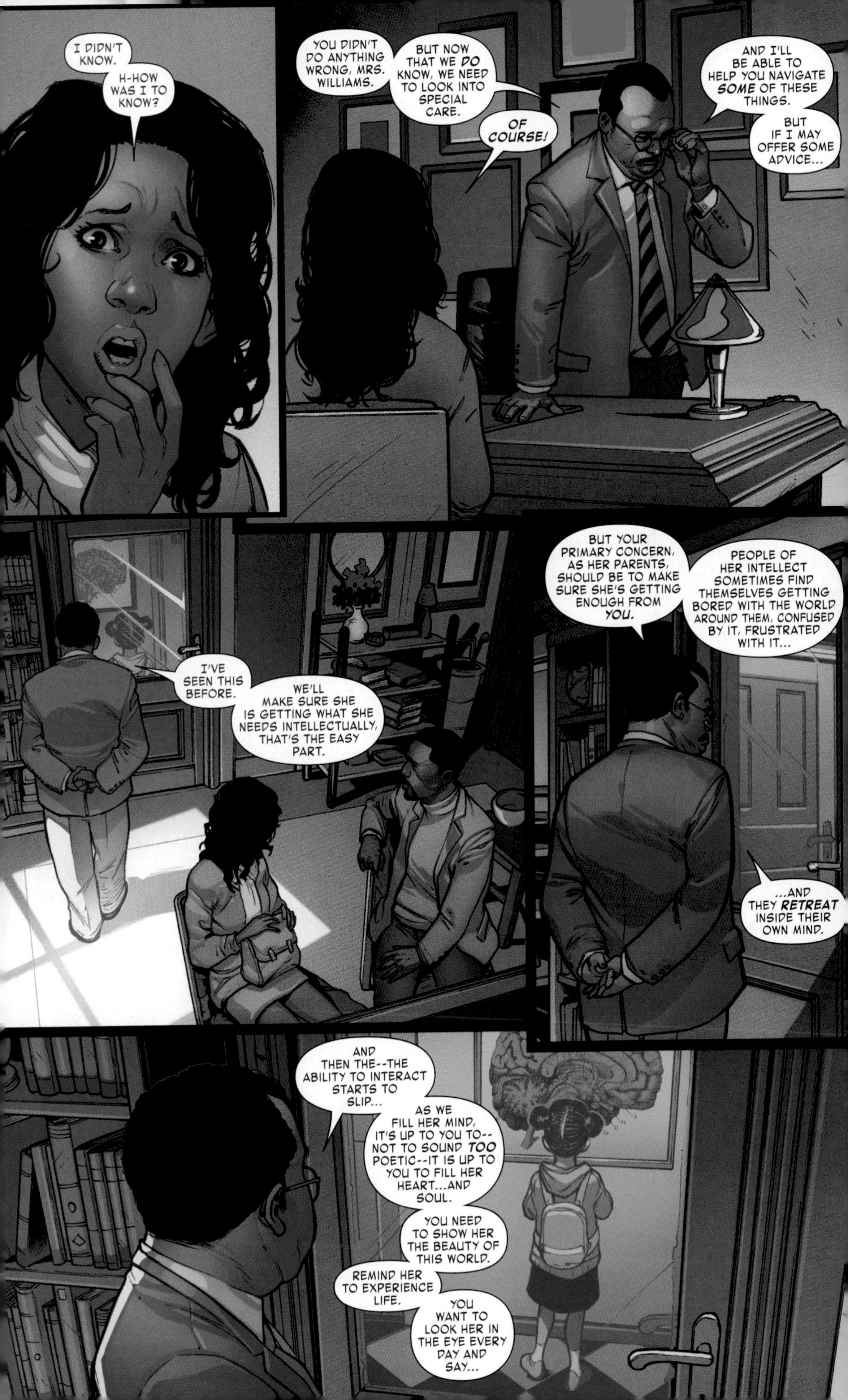
I DIDN'T KNOW.
H-HOW WAS I TO KNOW?
YOU DIDN'T DO ANYTHING WRONG, MRS. WILLIAMS.
BUT NOW THAT WE DO KNOW, WE NEED TO LOOK INTO SPECIAL CARE.
OF COURSE!
AND I'LL BE ABLE TO HELP YOU NAVIGATE SOME OF THESE THINGS.
BUT IF I MAY OFFER SOME ADVICE...
I'VE SEEN THIS BEFORE.
WE'LL MAKE SURE SHE IS GETTING WHAT SHE NEEDS INTELLECTUALLY, THAT'S THE EASY PART.
BUT YOUR PRIMARY CONCERN, AS HER PARENTS, SHOULD BE TO MAKE SURE SHE'S GETTING ENOUGH FROM YOU.
PEOPLE OF HER INTELLECT SOMETIMES FIND THEMSELVES GETTING BORED WITH THE WORLD AROUND THEM, CONFUSED BY IT, FRUSTRATED WITH IT...
...AND THEY RETREAT INSIDE THEIR OWN MIND.
AND THEN THE--THE ABILITY TO INTERACT STARTS TO SLIP...
AS WE FILL HER MIND, IT'S UP TO YOU TO--NOT TO SOUND TOO POETIC--IT IS UP TO YOU TO FILL HER HEART...AND SOUL.
YOU NEED TO SHOW HER THE BEAUTY OF THIS WORLD.
REMIND HER TO EXPERIENCE LIFE.
YOU WANT TO LOOK HER IN THE EYE EVERY DAY AND SAY...

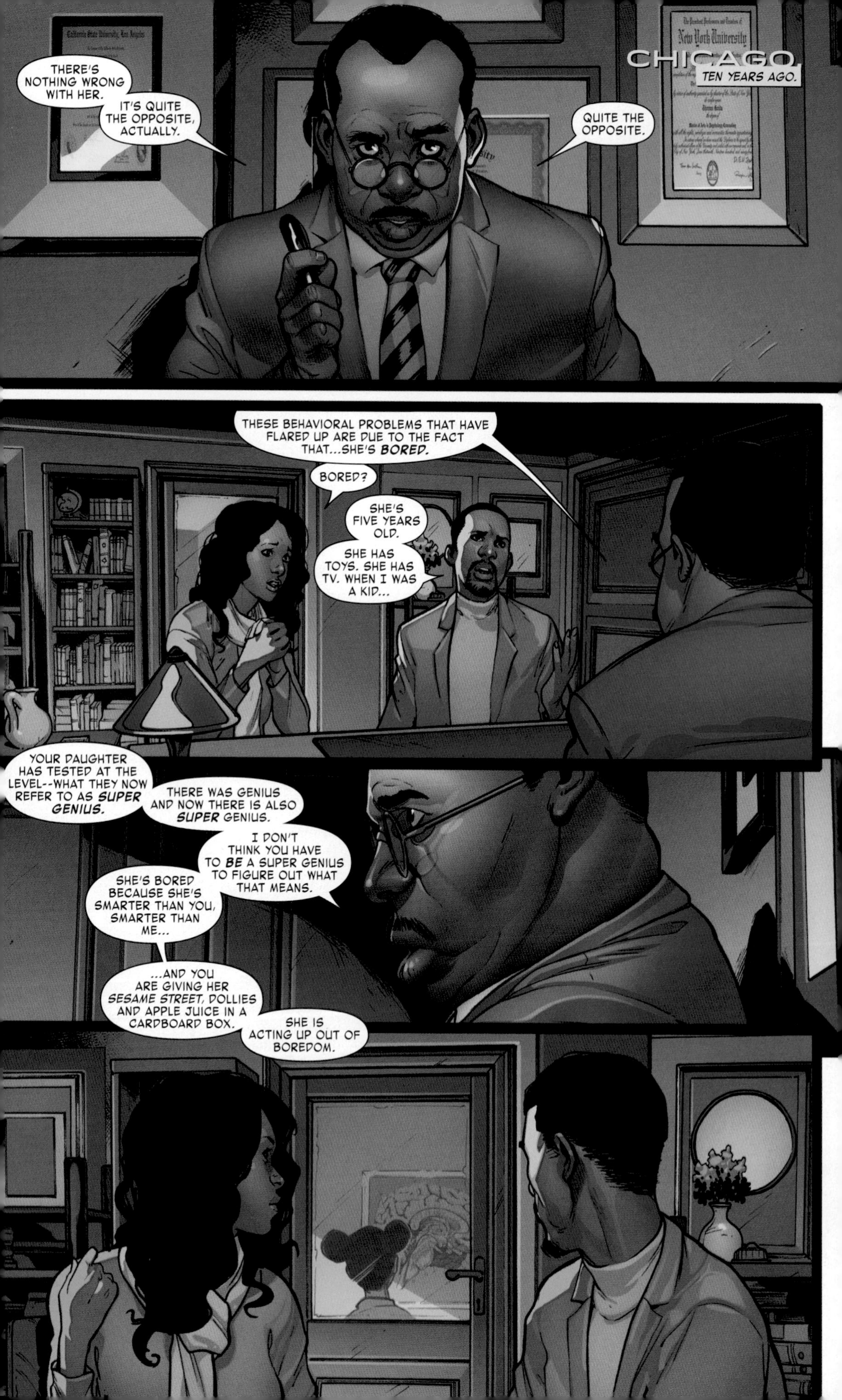
CHICAGO
TEN YEARS AGO.
THERE'S NOTHING WRONG WITH HER.
IT'S QUITE THE OPPOSITE, ACTUALLY.
QUITE THE OPPOSITE.
THESE BEHAVIORAL PROBLEMS THAT HAVE FLARED UP ARE DUE TO THE FACT THAT...SHE'S *BORED.*
BORED?
SHE'S FIVE YEARS OLD.
SHE HAS TOYS. SHE HAS TV. WHEN I WAS A KID...
YOUR DAUGHTER HAS TESTED AT THE LEVEL--WHAT THEY NOW REFER TO AS *SUPER GENIUS.*
THERE WAS GENIUS AND NOW THERE IS ALSO *SUPER* GENIUS.
I DON'T THINK YOU HAVE TO *BE* A SUPER GENIUS TO FIGURE OUT WHAT THAT MEANS.
SHE'S BORED BECAUSE SHE'S SMARTER THAN YOU, SMARTER THAN ME...
...AND YOU ARE GIVING HER *SESAME STREET,* DOLLIES AND APPLE JUICE IN A CARDBOARD BOX.
SHE IS ACTING UP OUT OF BOREDOM.

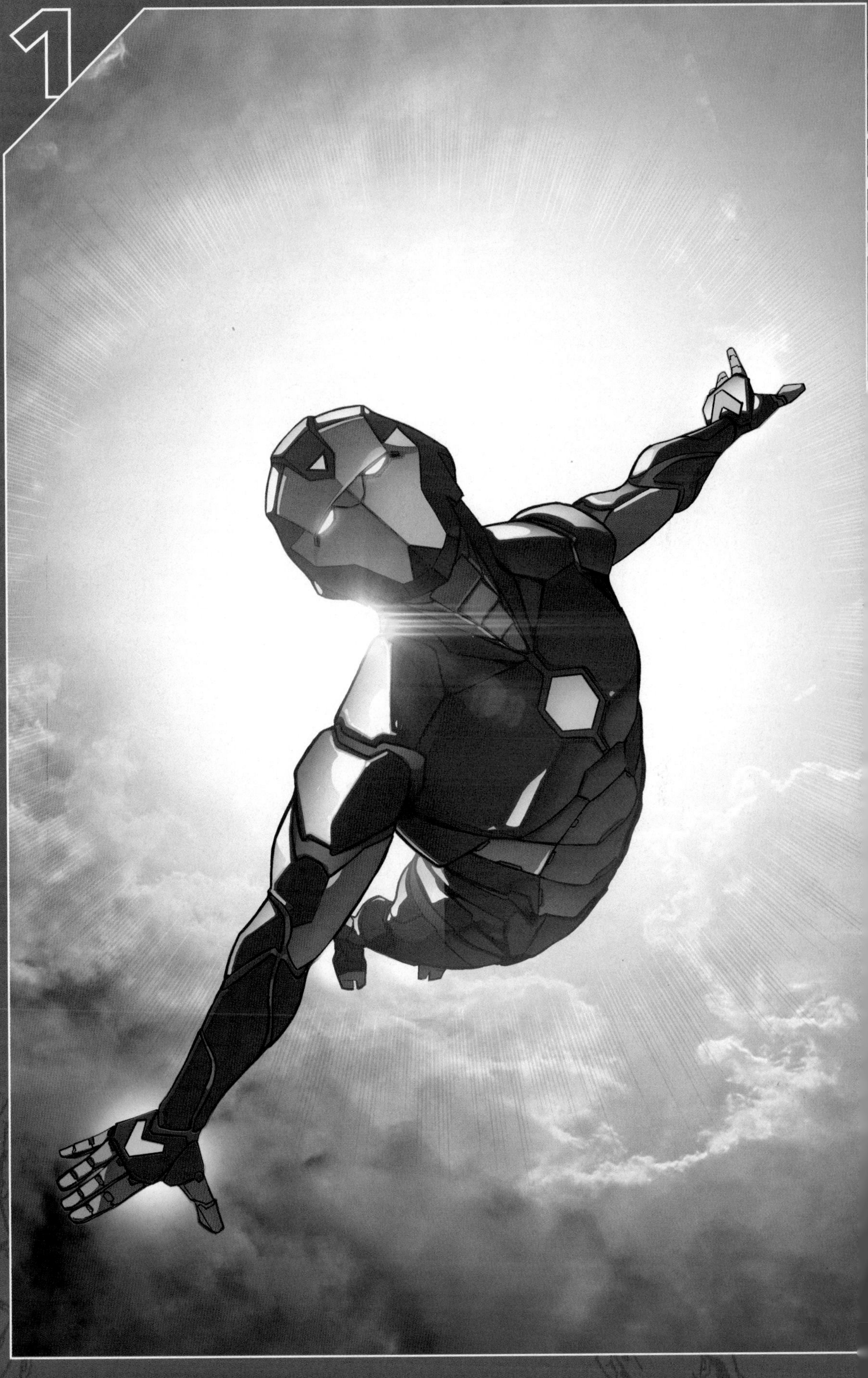
1

RIRI WILLIAMS

BRIAN MICHAEL BENDIS
WRITER

STEFANO CASELLI
ARTIST

MARTE GRACIA
COLOR ARTIST

VC's CLAYTON COWLES
LETTERER

STEFANO CASELLI & MARTE GRACIA
COVER ART

ALANNA SMITH
ASSISTANT EDITOR

TOM BREVOORT
EDITOR

IRON MAN CREATED BY STAN LEE, LARRY LIEBER, DON HECK & JACK KIRBY

COLLECTION EDITOR: JENNIFER GRÜNWALD
ASSISTANT EDITOR: CAITLIN O'CONNELL
ASSOCIATE MANAGING EDITOR: KATERI WOODY
EDITOR, SPECIAL PROJECTS: MARK D. BEAZLEY
VP PRODUCTION & SPECIAL PROJECTS: JEFF YOUNGQUIST
SVP PRINT, SALES & MARKETING: DAVID GABRIEL
BOOK DESIGNER: ADAM DEL RE

EDITOR IN CHIEF: AXEL ALONSO
CHIEF CREATIVE OFFICER: JOE QUESADA
PRESIDENT: DAN BUCKLEY
EXECUTIVE PRODUCER: ALAN FINE

INVINCIBLE IRON MAN: IRONHEART VOL. 1 — RIRI WILLIAMS PREMIERE. Contains material originally published in magazine form as INVINCIBLE IRON MAN #1-5. First printing 2017. ISBN# 978-1-302-90671-9. Published by MARVEL WORLDWIDE, INC., a subsidiary of MARVEL ENTERTAINMENT, LLC. OFFICE OF PUBLICATION: 135 West 50th Street, New York, NY 10020. Copyright © 2017 MARVEL No similarity between any of the names, characters, persons, and/or institutions in this magazine with those of any living or dead person or institution is intended, and any such similarity which may exist is purely coincidental. **Printed in the U.S.A.** DAN BUCKLEY, President, Marvel Entertainment; JOE QUESADA, Chief Creative Officer; TOM BREVOORT, SVP of Publishing; DAVID BOGART, SVP of Business Affairs & Operations, Publishing & Partnership; C.B. CEBULSKI, VP of Brand Management & Development, Asia; DAVID GABRIEL, SVP of Sales & Marketing, Publishing; JEFF YOUNGQUIST, VP of Production & Special Projects; DAN CARR, Executive Director of Publishing Technology; ALEX MORALES, Director of Publishing Operations; SUSAN CRESPI, Production Manager; STAN LEE, Chairman Emeritus. For information regarding advertising in Marvel Comics or on Marvel.com, please contact Vit DeBellis, Integrated Sales Manager, at vdebellis@marvel.com. For Marvel subscription inquiries, please call 888-511-5480. **Manufactured between 4/28/2017 and 5/30/2017 by LSC COMMUNICATIONS INC., SALEM, VA, USA.**

10 9 8 7 6 5 4 3 2 1

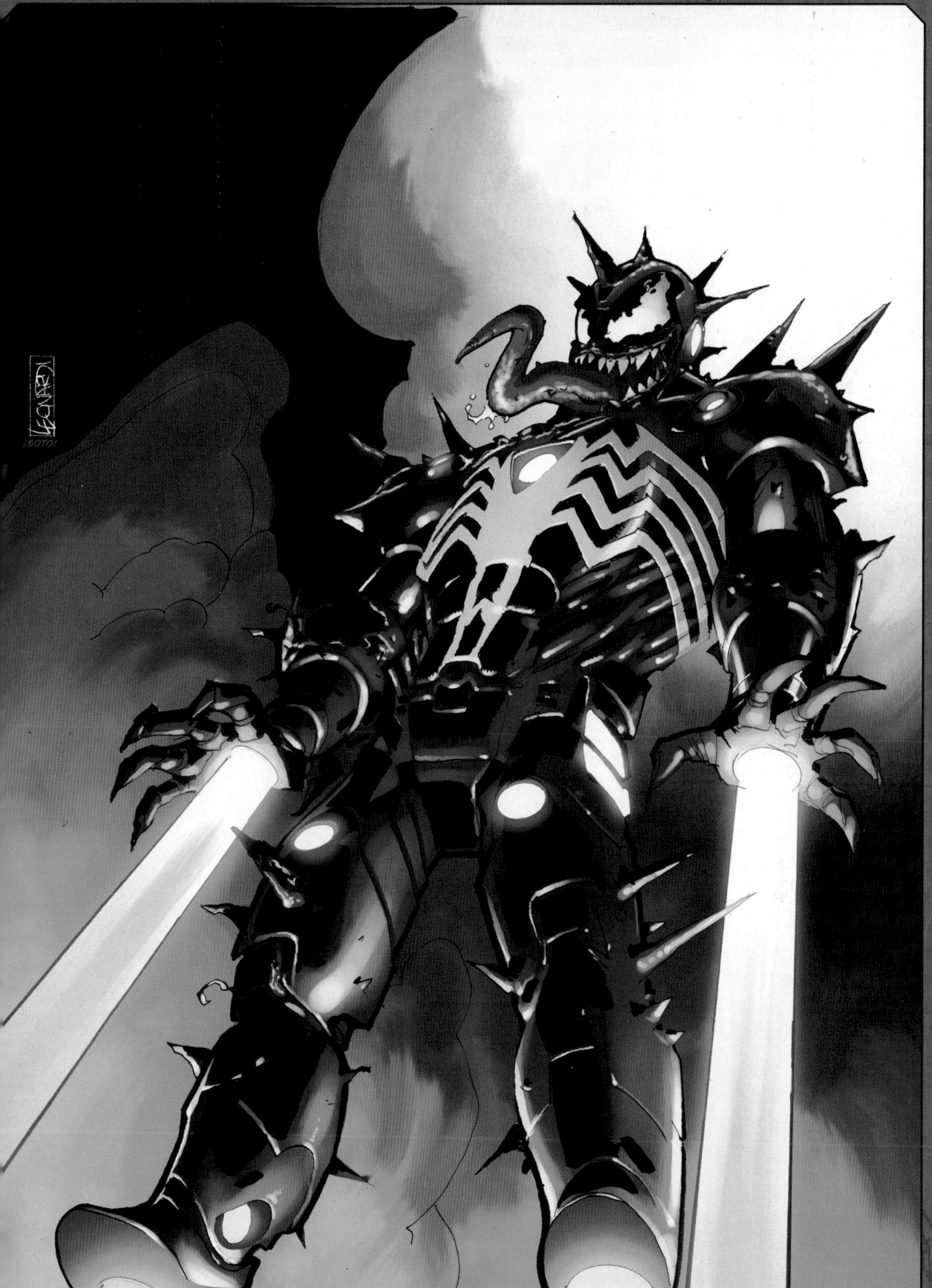

RICK LEONARDI & CHRIS SOTOMAYOR

5 VENOMIZED VARIANT

STEFANO CASELLI

RIRI & IRONHEART CONCEPT ART

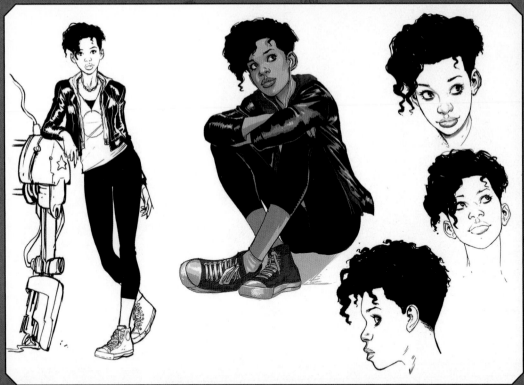

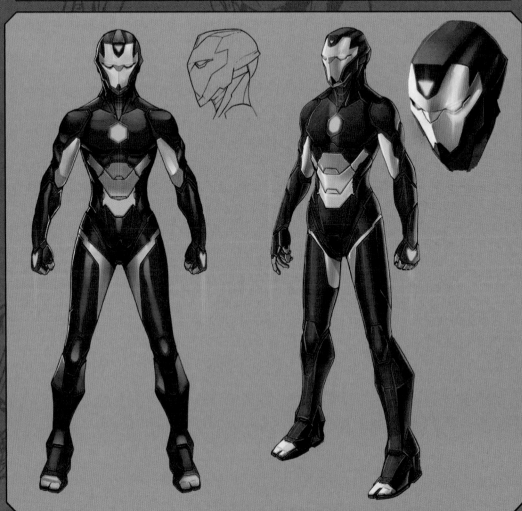

STEFANO CASELLI

ISSUE 1 COVER SKETCH & INKS

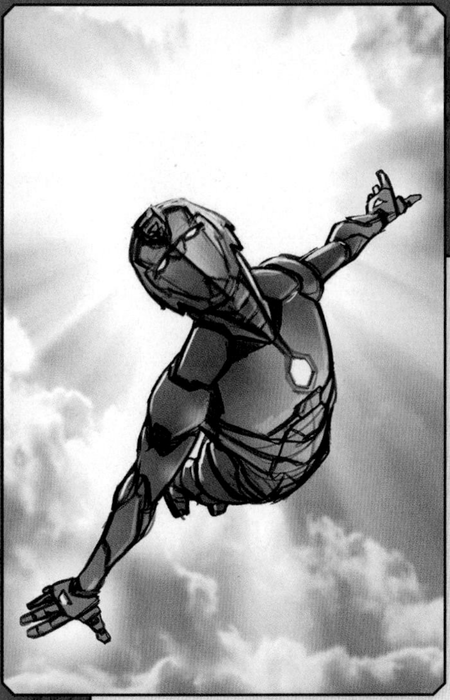

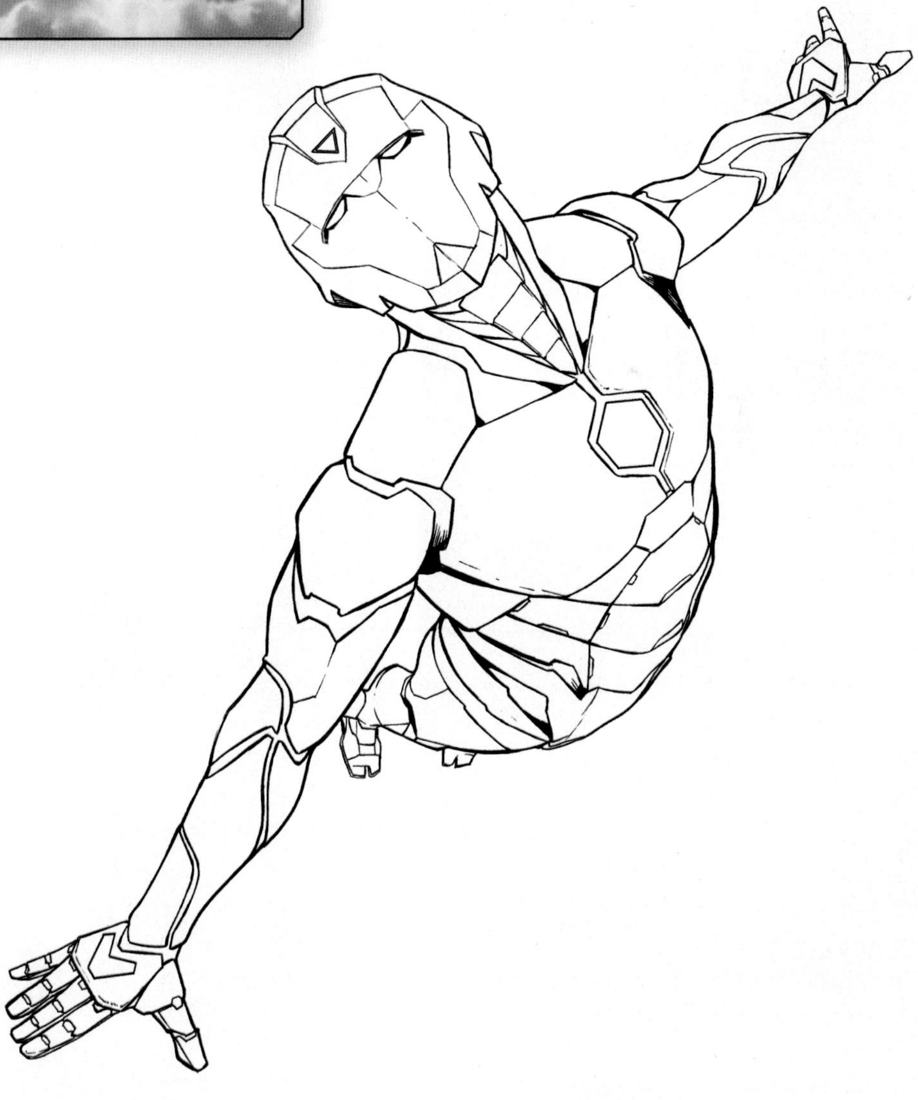

STEFANO CASELLI

ISSUES 2-3 COVER SKETCHES

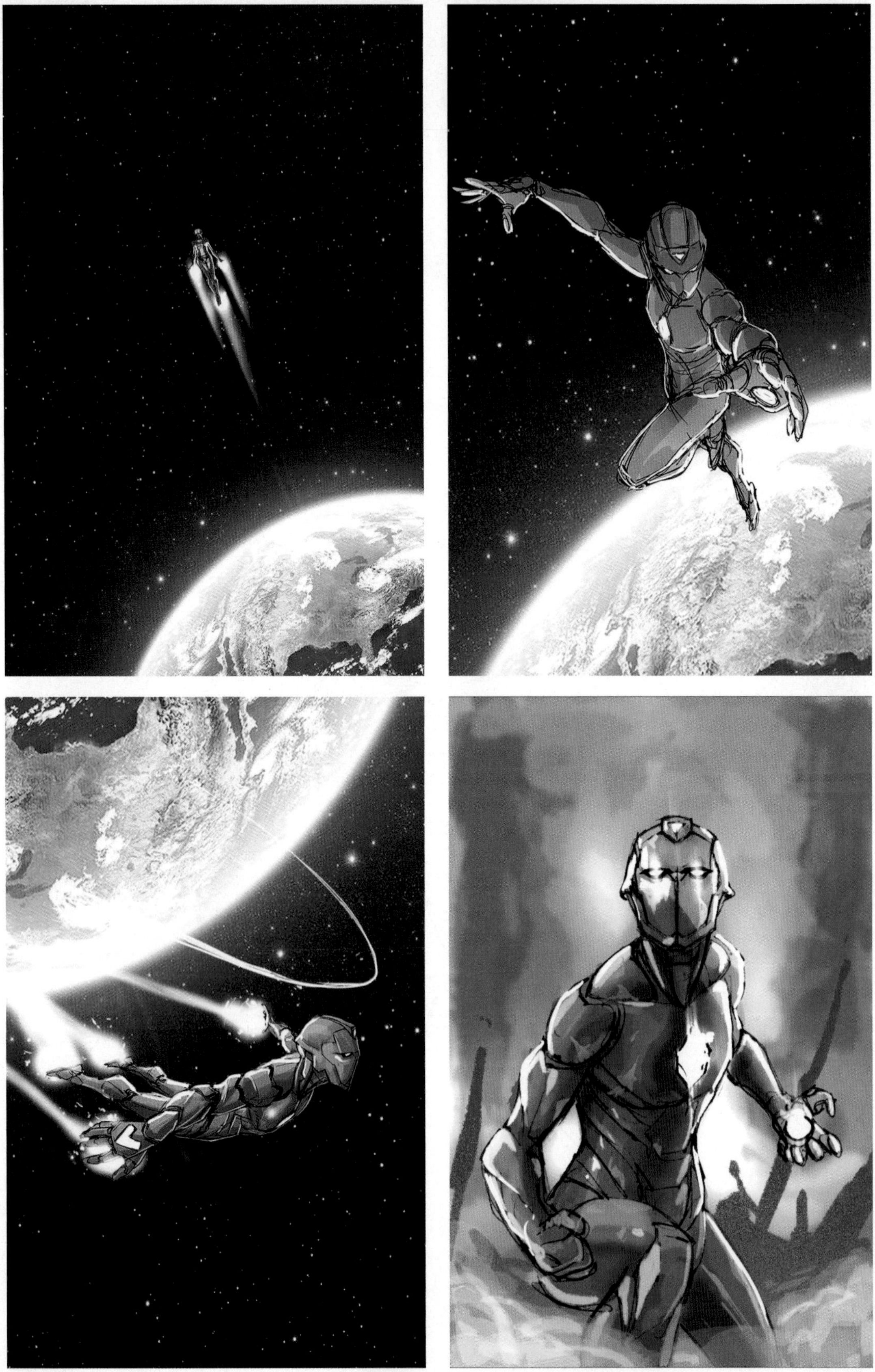

STEFANO CASELLI

ISSUE 2 COVER INKS

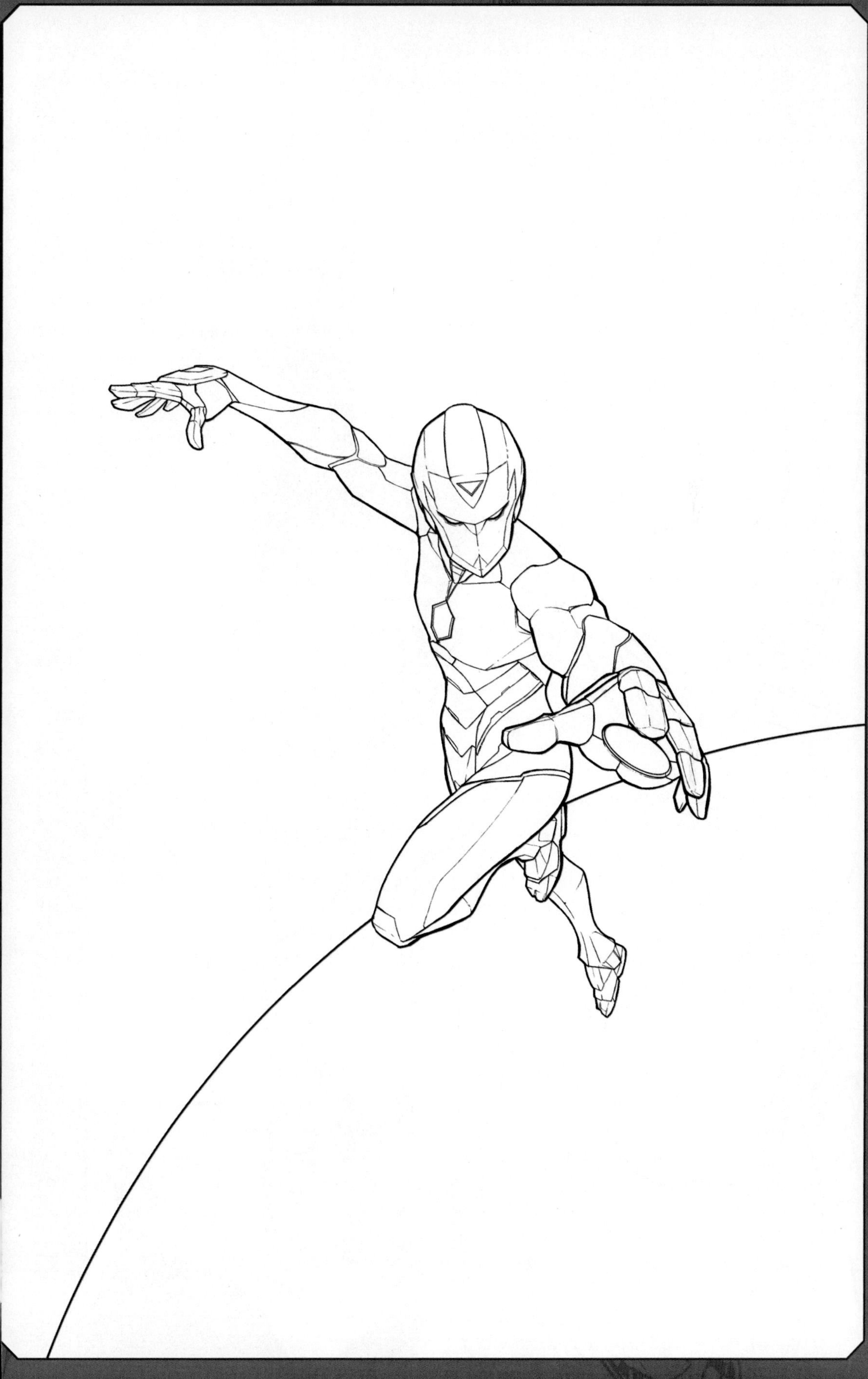

STEFANO CASELLI

ISSUE 4 COVER SKETCH & INKS

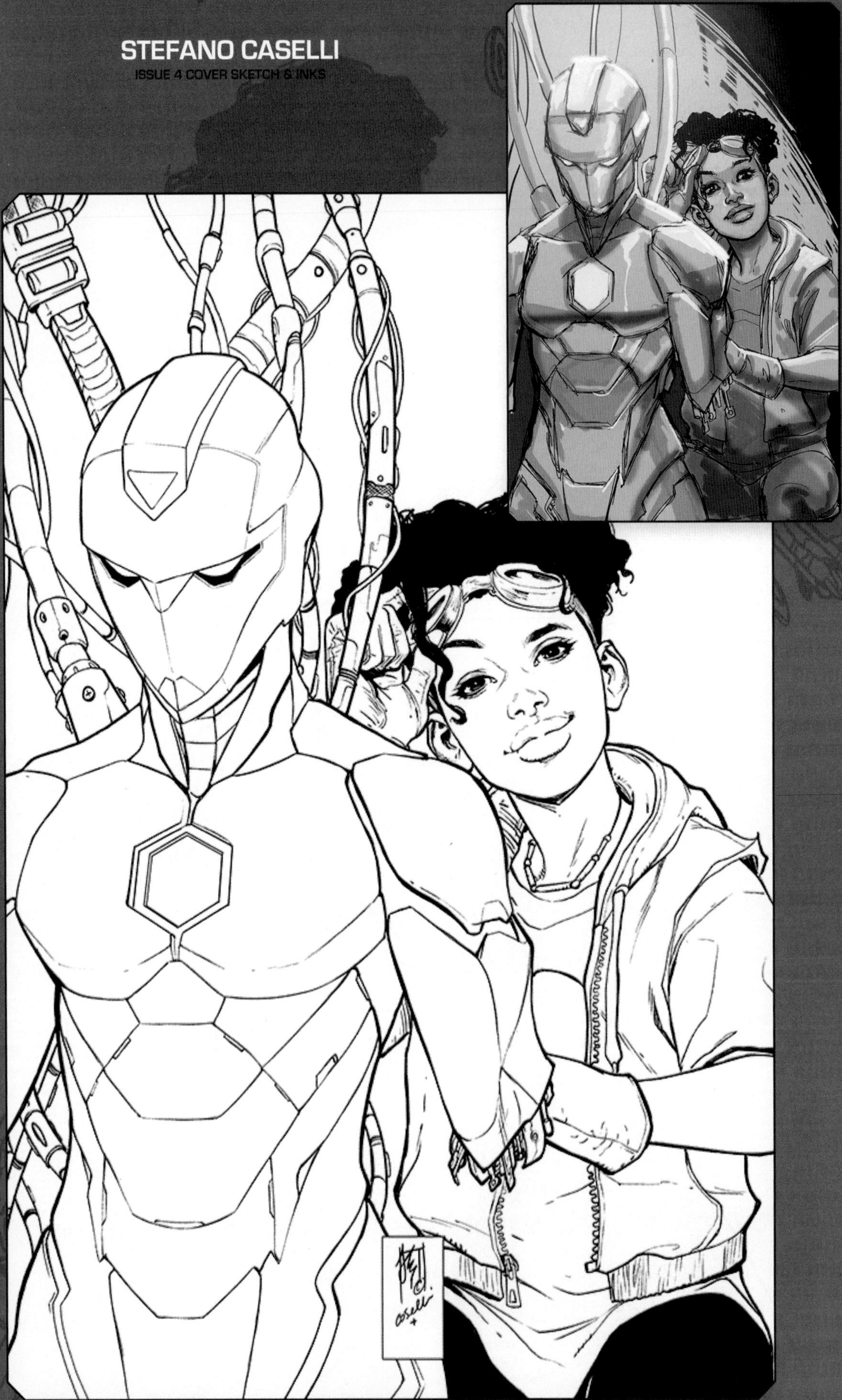

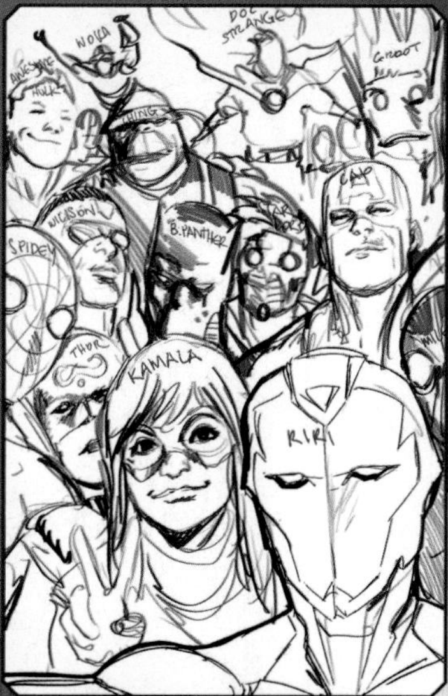
DOC STRANGE
GROOT
HULK
THING
CAP
WILSON
B.PANTHER
SPIDEY
THOR
KAMALA
RIRI

STEFANO CASELLI

ISSUE 5 COVER SKETCH & INKS

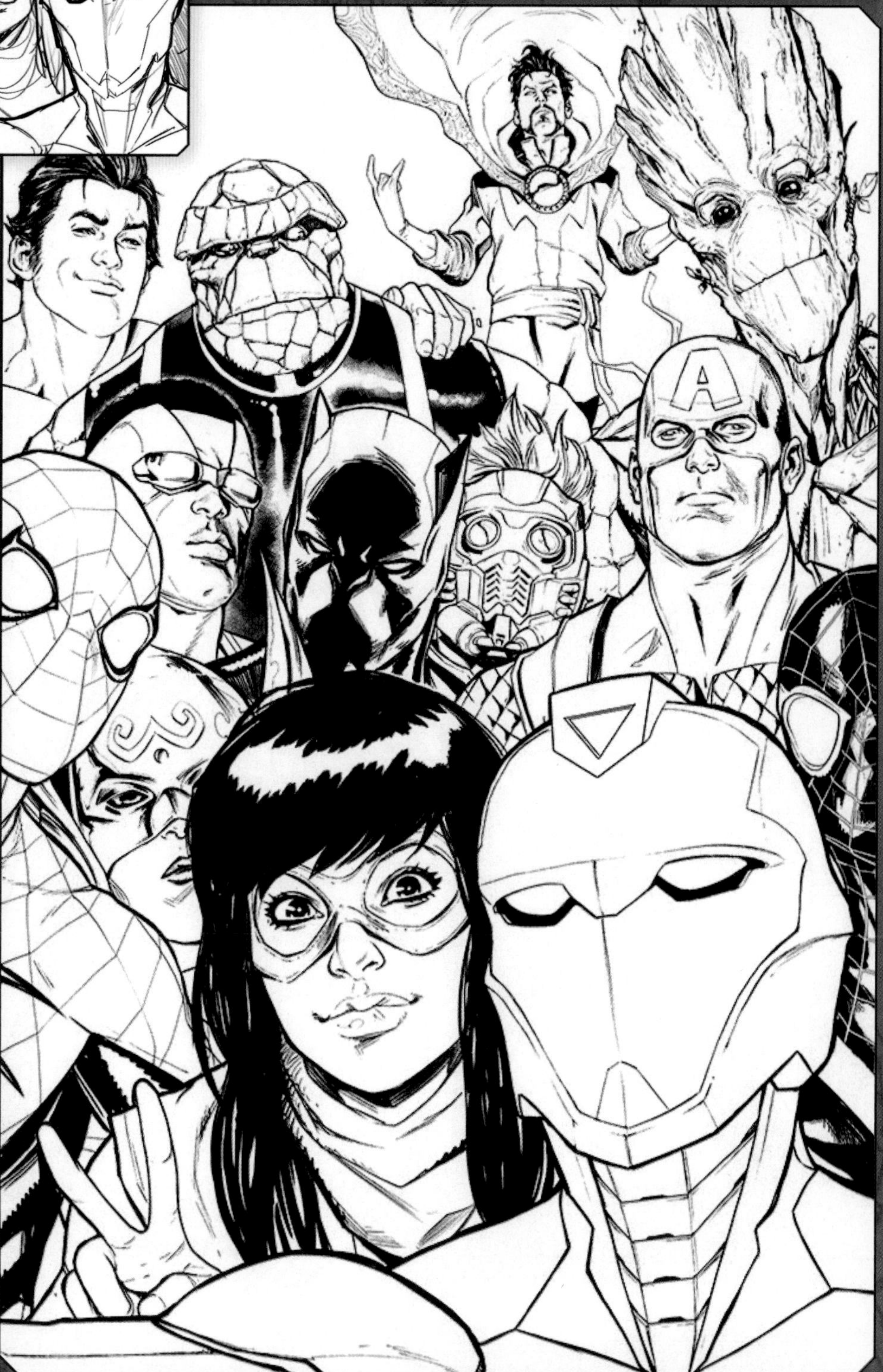

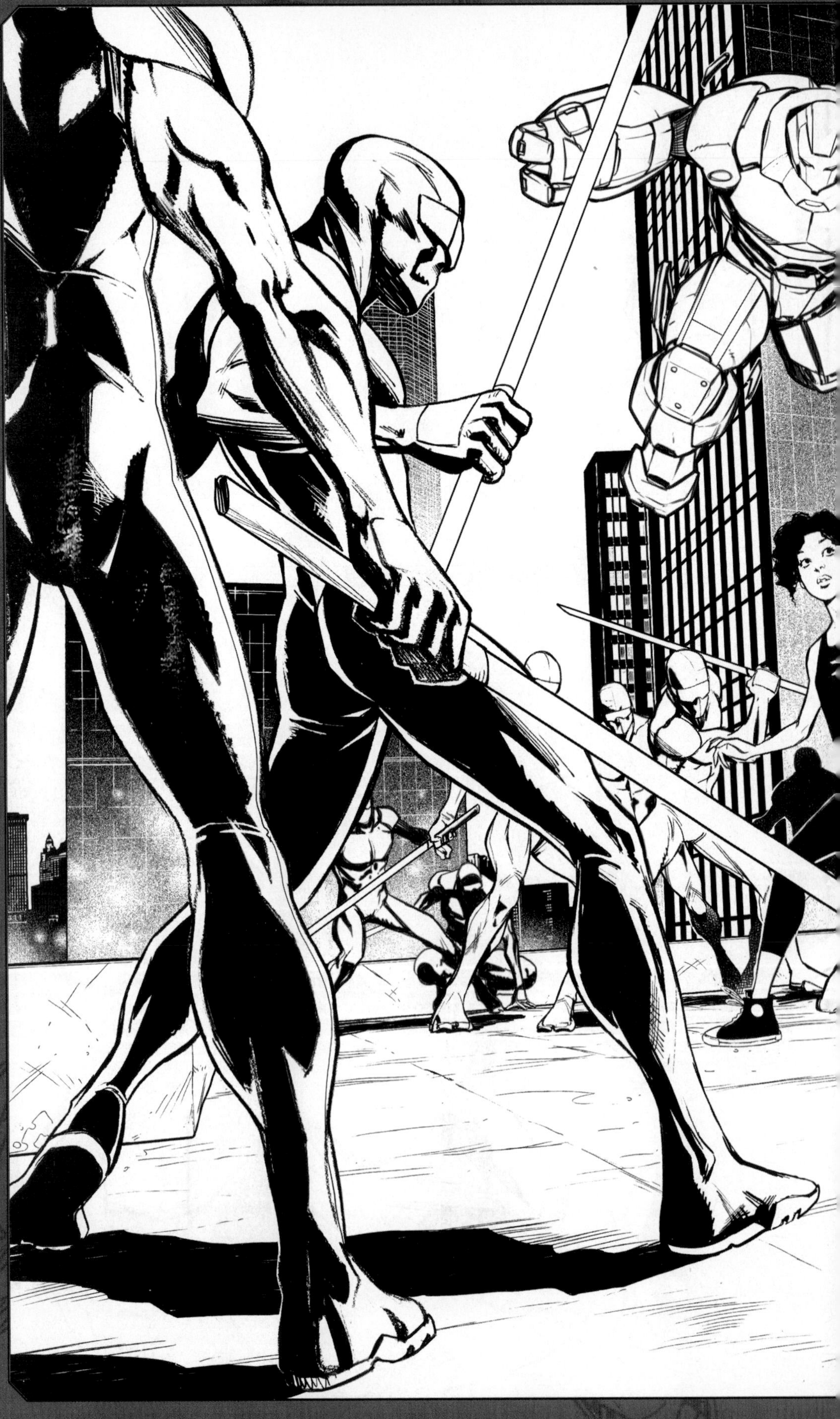

STEFANO CASELLI

ISSUE 4, PAGE2 2-3 ART

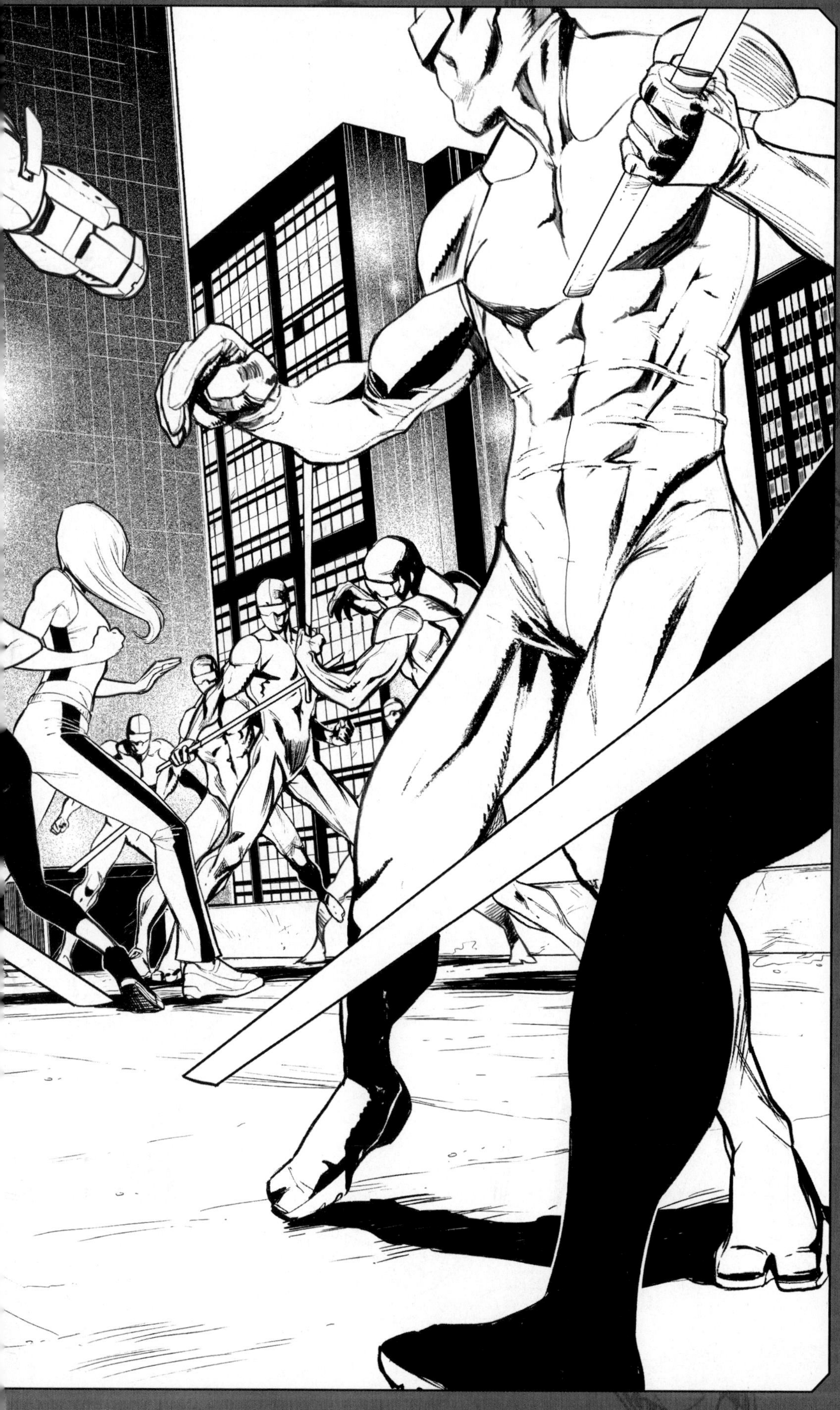

STEFANO CASELLI

ISSUE 1, PAGE 3 ART

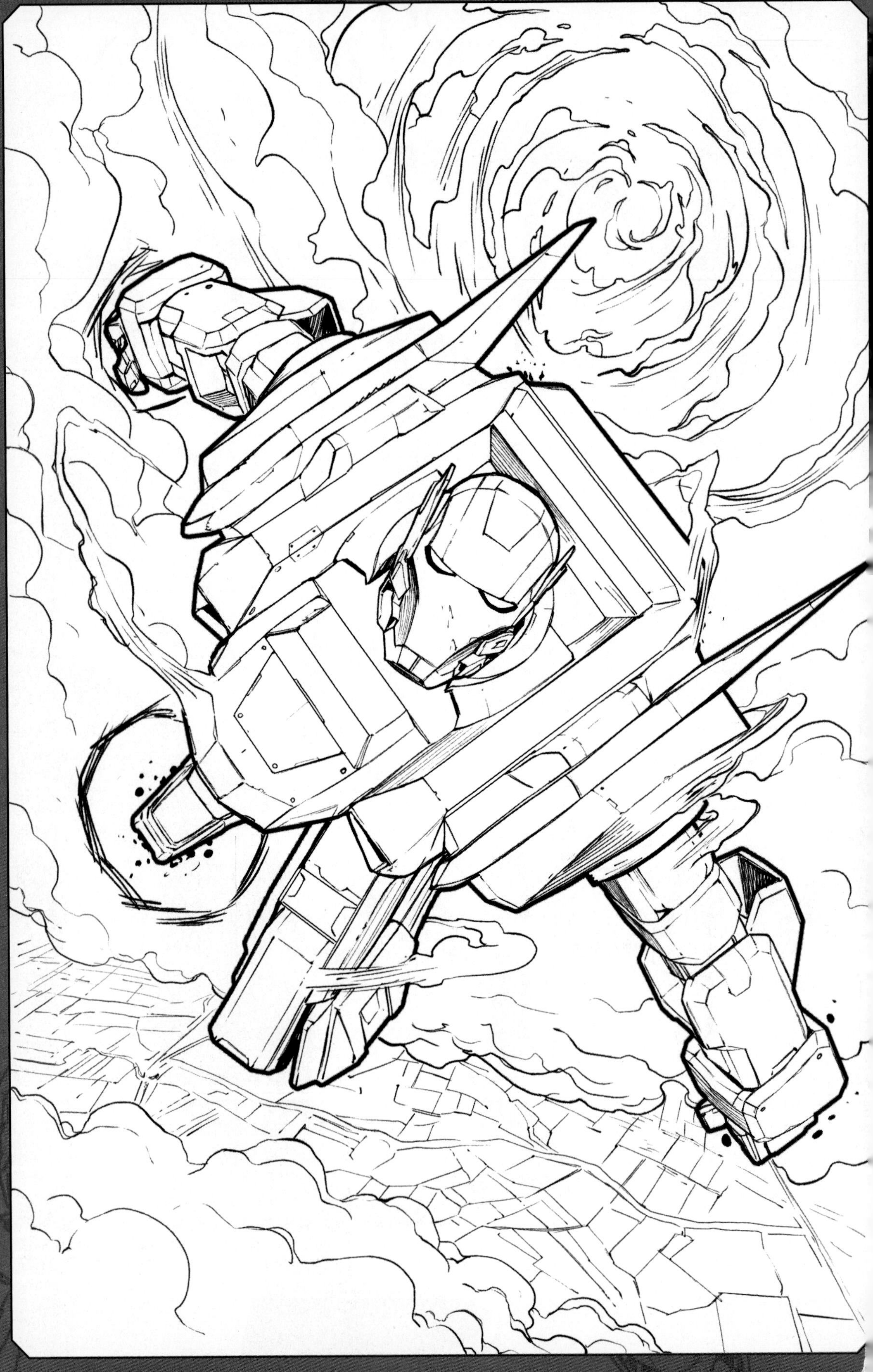